# Upper Palaeolithic and Epipalaeolithic Lithic Technologies at Raqefet Cave, Mount Carmel East, Israel

## György Lengyel

BAR International Series 1681
2007

Published in 2016 by
BAR Publishing, Oxford

BAR International Series 1681

*Upper Palaeolithic and Epipalaeolithic Lithic Technologies at Raqefet Cave, Mount Carmel East, Israel*

ISBN 9781407301198 paperback
ISBN 9781407331591 e-book

DOI https://doi.org/10.30861/9781407301198

A catalogue record for this book is available from the British Library

This book is available at www.barpublishing.com

BAR Publishing is the trading name of British Archaeological Reports (Oxford) Ltd.
British Archaeological Reports was first incorporated in 1974 to publish the BAR
Series, International and British. In 1992 Hadrian Books Ltd became part of the BAR
group. This volume was originally published by Archaeopress in conjunction with
British Archaeological Reports (Oxford) Ltd / Hadrian Books Ltd, the Series principal
publisher, in 2007. This present volume is published by BAR Publishing, 2016.

# BAR
PUBLISHING

BAR titles are available from:

BAR Publishing
122 Banbury Rd, Oxford, OX2 7BP, UK
EMAIL   info@barpublishing.com
PHONE   +44 (0)1865 310431
FAX   +44 (0)1865 316916
www.barpublishing.com

# TABLE OF CONTENTS

# LIST OF FIGURES

# LIST OF TABLES

# INTRODUCTION

This book is an update of a PhD thesis entitled Lithic technology of the Upper Palaeolithic and Epipalaeolithic of Raqefet Cave, Mount Carmel, Israel. The methodology was based upon a French research approach called *chaîne opératoire* (operational sequence), which entered the Levantine prehistoric research in the last decade. This approach regards lithic assemblages as remnants of past human behavior taken place by sequential steps enchained from raw material procurement to finishing tools.

The first lithic technology studies in the Levant 30 years ago without applying the approach of *chaîne opératoire* were made on assemblages of Negev. Then the aim of technology studies was to distinguish between cultures with a wider dataset than the lithic tool typology can offer. Synthesizing results (Marks 1981; Gilead 1981) led to the conclusion that Upper Palaeolithic sites could be classified among two distinct technological traditions: a blade dominated retouched blade and point maker (Ahmarian) and a flake dominated endscraper and burin maker (Levantine Aurignacian). This simple view widely conquered the Levantine Upper Palaeolithic archaeology and became long life among all that answered cultural questions straightforward. Other lithic technology studies, still without applying the *chaîne opératoire*, went into deeper level of understanding archaeological cultures and thus revealed differences within the traditions mentioned above. Ferring (1980; 1988) demonstrated two varieties of lithic production in the Ahmarian tradition, dividing it into an early and a late phase. After his work, the Early Ahmarian became characterized by a single, while the Late Ahmarian by a multiple lithic production strategy. In addition, he pointed out that increasing simplicity in lithic technology and surviving Upper Palaeolithic technological elements characterize the Epipalaeolithic. Similarly to the Ahmarian research, studies on the other Levantine Upper Palaeolithic entity, the Levantine Aurignacian, also demonstrated intra-cultural variability (Bergman 1987). It was argued for the masterpiece Aurignacian lithic assemblages of Ksar 'Aqil layers 13-6 in Lebanon that those are developmentally unrelated and lack lineage between them.

With the *chaîne opératoire* approach in the Levant further details of the lithic technology became studied (Marder 2002; Tostevin 2000; Williams 2003a, 2003b). Studies on the Early Ahmarian showed dissimilarities in sequential steps of the *chaîne opératoire* within this cultural entity, even between assemblages of the same site's two layers (Kebara Cave units III-IV) (Tostevin 2000). The degree of dissimilarity between the assemblages is even more pronounced than that between two different sites (Kebara III and Boker Tachtit 4). Other studies on this cultural entity also claimed dissimilarities in operational sequences between Early Ahmarian sites (Williams 2003a), thus Kebara III-IV assemblages were suggested to be separated as a sub-group definied "unnamed Leptolithic industries". Within the Levantine Aurignacian also variations in operational sequences were observed and thus this cultural entity was proposed to be divided into three groups (Williams 2003b).

Detailed *chaîne opératoire* studies, based on physical refitting of knapped stones of the operational sequences, on Negev Late Kebaran, Geometric Kebaran, Mushabian, Ramonian, and Terminal Ramonian/Early Natufian assemblages show that some assemblages are characterized by a single operational sequence in the lithic production, while greater variability was pointed out for other assemblages with up to five different operational sequences. Similarly to earlier results (Ferring 1980), the presence of Upper Palaeolithic technological features in the early Epipalaeolithic times is also illustrated by the *chaîne opératoire* studies (Marder 2002). Basically, comparing to each other the operational sequences, all Epipalaeolithic cultural entities seem belong to the same conservative technological tradition within which changes were gradual, and no clear chronological or cultural ordering could be recorded.

The question this book aims to answer somewhat different from that in earlier *chaîne opératoire* studies. There is a cave in Mount Carmel, Raqefet, which yielded a stratigraphy with a culturally indeterminate Early Upper Palaeolithic, a Levantine Aurignacian, a Late Kebaran, a Geometric Kebaran, and a Late Natufian assemblage. The Carmel area is abundant of different type of flint raw materials which can be found processed by knapping in the lithic assemblages of the cultural sequence. The answer this study is looking for is what operational sequences were used to produce stone tools from the Upper Palaeolithic to the Epipalaeolithic in the given stone raw material environment of the Carmel area, and how these operational sequences relate to each other.

This work never would have been accomplished without the help of many others. I am indebted to Árpád Ringer and Avraham Ronen for supervising me during my PhD. I especial thank Andrew Garrard who provided the complete archives of the excavations in 1970-1972 and Guy Bar-Oz for giving me permission to use his taphonomic observations made on the faunal remains of Raqefet. Further, I wish to thank the Zinman Institute of Archaeology at the University of Haifa for making all its equipment available for me, and my colleagues and friends, Mina Weistein-Evron, Michael Eisenberg, Dani Nadel, Daniel Kaufman, Alexander Tsatskin, Yossi Zaidner, Polina Spivak, Udi Grinberg, and Zsolt Mester who helped greatly carry out my research with their professional advices and amicable support. I also thank Anna Belfer-Cohen for giving me permission to study Hayonim D material, and her, again, and Adrian Nigel Goring-Morris for the unlimited help with professional literature. Least, I am most grateful to my parents, György and Judit, who supported me the most during my PhD.

# CHAPTER 1: RAQEFET CAVE

## Location

Raqefet cave is found on the southeastern side of Mount Carmel, in a wadi (called Raqefet) running north-west to south-east, 0.5 km upstream from the confluence with wadi Yoqne'am. This valley provides a major access route between the coast and the Plain of Jezreel, dividing the Cenomenian – Turonian limestones of Mount Carmel from the Eocene chalks of the Menashe Hills in the south (Figure 1.1.). A Terra Rossa soil has developed over much of the Carmel range supporting a Quercus calliprinus–Pistacia palestina open forest, although much of this has become degraded to maquis providing browsing for goat and sheep. A light colured redzina soil derived from the Cenomenian marls, is also found in shallow pockets within the Carmel range supporting a Pinus halepensis–Hypericum serphyllifolium association, although today these depressions are frequently ploughed for cereal cultivation. The Menashe Hills are largely covered by dark redzinas or brown forest soils which in their natural state might support Quercus ithaburensis, but again, much of this has been cleared for the cultivation of cereals. The alluvial soils of the Nahal Yoqneam and Jezreel Plain are very intensively cultivated, leaving no trace of their indigenous vegetation (Higgs *et al* 1975).

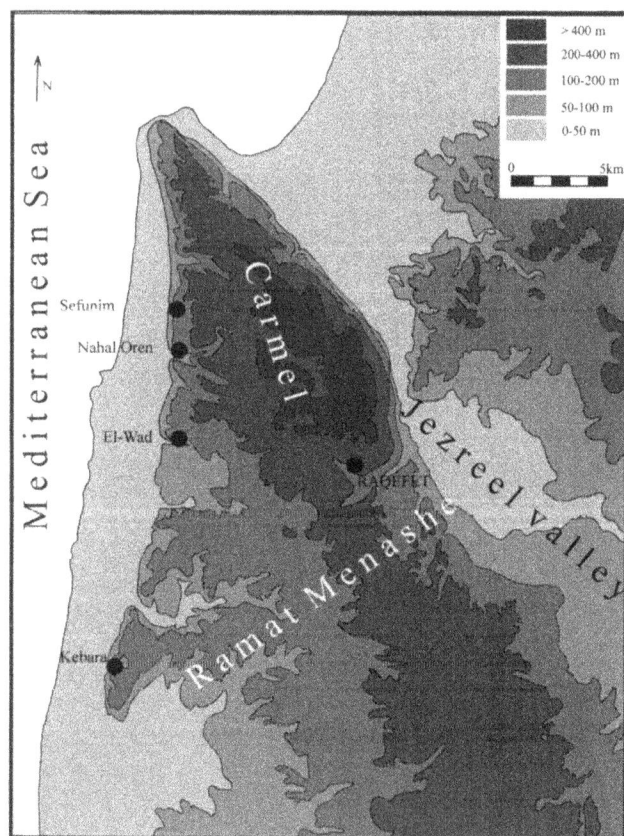

*Figure 1.1.* Location of Raqefet Cave with other Carmel sites.

The cave is located at an altitude of 230 m above sea level and approximately 50 m above the wadi bed. It is on the left bank, facing west, at the bottom of a cliff. The slope from the wadi bottom up to the cave is rocky and steep. In front of the cave below the entrance there is a narrow terrace. Five chambers form the cave, among which the rear has an open chimney. The cave is 50 m long and its area is *ca* 500 square m. At the front of the second chamber, there is a large rectangular block of rock (*ca* 5 m long) in a north-south orientation (Figure 1.3.), probably detached from the north wall.

## Research history

### Excavations in 1970-1972

The cave was discovered by Ya'aqov Olami in 1956 (Olami 1984). Eric Higgs of the University of Cambridge and Tamar Noy of the Israeli Museum conducted a joint excavation project at the cave between 1970 and 1972 (Noy and Higgs 1971; Higgs *et al* 1975).

The excavations were carried out in the first and the second chambers. A total of 75 square meters were excavated of the *ca* 500 square metres area of the cave. The three other inner chambers were left unexcavated (Figure 1.3.). Of the total occupation area of the cave, 126 square meters in the first chamber 42 square meters, in the second chamber, north and west to the rock 22 square meters and in the rear of this chamber 11 square meters were excavated. The excavated areas were indicated by square coordinates: in chamber 1 A-H/7-17, and trenches in chamber 2 B-G/18-23 and J-M/24-28 (Higgs *et al* 1975).

During the excavations two different grids were applied. In 1970 and at the beginning of 1971 13 rectangles of 3x1.5m were set up, numbered with Arabic numerals (Figure 1.4.). Each rectangle was divided into eastern and western half. In the second chamber only the top surface of the stratum was removed under this system. At the beginning of the 1971 season, the 3X1.5 rectangles were replaced by 1x1m grid that was used till the end of the excavations. Further division on the grid was made in 1972, when east and west and north and south halves of the 1x1 squares were distinguished.

For the purpose of horizontal division, deposits were distinguished from each other on the basis of color, texture and structure. In addition, ten centimeter thick artificial spit unit divisionwas applied to record artifacts. In the field, layers were given roman numerals. Roman capitals were used to denote pits and other intrusive elements. Levels of layers, e.g. sub-layers, were indicated by numbers and letters added to the layer number. The deposits were numbered in reverse stratigraphic order.

*Excavation in 2004*

In the summer of 2004 Raqefet Cave was revisited in order to verify the stratigraphy of the Upper Palaeolithic and Epipalaeolithic lithic assemblages. The field work reopened the B-G/18-23 trench and cleaned the first chamber down to the bedrock floor exposed previously. In addition, an unexcavated strip of the stratum in squares F/9-13 and additional small patches of sediment covering mortars and cupmarks in bedrock in squares G-H/12-13 were also excavated to bedrock (Figure 1.3.). The field work made use of 0.5x0.5 subsquares of the original 1970-1972 grid, and the deposits were removed by 5 cm artificial levels. All undisturbed sediment was dry sieved through a 2 mm mesh, and the sediments from bedrock mortars were wet sieved through 1 mm mesh.

The F/9-13 strip consisted of a 40 cm thick loose grayish-brown fine sediment with a very few sharp 10-20 cm large stones. A 6 cm thick root of a tree disturbed the sediment within which a few hundred potshards were found including those characteristic to the Pottery Neolithic, Late Chalcolithic, Early Bronze Age, Middle Bronze Age II, Middle Bronze Age IIb, Late Bronze Age, Iron Age I, Late Hellenistic and Roman periods (Lengyel *et al* 2005).

Three bedrock mortars, C-I, C-II, and C-XXIII, contained in situ sediments. In the C-I-II bedrock mortar complex the deposit was fine grained grey and brecciated near the bedrock. In the mortars a few 10-20 cm large sharp stones were found, probably placed there deliberately (Lengyel *et al* 2005) (Figure 1.2.). The flints are sharp, with no signs of rolling. Potsherds were found in the first 10 cm of the deposit, which covered the mortars. Within the mortars potsherds were absent.

In the large CXXIII mortar the deposit was fine grained loose grey sediment. No breccia was observed. The deposit contained sharp flints and a very few potsherds in the uppermost part of the mortar. Two erect stones were also encountered here.

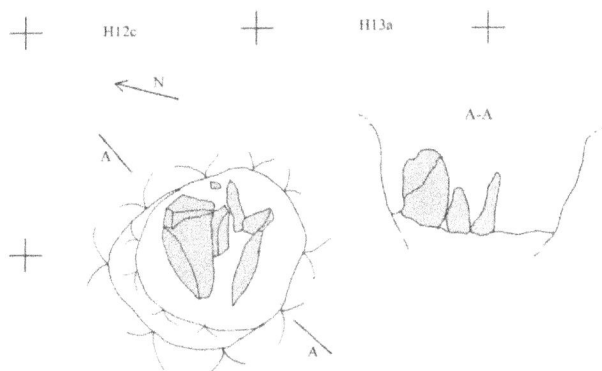

**Figure 1.2.** *C-I mortar with erect stones in subsquares H12c and 13a (subsquares are 50cm by 50 cm).*

*Studies on archaeological remains of Raqefet*

The archaeological material of the cave has never been completely published. The excavators prepared a paper that summarizes the results of their excavations, but remained unpublished (Higgs *et al* 1975). In this paper the authors survey the archaeological assemblages of all excavated areas of the cave and conclude that the site had been occupied during Mousterian, Middle to Upper Palaeolithic transition, Levantine Aurignacian, Kebaran, Natufian, Pre-Pottery and Pottery Neolithic and Bronze Age periods.

The first detailed study on archaeological material was made on Upper Palaeolithic assemblages of layers IV, III, and II in area B-G/18-23 by D. Ziffer (Ziffer 1978a, 1978b, 1981). He used metric data of knapped implements to see differences between Levantine Aurignacian appearences. On the basis of the results, Ziffer identified the Raqefet assemblages as Levantine Aurignacian Bii and showed similarities with assemblages of Ksar Akil, Kebara, Sefunim and El-Wad caves.

Contrary to the lithics, the whole Upper Pleistocene faunal remains of Raqefet went through analysis by A.N. Garrard in his PhD dissertation devoted to the study of Upper Pleistocene and Early Holocene man, animal, and plant relationships (Garrard 1980).

Lately, lithics of layers VIII-IV were studied by J. Sarel (2002, 2004) from the point of view of lithic technology. She claims that layers VIII-VI yielded industries with Mousterian modes of lithic production and Upper Palaeolithic type of blades, which all together are part of the Middle to Upper Palaeolithic Transition. Although Layer IV is present with data in her study, its assemblage is excluded from the analysis and conclusion.

In 2004, after studying the stratigraphy, the documents, and the entire archaeological assemblages of the cave, a slightly new division of the strata has been developed (Lengyel 2005; Lengyel *et al* 2005). The changes touch upon layer I, VII, and VIII of area B-G/18-23. It turned out that Layer I theoretically was excavated in two seasons, in 1971 and 1972. Indeed, layer II was mistaken for layer I in the 1972 excavation. On the original section drawings of square D20's southern wall, the upper part of layer II is consistently marked as layer I. Accordingly, in 1972, the upper part of Layer II in square D20 was excavated instead of layer I. The stone tools of Layer II upper part are non-microliths. Among them there are no typical Epipalaeolithic types, while the artifacts of Layer I from the 1971 excavation are typical for the Late Kebaran. Layers VII and VIII were not found in the section as different units. Accordingly, they are marked in the 2004 field report as a single layer (Lengyel *et al* 2005).

Basically, compared to the earlier excavators' observations, three additional archaeological entities have been pointed out in the cave. These are the Geometric Kebaran in layer VII of area J-M/24-28, and two culturally indeterminate assemblages: a Late Upper Palaeolithic in layer II and an Early Upper Palaeolithic in layer IV of area B-G/18-23. The late Upper Palaeolithic assemblage is scarce, atypical, its chronological position is based solely on the stratigraphy, and the question of its cultural division is unambatement at present. A similar problem was found with the Early Upper Palaeolithic assemblage of layer IV. Luckyly, its chronological position besides stratigraphic situation is based on [14]C AMS dating (see next paragraphs). A major dout is claimed herein concerning the presence of Middle to Upper Palaeolithic Transitional industries in layers VIII-V. Two types of debitages, Levallois and volumetric blade are mixed together. In addition, the hallmark of the Initial Upper Palaeolithic Emiren, an Emireh point is also included. As the next paragraphs on stratigraphy provide, the composition of these assemblages is due to heavy post-depositional disturbances. Thus, from archaeological point of view, identifying them as a single industry is far ambiguous. Two other entities of the cave were also reconsidered. The Kebaran and the Natufian are of late phase. Consequently, the prehistoric sequence of raqefet consists of Mousterian and Initial Upper Palaeolithic admixture, an indeterminate Early Upper Palaeolithic, Levantine Aurignacian, an Indeterminate Late Upper Palaeolithic, Late Kebaran, Geometric Kebaran, Late Natufian, PPNA, PPNB, and Pottery Neolithic.

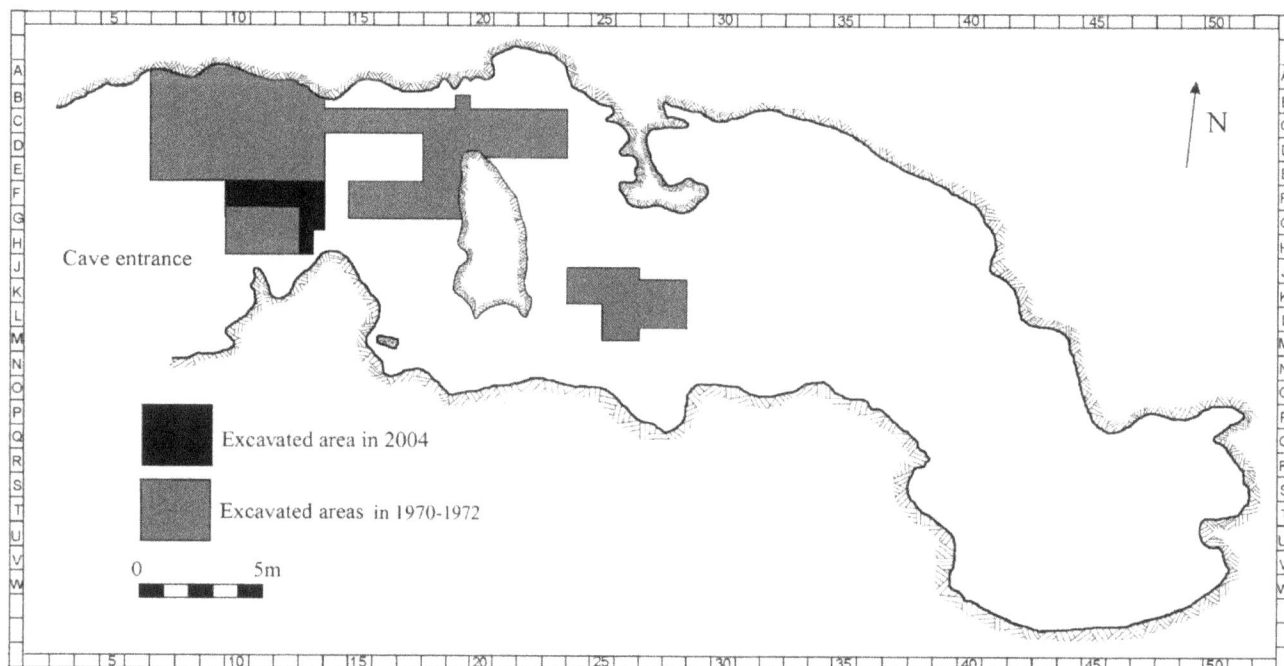

*Figure. 1.3.* Excavated areas of Raqefet (modified after Higgs et al 1975).

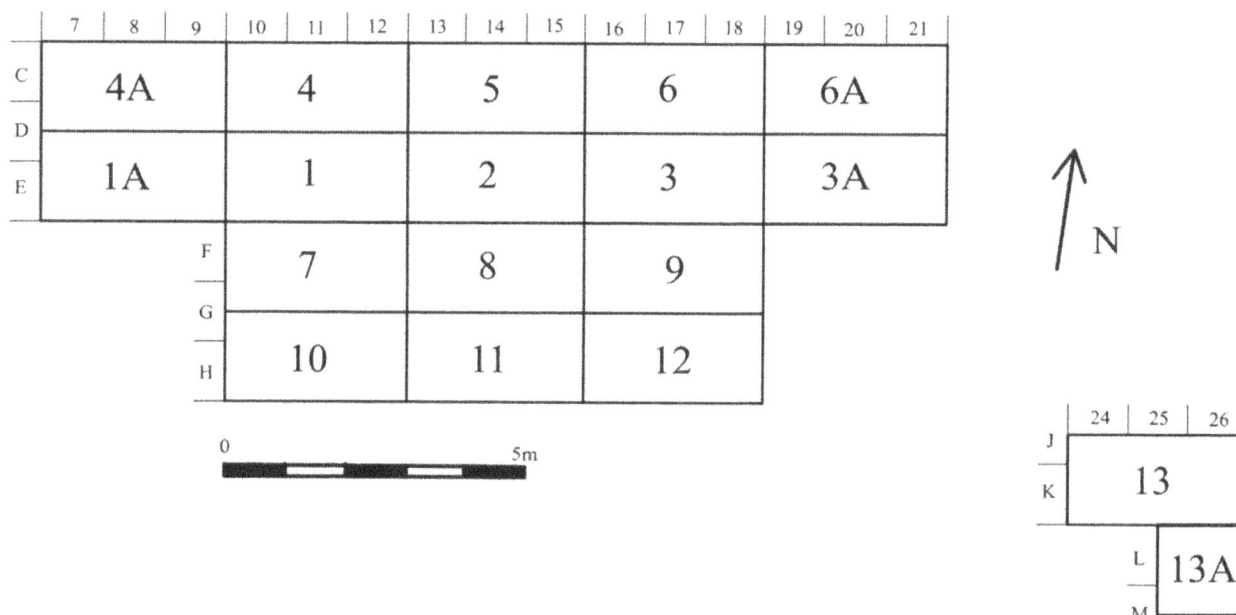

*Figure. 1.4.* Excavation rectangles 3x1.5 m of 1970 and early 1971.

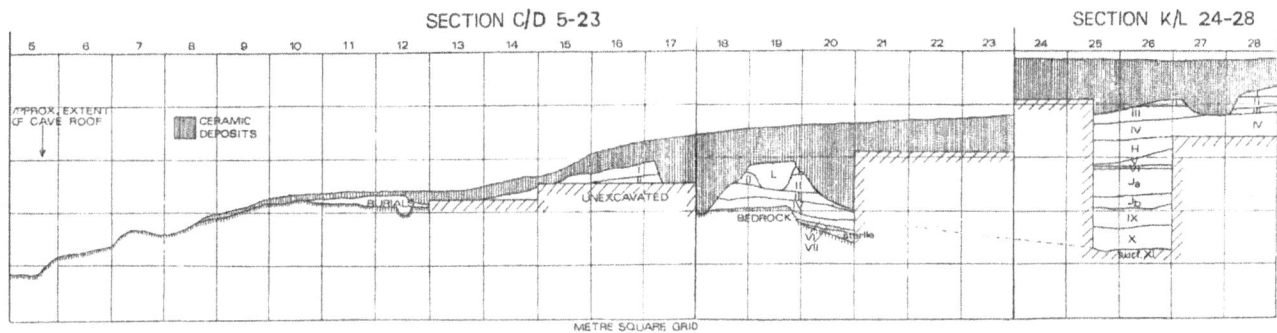

**Figure 1.5.** *Longitudinal section of the cave strata (Raqefet Archives).*

## Stratigraphy

Excavations at Raqefet Cave were carried out in three areas: A-H/7-17, B-G/18-23 and J-M/24-28. Crucial disturbances did not allow the 1970-1972 excavators to establish an exact stratigraphic connection between the areas. Therefore, the stratigraphy is described herein by excavation area. Different deposit sequences were recorded within area A-H/7-17. Its stratigraphy is presented by sub-areas marked by squares. The presentation of the layers of 1970 excavation on the basis of poor documentation is excluded.

The describtion of deposits is based on the 1970-1972 excavators' macroscopic observations (Raqefet Archive). Included are the location of the given stratigraphic unit, color, texture, particle size where possible, and the characteristic artifacts. The thickness of layers is given when the documents provide.

In this study, layers are indicated by roman numerals. Pits are marked by numbers in area A-H/7-17 and by capitals in areas B-G/18-23 and J-M/24-28. The presentation of deposits is in stratigraphic order, from top to bottom. Where stratigraphic correlation between pits and layers cannot be made pits are presented first and then layers. Some layers and pits were subdivided into levels. In such case each level is presented separately when its features considerably differ from the entire deposit unit. Otherwise, the levels are mentioned in the description of the main layer or pit. Additional data to the deposits of A-H/7-17 and B-G/18-23 from the 2004 revision appear separately presented in this chapter.

### Area A-H 7-17

Squares in this area, with the exception of C13-17, were excavated down to bedrock. This is the most disturbed part of the Pleistocene cave stratum, consisting of many intrusions from Holocene and historical periods.

### Sub-area C7-17, D-E/16-17

**Pits 1-2**
Extension: C17; D-E/16-17.
Features: red, stony deposit, which becomes increasingly stonier at its lower part.
Artifacts: potsherds and lithics including microliths (Kebara points), geometric microliths, and small backed lunates.

### Pit 3
Extension: C12-13.
Features: light brown-yellow, stony deposit.
Artifacts: potsherds and lithics including geometric microliths and small backed lunates.

### Pit 4
Extension: C-D/7-12.
Features: ashy, clay deposit with local hearths.
Artifacts: potsherds and a few flint flakes and blades without characteristic tool.

### Pit 5 (cut by pit 3)
Extension: C12-16.
Features: gold brown, sandy fill.
Artifacts: potsherds and lithics with geometric microliths including small backed lunates, plus an embedded incomplete structure made of flat stones.

### Layer I (correlated with Layer I in D-E/7-13)
Extension: C-D/7-12; C15-17.
Features: light brown, sandy deposit with few large stones.
Artifacts: potsherds and lithics with carinated end-scraper, narrow curved micro points, several microliths and backed sickle bladelets.

### Layer II
Extension: C12-13, C15-17.
Features: grey silt with few stones.
Artifacts: potsherds, lithics including small backed lunates, and PPN axes.

### Layer III
Extension: C14.
Features: brown stony deposit.
Artifacts: potsherds, and general lithics.

### Layer IV
Extension: C-D/7-12. Lies in small hollow in bedrock; relation to other deposits is unknown.
Features: very stony, brecciated deposit with localized ash pockets on bedrock.
Artifacts: very few potsherds and lithics including narrow curved micro points, backed and truncated bladelets and a backed sickle blade.

*Layer V*
Extension: in bedrock hollows, relation to other deposits is unknown.
Features: brecciated.
Artifacts: potsherds and lithics including a large amount of narrow curved micro points.

*Sub-area D-E/7-13* (Figure 1.6.)
*Pits 1-2 and 5*
Features: light brown very sandy with many stones.
Artifacts: potsherds and lithics including small backed lunates and trapeze-rectangles.

*Pit 3*
Features: yellow silt with large stones.
Artifacts: potsherds uncharacteristic lithics.

*Pit 4*
Features: yellow sand/grit.
Artifacts: potsherds and uncharacteristic lithics.

*Pit 6*
Features: loose, very stony fill.
Artifacts: potsherds and lithics with tools of geometric microliths including small backed lunates, and sickle blades.

*Layer I* (correlated with Layer I in D-E/7-13, and in G-H/10-12)
Features: 15-35 cm thick, light brown sandy deposit with few large stones.
Artifacts: lithics including geometric microliths, potsherds, and ancient glass fragments.

*Layer II*
Features: cream gritty deposit, slightly brecciated.
Artifacts: potsherds and lithics including a sickle blade and geometric microliths.

*Layer III* (correlated with burial deposits)
Features: 5-15 cm thick, very soft grey deposit containing stones.
Artifacts: general geometric microliths.

*Layer IV*
Features: 15-20 cm thick, golden brown stony deposit.
Artifacts: lithics including small backed lunates.

*Layer V*
Features: 15 cm thick, brown red deposit with two flat stones on its surface.
Artifacts: lithics including small backed lunates.

*Layer VI* (correlated with Layer III in G-H/10-12)
Location: in bedrock hollows.
Features: loose silty deposit.
Artifacts: general geometric microliths and 1 potsherd.

*Sub-area G-H/10-12* (Figure 1.7.)
*Pit 1*
Features: light brown sandy deposits with a few large stones.
Artifacts: potsherds, ancient glass fragments, and lithics with geometric microliths including small backed lunates.

*Layer I*
Features: light brown sandy deposits with a few large stones.
Artifacts: potsherds, ancient glass fragments and lithics with geometric microliths including small backed lunates.

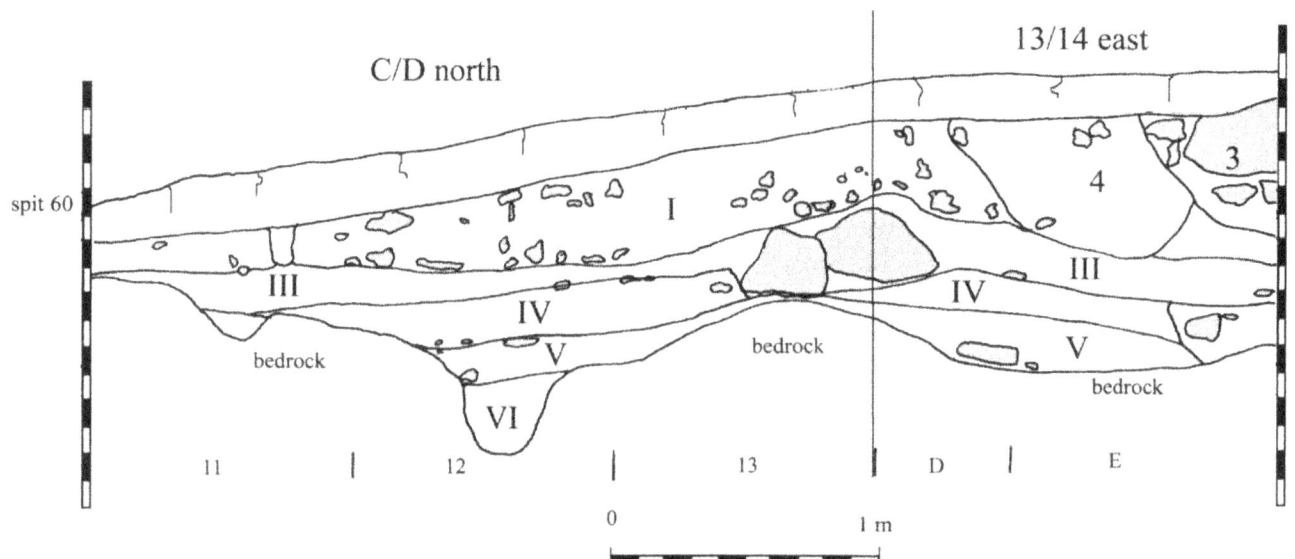

**Figure. 1.6.** *Section of D-E/11-13. Grey shading indicates stones within the deposit (on every figure of stratigraphy).*

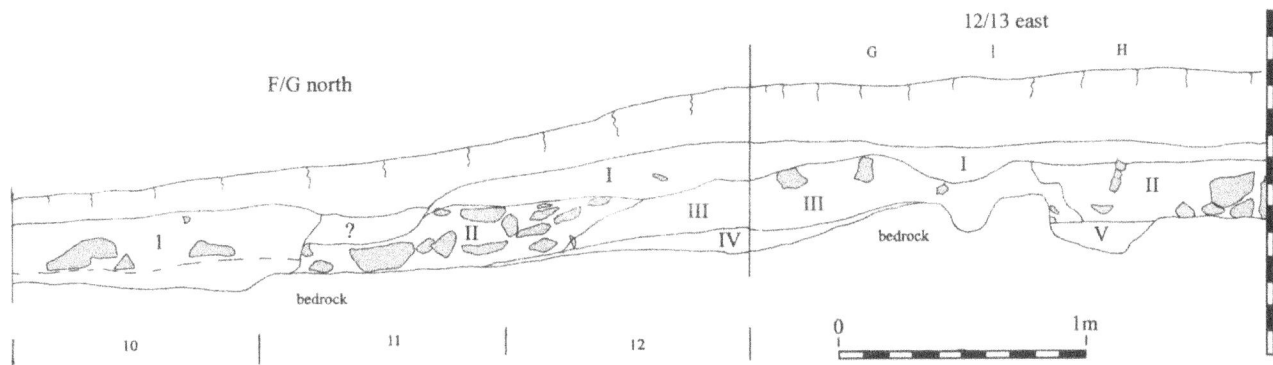

**Figure. 1.7.** *Sections of squares G-H/10-12.*

*Layer II*
Features: 10-20 cm thick, loose very stony fill.
Artifacts: potsherds, fragments of ancient glass, and lithics with geometric microliths including small backed lunates, and a backed sickle blade

*Layer III*
Features: 20-30 cm thick grey sandy deposit with a few stones.
Artifacts: potsherds and microlithic stone tools.

*Layer IV*
Features: 5 cm thick, cream gritty slightly brecciated deposit adjacent to bedrock.
Artifacts: very few potsherds and geometric microliths.

*Layer V*
Location: hollows and cup marks in the bedrock.
Features: unknown.
Artifacts: uncharacteristic stone tools, generally microliths including a few geometrics.

*Burial deposits in B-C/10-12*
    *Grave of Homo 2*
This skeleton was found in squares B-C/10-11 at the north wall of the cave, near the entrance in a basin in yellow deposit. The skeleton was covered with a large number of stones (Figure 1.8.). The deposit did not contain potsherds, the stone tools are small backed lunates and a few sickle blades.

    *Grave of Homo 3*
The feature of the deposit is unknown. The filling contained several potsherds.

Under the skeletons a stone structure was found (Figures 1.9-10.). Under the stone structure a hard red layer covered the bedrock floor. This layer is associated with small backed lunates and basalt implements (Figure 1.11.).

**Figure. 1.8.** *The stone cover of burial H2. North view. Scale 1 m (Raqefet Archives).*

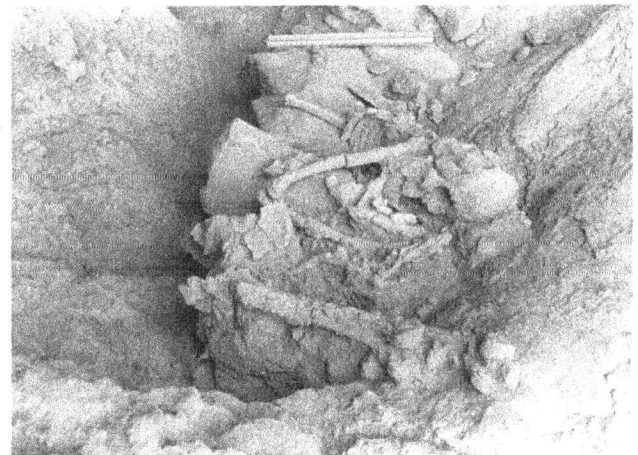

**Figure 1.9.***Homo 2 on stone structure. East view. Scale 30 cm (Raqefet Archives).*

7

**Figure 1.10.** *Homo 3 on stone structure. North view. Scale 30 cm. (Raqefet Archives).*

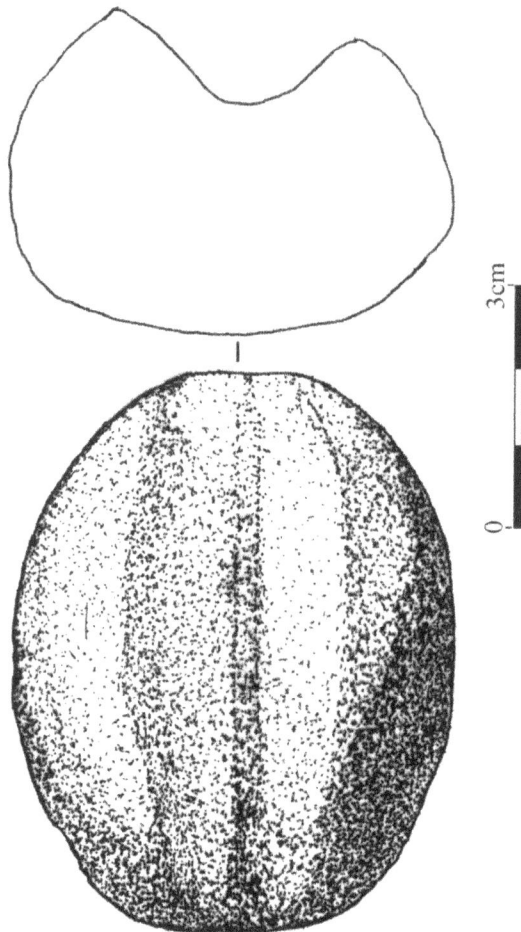

**Figure 1.11.** *Basalt shaft straightener from the grave of Homo 3.*

## Area B-G/18-23

Squares D-E-F-G/18-19 were excavated down to bedrock. Squares C-D/21-23 were partially excavated on account of deep ceramic intrusions.

*Top layer*
Features: silver gray and orange silt, very variable and stony, only a few centimeters thick; at its top it is orange brown clay, between 1-5 cm thick, covering square D21.
Artifact: potsherds, general lithics and a bone point.

*Pit A* (cuts pit E and D)
Extension: C-D/20-23.
Features: loose silver silt, packed with stones.
Artifacts: few flints, and potsherds.

*Pit B*
Extension: D-E/18-19, from the bottom of top layer cut through Pit Ca down to spit 54 in Pit F (Figure 1.13.).
Features: unknown.
Artifacts: a red pottery characteristic to the Neolithic Yarmukian culture, potteries and flints.

*Pit C a-d*
Extension: C-D/18-19, from the base of top layer down to bedrock at spit 64.5 (Figures 1.12, 13, 15.).

*Level a*
Features: red, very loose and sandy.
Artifacts: large amount of potsherds, lithics including microliths, sickle blades, and a few helwan lunates.

*Level b*
Extension: local to E and C18-19
Features: brecciated orange tongue extending into pit.
Artifacts: flints including Kebara points.

*Level c-d*
Features: extremely stony loose bright red grey silt; cuts down to bedrock breccia.
Artifacts: flints, microliths, triangles, axe, and no potteries.

*Pit Da-c*
Extension: C-D/20-23 (Figures 1.14-16.).

*Level a*
Features: brick red silt.
Artifacts: iron, bones and potsherds.

*Level b*
Features: silver grey loose silt.
Artifacts: lithics including many small backed lunates, backed and truncated microliths, and a dentalium bead.

*Level c*
Features: stony brown grey silt.
Artifacts: flints including a sickle blade.

*Pit Ea-c*
Extension: large covering much of C-D/21-23.

8

*Level a*
Features: yellow orange loose silt.
Artifacts: few flints and potsherds.

*Level b*
Features: grey fine, stony silt.
Artifacts: potsherds and a few stone tools.

*Level c*
Features: grey orange loose silt.
Artifacts: few flints and potteries.

*Pit F*
Extension: E-F/18-19, from spit 53 down to 56.
Features: it is a sandy red fill.
Artifacts: few potsherds, dentalium beads, and flints including a Helwan lunate, backed sickle blade and bladelets, Kebaran points, small backed lunate, trapeze-rectangles, and a microburin.

*Pit Ga-e.*
It is unusual in having perfectly vertical sides, it is

probable that it was lined, although no evidence of the lining has been found. It was cut into the bedrock breccia.
Extension: E-F/18-19 from spit 56 down to bedrock at spit 66.

*Level a*
Features: yellow brown gritty soil with ash laminae.
Artifacts: flints including a helwan lunate, a microburin, and microliths.

*Level b*
Features: laminated ash and silt.
Artifacts: few flints.

*Level c*
Features: ash and charcoal with yellow grit lenses.
Artifacts: few flints.

*Level d-e*
Features: ash and charcoal laminae with grit.
Artifacts: uncharacteristic stone tools and a bronze fibula.

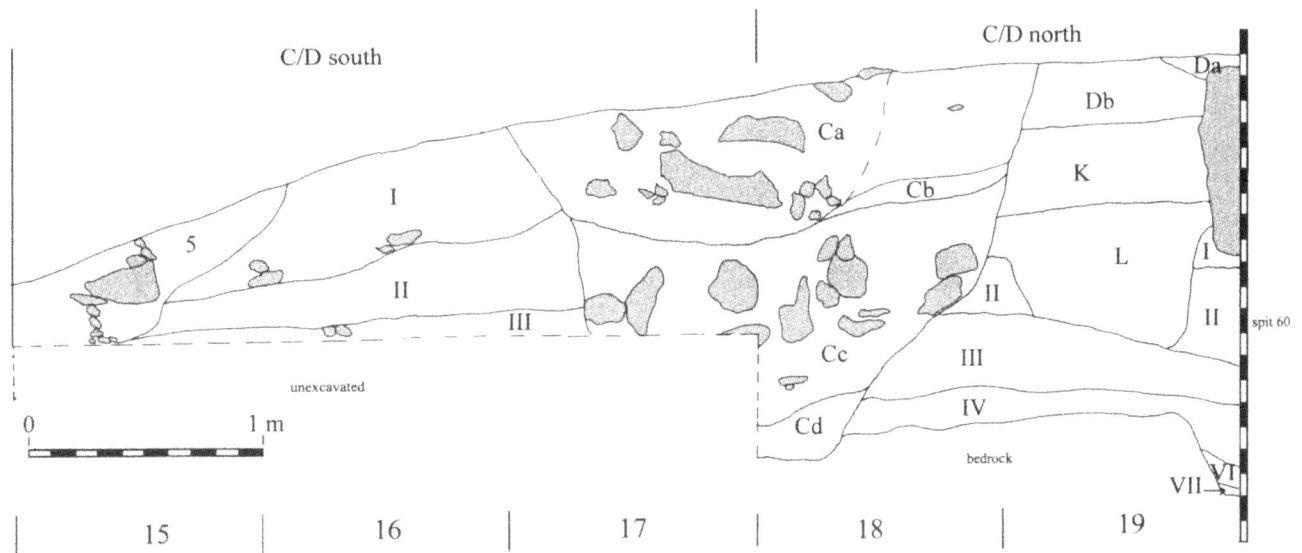

*Figure 1.12. Section of C/D 15-19. Note that the deposit numbers in squares 15-17 correspond with area A-H/7-17 deposits.*

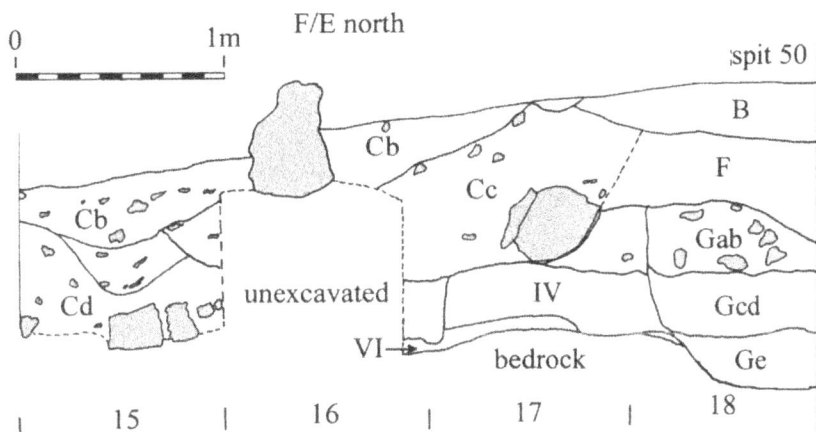

*Figure 1.13. Section of F/E north in squares 15-18.*

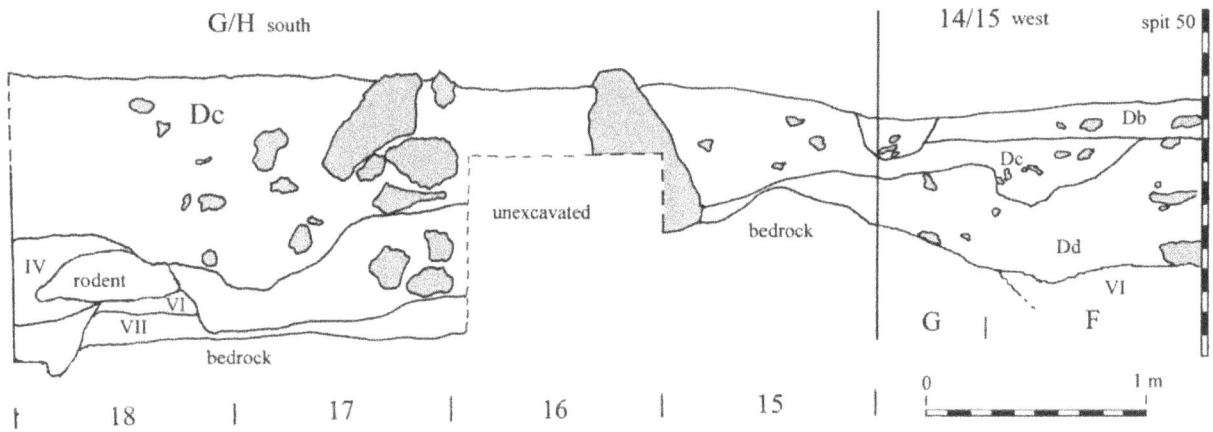

**Figure 1.14.** *Sections of squares F-G/15-18.*

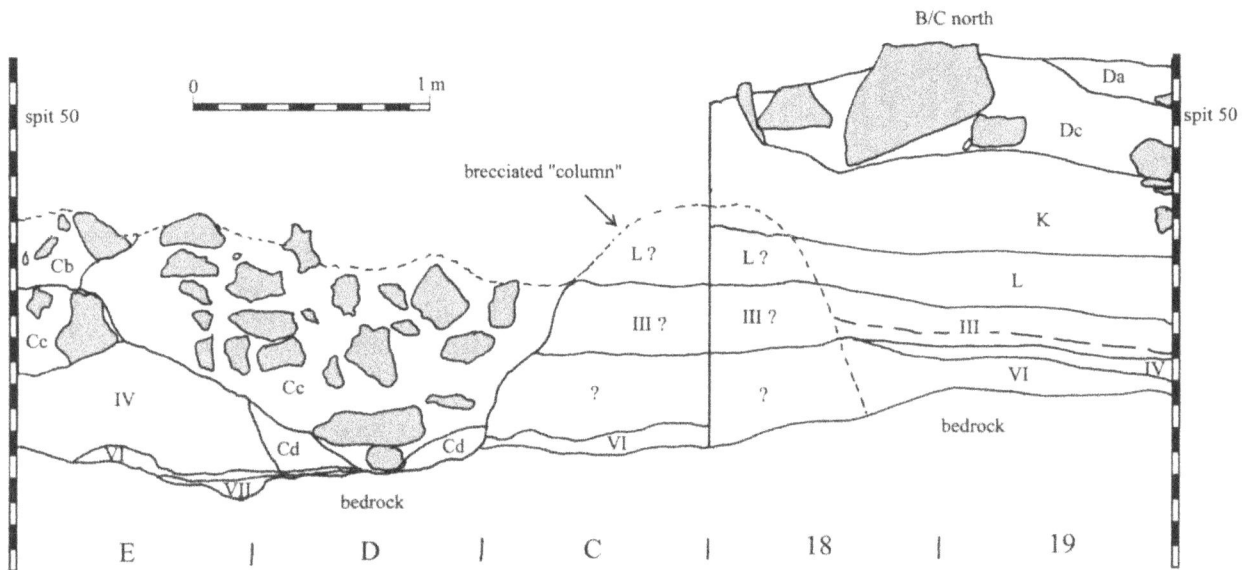

**Figure 1.15.** *Section in squares C-E/18-19.*

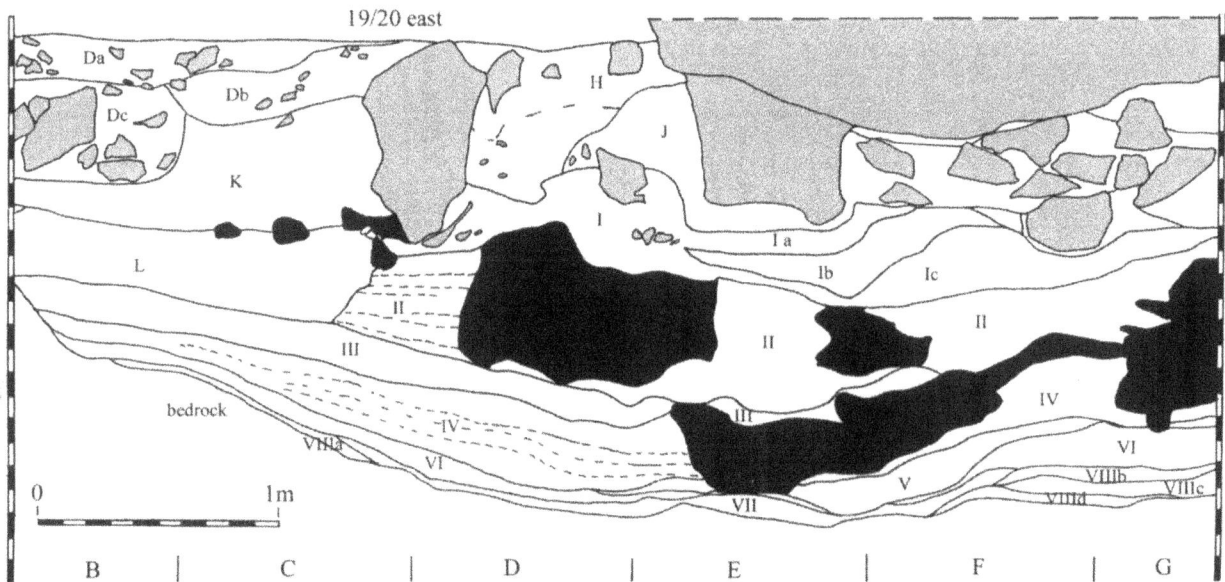

**Figure 1.16.** *Section of squares B-G/19 east. (Black shaded parts indicate animal burrows).*

## Pits H and J

These pits were not separated during excavation as the distinction between the two extremely unclear. In section a line can be discerned separating the two deposits. Both intrusions have extremely variables fills and the animal burrows pierce the lower part of H. These pits are earlier than Pit G.

Extension: C19, C-D/20-22, from the bottom of top layer down to spit 52.

### Pit H

Features: heavily brecciated.
Artifacts: flints including an el-Khiam point (Figure 1.17.).

### Pit J

Its relationship to K is unknown but earlier than H.
Features: red brown filled, flecked charcoal and ochre with a few stones bigger than 20 cm.
Artifacts: flints including microliths, rectangle, obliquely truncated backed bladelet, many small backed lunates, el-Khiam point, sickle blades, and dentalium beads.

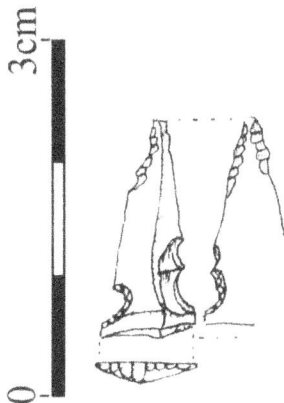

**Figure 1.17.** *El-khiam point of Pit J in area B-G/18-23. (drawing of Raqefet Archives).*

## Pit K

Extension: B-C-D/19-21 from spit 54 down to spit 56 and in C20 it cuts layer VI (Figure 1.18.).
Features: brown grey silt, and very similar in color and texture to pit L and probably contains material derived from that earlier fill.
Artifacts: uncharacteristic flint artifacts.

## Pit L

Extension: forms a gully at least 2x1.5 metre in area, along the north wall of the cave. It cuts through layers I and II. B-C-D/19-21 from spit 55 down to spit 59 (Figure 1.16.).
Features: contains a grey brown fill with fine ash lenses including charcoals. Slightly laminated and brecciated with local burnt areas. In C18-19 red and grey lamination appeared. Two large stones possibly contemporary with pit L have been sunk vertically into small pits cut into the surface of layer I.

Artifacts: large number of Levantine Aurignacian material since cut through layer II. In addition, bronze or cooper fragment, trapeze, backed and truncated bladelets, small backed lunate, sickle blades with backing, helwan lunates, 1 bone point, Kebara point are also found among the lithics.

## Layer Ia-c

Extension: C-E/18-19 (Figure 1.16.).
Features: 20-50 cm thick relatively hard unlaminated clayey loam that was subdivided into the upper sub-layer Ia of grayish hue, the middle sub-layer Ib of darker gray and the lower sub-layer Ic of brownish gray color. The layer contains scattered lenses 5-7 cm thick and up to 30 cm wide, of soft to hard yellow nodules possibly composed of phosphates, and few pieces of ochre. Occasionally, sinuous laminae are present with a dip of *ca* 10° north. The lower boundary is gradual. Charcoal is abundant.
Artifacts: flints of a Kebaran industry with obliquely truncated backed bladelets.

## Layer II

Extension: C-G/18-20 (Figure 1.16, 1.18.).
Features: 40-90 cm thick a grey-yellow brecciated deposit with charcoal flecks and some grit lenses divided by thirteen to fifteen 1-3 mm thick dark ash laminations in C-D/19-20. Only four of these could be traced for more than 10-20 cm horizontally and those were used as marker bands in sub-layer separation. The bands here are dipping at approximately go to South-East, South. Much of the horizon in C-D/19-20 has been lost a consequence of animal burrowing and a cutting Pit J. The contents of the large animal burrows that cut extensively into this level were easily separated, on account of color and textural differences.
Artifacts: the upper part of the layer contains an industry that has no characteristic elements of any Palaeolithic cultures, as it consists of an unidentified blade industry. The lower part in C-E/18-20 contains stone tools characteristic to Levantine Aurignacian.

## Disturbances in Layers II and III

These deposits were totally removed during the excavation, and they have no markers in the section. Their description follows the excavators' observations.
Extension: C-D/19-18.

### D1

Its sediment was distinct from the charcoal laminated deposit, although it was grey slightly brecciated with laminations as well. It was equivalent to the base of Layer II and the surface of Layer III.

### D2

It was dominantly dark grey, at its base yellow. It was almost certainly equivalent to layer II, its base was probably equivalent to the surface of layer III.
D3 lies between pits D, F, J and Layer I, its sediment is similar to D2.

*Layer III*

Extension: B-C-D-E/18-20 (Figure 1.16, 1.18.).

Features: 10-20 cm thick, heavily brecciated silver/grey deposit containing fine sand laminations and split by two darkish bands in C-D/19-20. It contains charcoal flecks. On the top surface of this deposit in C-D/18-20 are a large number of artifacts. At the base of the layer in B-C/18-20 was a red deposit varying in thickness from 1-5 cm (IIIa). In F-G/19 it is not possible to trace the layer. In C18 there was a heavily brecciated column containing abundant bone material; its upper part contains material from the pit (L) situating above and this layer.

Artifacts: flints of Levantine Aurignacian.

*Layer IV*

Extension: The entire area except square G (Figure 1.16, 1.18.).

Features: in F it is reworked by a huge burrow, in-filled with relatively soft unlaminated loam. The layer is 20-40 cm thick light-grayish laminated gley with scattered charcoal and a discontinuous charcoal strip less than 1 cm thick at its lower boundary. Charcoal is abundant especially in the dark bands of lamination. In B19 the lamination disappears. Flint artifacts are distributed scattered in the layer. The equivalent of layer IV in square C18 (by the cave wall) was a deposit heavily cemented with calcite.

Artifacts: flint tools including fine blades and bladelets in the middle of the layer, and a few intrusive Aurignacian elements on the top of the layer and eroded Mousterian items close to the bottom.

*Layer V*

Extension: E-F-G 19 (Figure 1.16.).

Features: 10-20 cm thick deposit, the upper surface defined by narrow (½cm) ash line that runs uninterrupted over its entire surface (3 meters). It is red brown homogenous silt.

Artifacts: few flints, 56.8% of the material is abraded (Sarel 2002, 2004).

*Layer VI*

Extension: the entire area (Figure 1.16, 1.18.).

Features: heavily brecciated light grey silt containing laminae of grit 5-10 cm thick in B-D, 1 cm in E and 15 cm in F-G. It likewise contains lenses of partially abraded artifacts at its base, but the majority of flint implements are fresh. Layer VI sits directly over layer VII, but in places making contact with bedrock where the latter is higher. Its upper surface was sculptured by meandering runnels, which might have resulted from water scouring or animal burrowing.

Artifacts: levallois flakes, flakes, blades and an Emireh point (Higgs *et al* 1975) (Figure 1.19.). A total of 51% of flint implements are abraded (Sarel 2002, 2004).

*Layer VII*

Extension: the entire area (Figure 1.16, 1.18.).

Features: 5-10 cm thick deposit. It consists almost entirely of flint artifacts with only a very sparse matrix of fine silver grey-yellow brecciated silt or clay. Linear orientation of artifacts in E-W direction in E 19 along the channel bed was observed. The deposit lies deepest in the cavities of the underlying bedrock especially in D-E/19 and D20. Deposit thickest in hollows of underlying bedrock absent at points where bedrock is rising. Layer VII partially covered layer VIII in squares C and F.

Artifacts: flints of levallois flakes, flakes, blades, 19.8% of the material is fresh, the rest is eroded (Figure 1.19.) (Sarel 2002, 2004).

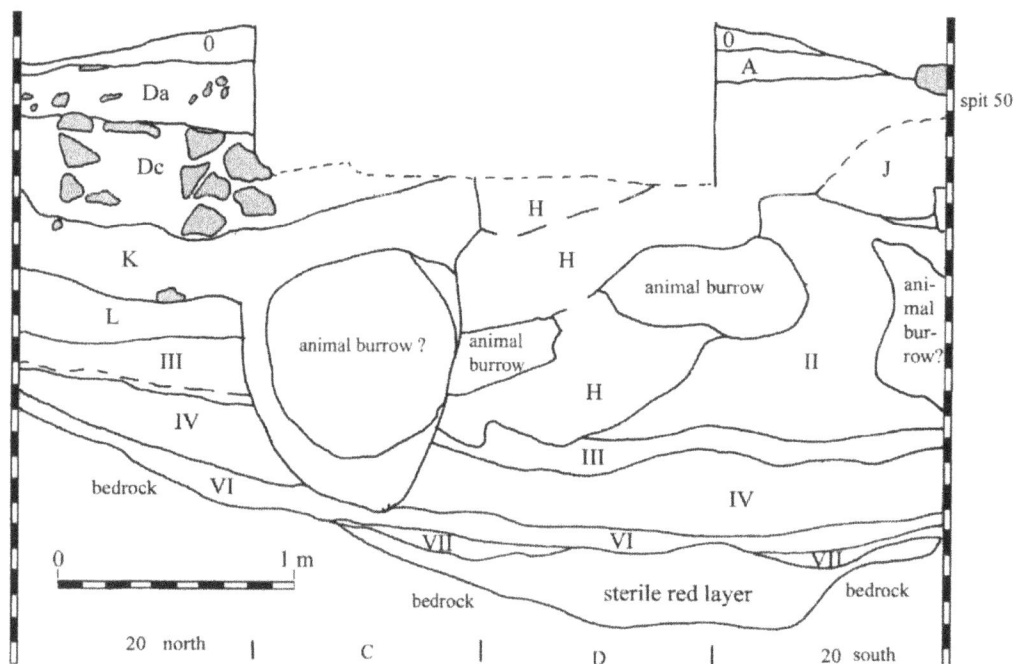

**Figure 1.18.** Section of squares C-D/20.

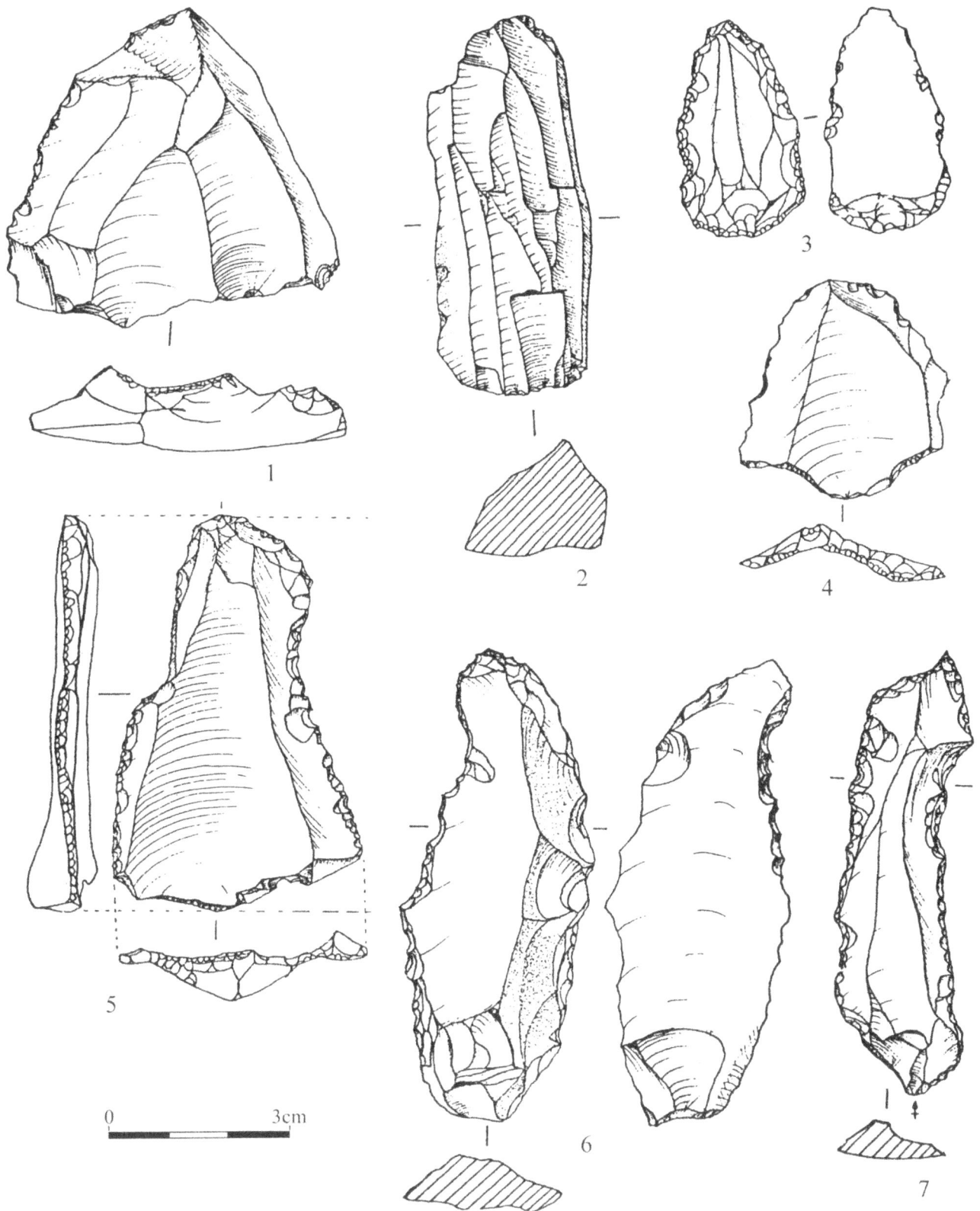

**Figure 1.19.** *Flint artifacts from the Late Mousterian or Middle to Upper Palaeolithic Transition layers, VIII-VI. Layer VI: 1, Levallois core; 2 prismatic, bipolar blade core; 3, Emireh point. LayerVII-VIII: 4, Levallois flake; 5, retouched Levallois flake; 6 denticulated blade; 7, retouched blade (modified after Higgs et al 1975).*

*Layer VIIIa-d*
Extension: the entire area except square G.
Features: earliest deposit with evidence of human occupation was a 5 cm thick highly breciated skin covering the bedrock in B-D/18-19 and C-D/20-21 (layer VIII a) and F-G/19 (layer VIII b-d). Layer VIIIa was very thin in C20, and only partially excavated as covered in firm. It cut by pit D in D18 and in D-F/18-19 pit F cut breccia respectively. Layer VIII b was light grey breccia, layer VIII c was dark grey breccia and layer VIII d was yellow breccia. All of them were thin not exceeding 5 cm.
Artifacts: flints of levallois flakes, flakes, blades, 17.3% of the material is fresh (Figure 1.19.) (Sarel 2002, 2004).

*Bedrock features*
The bedrock was very soft yellow-colored. It was covered in C-D-E/19-20 with a 5-15 cm thick sterile red silty layer, which is probably the weathered bedrock, but its exact origin is obscure.

## *Area J-M/24-28* (Figure 1.22.)
Squares J-M/25-26 were excavated down to the surface of layer XIII at a depth of 3.70m, squares K-L/27-28 down to layer VII at a depth of 1.50m and J-K/24-25 only superficial ceramic deposits were removed. The bedrock was not reached in any of the squares.

*Pit A*
Extension: J 26.
Features: thick light grey clay, contains large flat stones.
Artifacts: flints and potsherds.

*Pit B*
Extension: J/25-26.
Features: pit of ash and clay and fire-burnt deposit.
Artifacts: flints and potsherds.

*Pit C*
Extension: K 28.
Features: unknown.

*Layer Ia-d*
Extension: J-K/24-26.
Features: 40 cm thick grey orange gritty clay deposit, which is becoming less clayey in level c and level d. In level c hearth remains were found, here the deposit lighter and looser and sandier.
Artifacts: flints and a large amount of potsherds.

*Layer IIa-b*
Extension: J-K/24-26.

*Layer IIa*
Features: 15-25 cm thick, a series of ash and hardened bands, and hearths were found between stony bands.

Artifacts: potsherds and flints including Neolithic axes.
*Layer IIb*
Features: 15-30 cm thick red, at some places brown loose soil full of exceptionally large stones down cutting in L-M/25-26. At its SW corner it is sandy.
Artifacts: potsherds and flints.

*Pit Da-e*
Extension: J-K/25-26.

*Level a-b*
Features: loose red speckled with decayed limestone.
Artifacts: potsherds and flints including a Jericho point (Figure 1.20.) and an axe (Figure 1.21.).

*Level c*
Features: red grit with charcoal flecks.
Artifacts: potsherds and flints.

*Level d*
Features: loose red soil.
Artifacts: potsherds and flints.

*Level e*
Features: base of pit.
Artifacts: many potsherds including painted Neolithic ware and lithics.

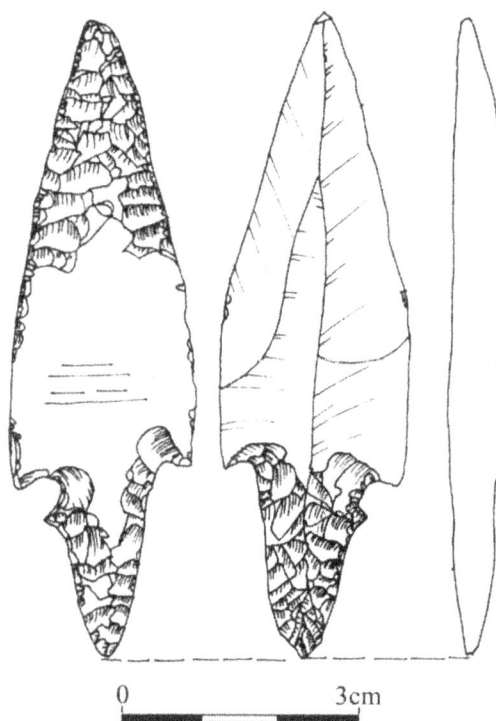

**Figure 1.20.** *A Jericho point of Pit Da-e in Area J-M/24-28 (drawing of Raqefet Archives).*

*Pits E, F, G*
Extension: a complex of large intrusions in K-L/27-28 which is stratigraphically later than Layer III and earlier than Layer II.

*Pit E*
Features: red brown silt with few stones, circular pit cutting from base Layer II.
Artifacts: potshards and flints.

*Pit F*
Features: red extremely hard clay.
Artifacts: glasses, potsherds, flints including a flint "leaf point".

*Pit G*
Features: very loose fill, full of large stones which are randomly thrown in.
Artifacts: potsherds, flints and a cooper bead.

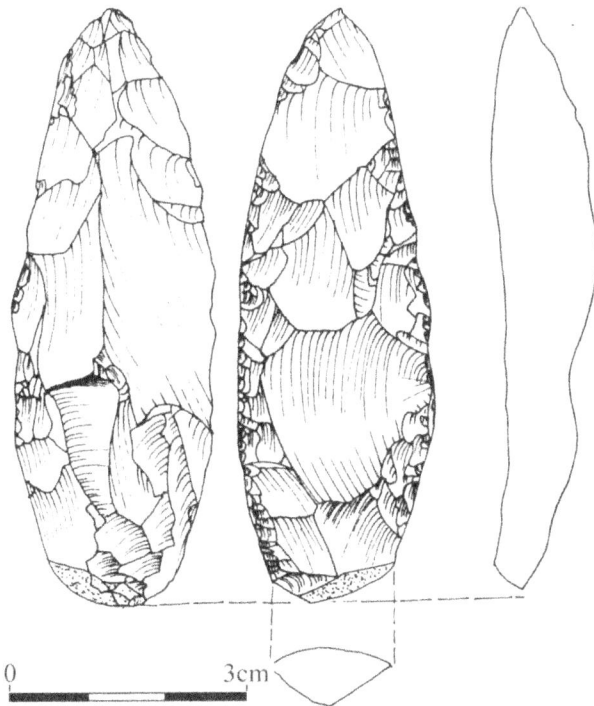

**Figure 1.21.** *Neolithic axe of Pit Da-e in Area J-M/24-28 (drawing of Raqefet Archives).*

*Layer III*
Extension: J-K/24-26.
Features: 10-20 cm thick light brown clay fairly stony, at some parts it is red.
Artifacts: potsherds and flints.

*Layer IV*
Extension: J-M/25-28.
Features: 20 cm thick dark brown loose silt with local clayey areas; thick clay band extending locally from east end.

Artifacts: potsherds and flints including axes.

*Layer V*
Extension: J-K/25-28.
Features: 20 cm thick hard compact encrusted; clayey silt and grit, brown-yellow > red-brown deposit.
Artifacts: few potsherds found in J-M/26-24, and flints including a Kebara point, trapeze-rectangles, sickle blades, and an axe.

*Layer VI*
Extension: J-M/25-28.
Features: 25-30 cm thick deposit, its top was dark slightly gritty deposit very hard brecciated. In the middle it became looser dark brown, downer became yellowish brown crumbly and small hearths and ashy patches appeared. At the base was a black ashy hearth deposit – limited to south end of L-M/26.
Artifacts: a basalt mortar, flints including backed lunates, trapezes, obliquely truncated backed bladelets, microburins, curved backed items, an axe, and a sickle blade. A very few potsherds were found in J-M/24-26.

*Layer VII*
Extension: J-M/24-28
Features: 20-30 cm thick light brown clayey silt deposit with local breccia. At its base it becomes dark grey with a series of hearth deposits in L-M/28-27. These are concentrated around a series of large stones intrusive from Pit E situating beneath Layer VII.
Artifacts: flints including geometric microliths, and 2 potsherds with a few dozens abraded Levallois artifacts in J-M/24-26. On some of the artifacts travertine coating is found.

*Pit H*
Extension: J-M/25-26.
Features: brown and black with ash concentrations at base becoming lighter and sandier above.
Artifacts: flints including obliquely truncated backed bladelets, trapeze rectangles, a lunate, trapeze, and a piece of potsherd.

*Layer VIII*
Extension: J-M/25-28.
This deposit was mixed in excavation with neighboring base Pit De.
Features: 40-45 cm thick loose, light very stony soil with small hearth areas.
Artifacts: potsherds and flints including backed lunates and backed bladelets, few obliquely truncated bladelets, a sickle blade, lunates and a Helwan lunate.

*Layer IX*
Extension: J-M/25-26.
Features: 5-15 cm thick deposit; the upper part is a dark grey layer very gritty, the lower is red stony deposit containing "rotten limestone" fragments and slightly brecciated.

15

Artifacts: flints including backed bladelets.

*Pit J*
Extension: J-M/25-26.
Features: at is upper part it is brown black loose silt which is becoming clayey at surface. At its lower part it is crisp light brown soil.
Artifacts: flints including Levantine Aurignacian endscrapers.

*Layer X*
Extension: J-M/25-26.
Features: 40-45 cm thick semi brecciated dark grey gritty deposit flecked, laminated with charcoal and ash and yellow nodular material.
Artifacts: flints including Levantine Aurignacian endscrapers and eroded Levallois implements.

*Pit K*
Extension: J-M/25-26.
Features: generally red grey colored; at the top it was heavily brecciated dark soil with grit laminae, flecked locally with gritty brown silt, in the middle it becomes reddish grey brecciated soil.

Artifacts: the lowest level contained abraded flint implements of Mousterian and blades.

*Layer XI*
Extension: J-M/25-26.
Features: 30-40 cm thick deposit; at the surface of this deposit was an extremely tough firmly brecciated crust of fine silt/clay. Lower down, gradually softer, it became less brecciated but at the same time more clayey and there was a steady gradation into layer XII.

*Layer XII*
Extension: J-M/25-26.
Features: 40-45 cm thick grey clay flecked with charcoal and banded with dark ashy lines and charcoal.
Artifacts: heavily eroded Levallois items.

*Layer XIII*
As mentioned earlier the excavation stopped at the very distinct upper brecciated surface at the depth of spit 71. The deposit has an extremely hard brecciated surface of light grey clay with grit laminae.

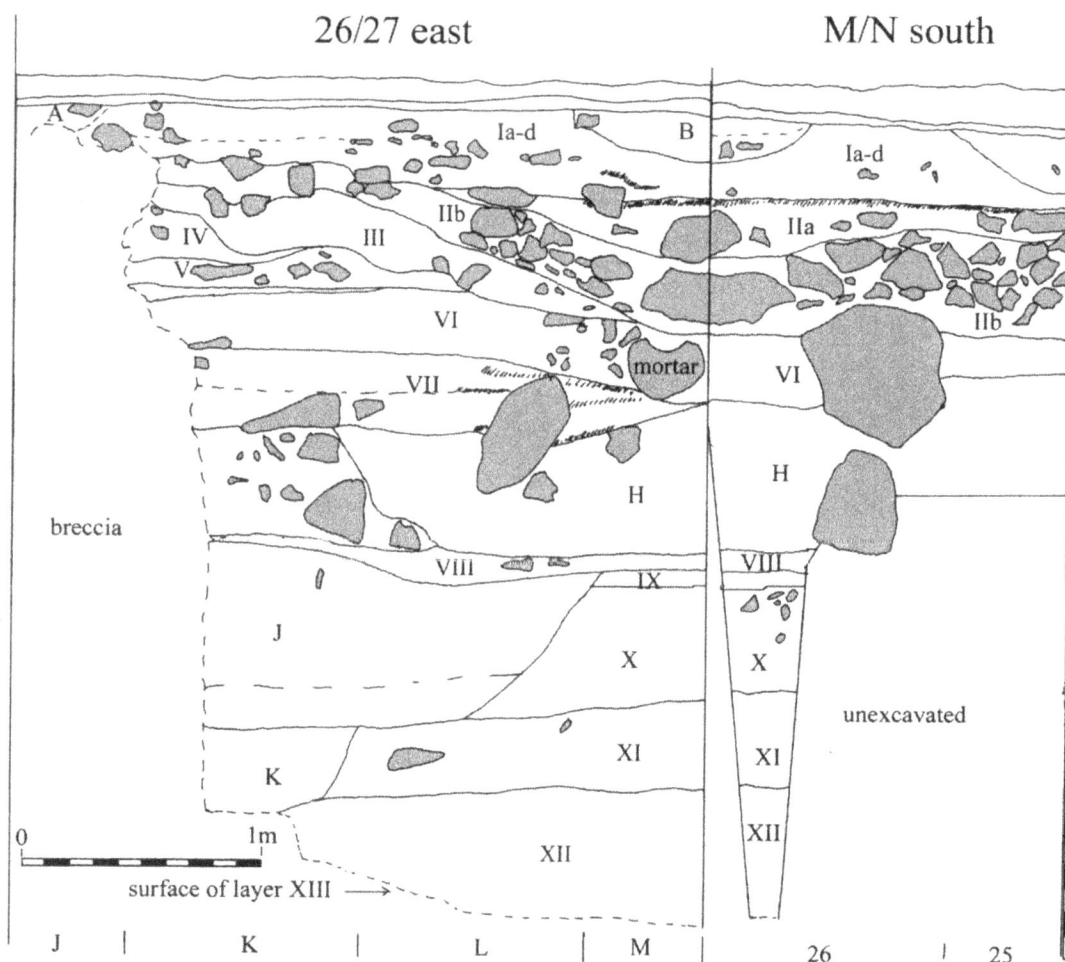

**Figure 1.22.** *Section of squares J-M/25-26.*

## Radiocarbon dating of layers in Raqefet

The layers of the cave were dated after the 1970-1972 excavations. Recently in 2004 from samples collected by the excavators in 1970-1972 new dates have been obtained. The 1970-1972 dates were made on charcoals and bones with decay counting method, while all 2004 dates are on charcoals obtained by AMS.

### *The conventional dates (after Raqefet Archives)*
*Area B-G/18-23*
  *Pit L*
Sample: bone from square C20.
Date: 10,980±260 uncal. BP. (I-7032) – δC¹⁴: 745±8.
Comments: the larger than normal statistical uncertainty was due to the low collagen content of the sample.

*Layer II Upper part*
Sample 1: charcoals from squares C-D/20.
Date: 18,910±330 uncal BP (I-6865), – δC¹⁴: 905±4.
Comments: the sample could not have been treated for the removal of humic acids.

Sample 2: charcoals from squares C-D/20.
Date: 15,460±200 uncal BP (I-7031), – δC¹⁴: 854±4.
Comments: the pretreatment for removal of humic acid for the sample was shortened because of its solubility in NaOH solution.
Note: I-6865 was published elsewhere as belonging to the Kebaran layer of the site (Noy *et al* 1973: 96).

*Layer III*
Sample 1: charcoals from squares C-D/20.
Date: 33,810±1740 uncal BP years (I-6866), – δC¹⁴: 985±3.
Comments: The sample received complete treatment for removal of humic acids.

*Layer IV*
Sample 1: Charcoals from square D/20 west, east and C-D/20, bottom of the layer.
Date: 33,810±1740 uncal BP (I-6867), – δC¹⁴: 985±3.
Comments: The sample received complete treatment for removal of humic acids.

*Layer VI*
Sample: charcoals from square C20, D20 west and east.
Date: 26,060±840 uncal BP years, - δC¹⁴: 961 ± 4.
Comments: The sample received abbreviated pretreatments because of its solubility in NaOH solution.

*Layer VII*
Sample: charcoals from D/20 west and east.
Date: 34,600±1900 uncal BP, - δC¹⁴: 987 ±3.
Comments: The sample received abbreviated pretreatments because of its solubility in NaOH solution.

*Area J-M/24-28*
Sample: charcoals from square K28's Layer IV, VI, and VII.
Date: 10,580±140 uncal BP (I-7030) – δC¹⁴: 732±5.
Comments: The sample received a complete pretreatment for removal of humic acids.

The dates of 15,460±200 BP and 18,910±330 BP are not in accordance with the archaeo-stratigraphic position, because they derive from layer II upper part which is associated with a non-Epipalaeolithic industry. The amount of charcoal in this layer is small. The sample of dating was collected from scattered spots instead of closely enclosed group of charcoals (Raqefet Archive). Probably, many of them penetrated from the Late Kebaran layer situating above.

The dates of the two Upper Palaeolithic layers (I-6866 and I-6867) are identical. This may be due to vertical movement of charred remains. These dates should be used with high degree of caution.

The dates of 26,060±840 BP and 34,600±1900 BP from layers VI and VII beneath the Upper Palaeolithic are extremely late in terms of association with Mousterian artifacts. Since both layers contain a large number of eroded flint artifacts (especially in layer VII) which is the result of postdepositional disturbances of origin of flow, the charcoal samples obviously could have not been contemporaneous with the flint tools.

The date of area J-M/24-28 stem from charcoal samples of several layers. This date has unclear archaeological context.

### *The AMS dating* (Lengyel *et al* 2006)
The samples of AMS dating are wood charcoals. They originate from layer III and IV. The charcoals were collected by Eric Higgs and Tamar Noy during the 1970-1972 excavations and stored at the University of Cambridge, Department of Archaeology. The charcoal samples have been kept in tightly closed nylon bags. The charcoals are in a good state of preservation; some of the pieces are 1-2 cm large. The weight of the collected samples ranged between 0.6 and 22 grams. Each sample consisted of several species of wood, among which *Amygdalus sp. af A. korchinsky* was the most common (identification by L. Fabre).

From each sample a single piece of *Amygdalus* was used for dating. The samples were submitted to the Radiocarbon Laboratory of the Weizmann Institute of Science in Israel and were all measured by Accelerator Mass Spectrometry. Samples were pre-treated using the Acid, Base, Acid protocol in order to remove the environmental contaminants and obtain pure charcoal for dating (Alon *et al.* 2002; Yizhaq *et al.* 2005). The pure charcoal content of the samples ranged between 60-80%, which is characteristic of well-preserved charcoal. All calculated ¹⁴C ages have been corrected for the fractionation so as to refer the results to be equivalent with the standard δ¹³C value of -25‰ (wood).

*Table 1.1: AMS $^{14}$C dates of layer III and IV.*

| Sample | square | layer | level | $^{14}$C Age ± 1σ year BP AMS | Lab No | δ$^{13}$C‰ |
|--------|--------|-------|-------|-------------------------------|--------|-------------|
| 1 | B19 | III | bottom | 30,540±440 | (RTT4945) | -24.2 |
| 2 | CD20 | IV | 1 | 30,610±400 | (RTT4940) | -24,8 |
| 3 | CD20 | IV | 2 | 31,800±470 | (RTT4944) | -24,3 |
| 4 | C20 | IV | 2 | 31,340±480 | (RTT4942) | -24,3 |
| 5 | E19 | IV | 3 | 32,100±450 | (RTT4941) | -24,5 |
| 6 | C20 east | IV | 4 | 31,070±430 | (RTT4939) | -24,5 |
| 7 | E19 | IV | 4 | 32,560±520 | (RTT4938) | -25,3 |
| 8 | C20 west | IV | 5 | 31,920±480 | (RTT4943) | -25,2 |
| 9 | D20 west | IV | 5 | 33,040±550 | (RTT4937) | -24,6 |

All the dates obtained for layer IV are all very close and most likely represent the same event (Table 1.1.). Although there is a great agreement between the stratigraphy and the sequence of radiocarbon dates, two dates from the lower levels, 31070 ± 430 (RTT-4939) from level 4 and 31920 ± 480 (RTT-4943) from level 5, are slightly younger than expected. This might be due to downward movement of charcoal pieces from the upper levels. Also some sample contamination, especially in square C/20, from the post-Natufian pit K cutting through layers III and IV in square C/20 cannot be excluded.

## Site formation processes at Raqefet

In order to identify the depositional and post-depositional processes contributed to the site formation of Raqefet, detailed laboratory studies, including mineralogical and micro-morphological analyses, are yet to be performed. However, some basic ascertainment based on the visible features of the sedimentary structures of the cave strata may be made.

In the entire cave stratum the agency of sedimentation is best recognized from area B-G/18-23. Here, laminated deposits constitute the largest part of the stratigraphy, which reflect slight changes in the depositional environment or pulsation in the velocity of the transport agent. Their origin is believed to stem from water penetration associated with either particular events or seasons, subtle changes in grain size that retard downward movement of water, or flocculation of clay under particular subsurface conditions (Stein 1987). Laminations in deposits in other Levantine caves are already well known from Hayonim and especially from Kebara (Goldberg and Bar-Yosef 1998; Goldberg and Laville 1988, 1991).

The low velocity water activity in the cave indicated by laminations in strata starts at layer IV and ends up at the top of layer II. The lower part, layer IV, is composed of a very gleyey material with scattered charcoal and a discontinuous charcoal strip less than 1 cm thick at its lower boundary. Charcoal is abundant especially in the dark bands of lamination. The upper part of the laminated deposit, layer III and II, is more clayey but loamy. The lamination at the base of this upper part is more uniform

than at the top. It contains thick, 1-2 cm, regular sinuous laminae dipping northward. From the middle of the laminated deposit, starting about at the top of layer III, the deposit becomes brecciated and remains very solid up to the top of layer II.

The low energy runoff did not abrade the artifacts, the erosion effect must have been weak, although through the whole deposit the *in situ* anthropogenic structures, such as hearths, have been distorted. The water stopped being the main agency of sedimentation by the time of the Epipalaeolithic, as it is indicated by the limited lamination feature of layer I containing Late Kebaran material. However, the water appeared temporally with no or low velocity as is evidenced by the presence of travertine coating on some Geometric Kebaran artifacts in area J-M/24-28 layer VII.

### Anthropogenic disturbances

Most of the excavated sediments in Raqefet exhibit anthropogenic postdepositional disturbances. These frequently occur as pits in the strata. Their fillings are usually loose and structurally uniform, containing archaeological remains of several periods. These are with high frequency in areas A-H/7-17and J-M/24-28.

In area A-H/7-17 the stratum was originally thin, therefore the disturbances often reached the bedrock floor. At this part of the cave the first evidences for anthropogenic disturbances are from the Natufian period, when entire deposits were removed in order to reach the bedrock to cut cup marks and mortars into the cave floor near the cave entrance (Lengyel *et al* 2005). The removed deposits were mostly of Late Kebaran and Geometric Kebaran, as evidenced by the high frequency of their typologically significant stone tools in backfill sediments. Some parts of cave floor were re-filled with Late Natufian material (CI, CII and CXXIII bedrock mortars), probably parallel with the formation of layers IV-VI in D-E/7-13. The layer formation was a fast embedding process, since the deposits are structurally uniform, and the bones show low rate of weathering (in layer IV of squares D-E/7-13 2 bones out of 11 were recorded beyond Behrensmeyer stage 2 [taphonomic observations of G. Bar-Oz ]). Then, burial pits were dug through these layers down to the bedrock. These deposits were also intensively disturbed beginning from the Pottery Neolithic up to date.

In J-M/24-28 most disturbances are anthropogenic. These go through the entire section, leaving only some parts of the deposits intact. The earliest pit in cave, Pit K, was probably cut during the Upper Palaeolithic deep into eroded Middle Palaeolithic layers. A later pit, Pit J, contains no eroded Levallois artifacts but a few items characteristic to the Aurignacian.

Pits of anthropogenic origin were not always filled up rapidly, resulting uniform filling. For instance, in area B-G/18-23, Pit G exhibits five members, all of which are featured by lamination consisting of charcoal, ash and silt. This pit might have been open for relatively long time and its filling up took place gradually with human made fire residues and pit wall collapsing.

## Biogenic disturbances

Biogenic disturbances are easily recognizable in regularly ordered strata. They are usually caused by burrowing animals. These features are well visible in the laminated strata of area B-G/18-23. Taphonomical observations on bones also show rodent gnaw marks (by G. Bar-Oz).

Other biogenic disturbances are connected to plant root penetrating into the deposits. Extensive and obvious root etching on bones was observed from layer IV of D-E/7-13 in the first chamber near the entrance (8% of 65 examined bones) (by G. Bar-Oz). In addition, during 2004 field work direct evidences of plant root disturbances were found in F/9-13 deposit.

## Geogenic disturbances

The most common natural disturbance in cave sediments is caused by water. This phenomenon was recognized in Levantine caves (Bar-Yosef and Vandermeersch 1972).

The earliest deposits in Raqefet are layers VIII, VII and VI in B-G/18-23, which contain Mousterian industry with a small amount of blade elements (Sarel 2002, 2004). The two lower layers (VIII and VII) consist of artifacts deposited in linear E-W orientation. The artifacts are highly abraded. Sharp edges or ridges can be found only in exceptional cases (Figure 1.23.). The number of fresh material is low in layers VIII and VII (17.3% and 19.8% of the material, respectively). In layer VI the fresh material accounts for 47.5% (Sarel 2002, 2004). These suggest that the original deposit was washed away by water, and the artifacts were accumulated and spread on the bottom of the cave. In this area the cave floor rises up steeply, which was the reason for strong artifact accumulation at this part. Consequently, the sedimentation in the cave stopped shortly after the Mousterian by strong water erosion, and, as is displayed through the increasing fresh material at the expense of

abraded material, the karstic activity decreased and the deposit formation started again.

***Figure 1.23.*** *Heavily abraded Mousterian artifacts. Scale 5 cm.*

## Diagenetic transformations

The distribution of bat guano in caves correlates well with the presence or absence of bones in the sediment, and they are one of the main agencies of diagenetic transformations of organic materials (Shahack-Gross *et al* 2004).

From layer III through layer I of area B-G/18-23 at Raqefet, yellow, phosphate-rich stripes and nodules increasingly towards up continuously appear. They are in the largest amount in the upper part of Layer II. The bone preservation is extremely poor in the laminated strata. These may illustrate that chemical alterations were also responsible for site formation processes, possibly due to acid penetration into the deposit from bat guano that is still present in the cave in large quantity.

## Breccia formation

A very hard breccia was found in the entrance of the cave, which bears Mousterian implements and those of typical to the Epipalaeolithic.

The top of layer III in B-G/18-23 is also heavily brecciated, and in square C18 which is situated by the cave wall, a thick soft breccia was formed. This "brecciated column" contains material from Pit L on the top, than from layer III and IV. Since the material of Pit L is in the "column", the formation of this breccia must be very late, around at the end of the Epipalaeolithic. This breccia bearing flint artifacts uncharacteristic to the Mousterian was also found on the wall of the first chamber near the bedrock floor. In addition, in one of the Natufian bedrock mortars in the first chamber (CI) Natufian flint artifacts were found embedded within this type of breccia.

# CHAPTER 2: METHODOLOGY FOR LITHIC TECHNOLOGY

## Sampling the archaeological material

The approach to study Raqefet lithic assemblages is the lithic technology, which requires well definable "clean" assemblages and avoids mixtures containing considerable "noise" from other assemblages. Based on this reason, the sampling procedure of Raqefet archaeological material uses the observations made on the site formation processes. Therefore, assemblages coming from the least disturbed sequences and undisturbed deposits are selected for study. There are three criterions for sampling the archaeological material.

1) A given deposit or stratigraphic unit may contain artifacts of several periods due to post-depositional disturbances. One of the appearances of the disturbed deposit is the pit. Pit assemblages can easily be recognized on the basis of stratigraphy. Assemblages from pits are eliminated from the present study.

2) Besides pits, layers also may contain mixed assemblages. In this case the deposit features do not show mixture, vertical and horizontal displacement by taphonomic agencies is a major problem. Hence the compositions of the assemblages may operate the sampling process. This examination can recognize and eventually eliminate compound assemblages which are mixtures of two or more distinct prehistoric cultures or periods.

3) Reliable assemblages with low artifact number (lower than 100) are also eliminated from the study.

### The sample assemblages

According to the observations on the site formation processes area B-G/18-23 contained the least disturbed sequence of layers. Post-depositional disturbances in this sequence were easily recognizable because most layers were laminated and the pits were very distinct in color, structure and compaction. Eventually, 21% of the assemblages are reliable for study. These are an indeterminate Early Upper Palaeolithic from layer IV, Levantine Aurignacian from layer III, and Late Kebaran from layer I (Table 2.1.).

### Indeterminate Early Upper Palaeolithic

Although layer IV contains a few items of eroded Levallois implements, the assemblage is used in the study since these intrusive elements are heavily eroded and can be easily separated from the sharp technologically and typologically distinct Upper Palaeolithic artifacts.

This industry is the earliest in the studied sequence. Its chronological position, according to the stratigraphy, is earlier than the Levantine Aurignacian and later than the Initial Upper Palaeolithic and Mousterian remains in layers V-VIII. According to [14]C dates (33-31 kyear BP) it falls within the radiocarbon age of Kebara Unit I-II Aurignacian, Ksar 'Aqil layers 11-12 Aurignacian

(Tixier's excavation) and Üçagizli layer B Early Upper Palaeolithic (Bar-Yosef *et al* 1996; Mellars and Tixier 1989; Kuhn *et al* 2003). This period is associated with Early Ahmarian in the southern Levant (Belfer-Cohen and Goring-Morris 2003).

Raqefet layer IV is characterized by a fine blade and bladelet production although flakes outnumber the blade/lets in the assemblage. The industry lacks the best hallmark of the Early Ahmarian, the el-Wad point, and also Levantine Aurignacian lithic elements. The only typological resemblance to the Early Ahmarian is that endscrapers were made on core tablets and cortical flake blanks (Davidzon and Goring-Morris 2003; Monigal 2003). This composition of tool kit does not clearly allow classifying this industry as Early Ahmarian. Henceforth, it is called indeterminate Early Upper Palaeolithic assemblage.

*Table 2.1. Cultural sequence of area B-G/18-23 by stratigraphic units. Pottery covers unidentified potsherds. Flint covers general lithics without characteristic tools. Capitals mark pits, Roman numerals mark layers.*

| Area B-G/18-23 | |
|---|---|
| A | Pottery, flint |
| B | Pottery Neolithic |
| C | Pottery, Late Natufian, Late Kebaran, PPN |
| D | Iron age, Late Natufian, Geometric Kebaran |
| E | Pottery, flints |
| F | Pottery, Late Natufian, Late Kebaran, Geometric Kebaran |
| G | Bronze Age, Late Natufian |
| H | PPNA |
| J | PPNA, Late Natufian |
| K | Flint |
| L | Bronze Age, Late Natufian, Geometric Kebaran, Levantine Aurignacian |
| I | Late Kebaran |
| II | Indeterminate Late Upper Palaeolithic |
| III | Levantine Aurignacian |
| IV | Indeterminate Early Upper Palaeolithic |
| V | Sterile |
| VI | Middle and Upper Palaeolithic with traits of Emiren |
| VII | Middle and Upper Palaeolithic with traits of Emiren |
| VIII | Middle and Upper Palaeolithic with traits of Emiren |

### Levantine Aurignacian

The distribution of Levantine Aurignacian artifacts in the stratum concentrates within a 30 cm thick level including the entire layer III, and only the very base of layer II in squares C-D/20 and the very top of layer IV in square C20 with a few dozens of artifacts. In the study layer III is included.

This industry of Raqefet can be compared without difficulties to other Levantine Aurignacian assemblages. According to the high frequency of nosed, shouldered and carinated endscrapers, and typical Aurignacian retouch forms, Raqefet Aurignacian resembles most to the classic Levantine Aurignacian of Ksar 'Aqil 8 (Dortch 1970; Bergman 1987; personal observations), Hayonim D

(Belfer-Cohen and Bar-Yosef 1981; personal observations), Kebara D (Garrod 1954; Ziffer 1978a, 1978b), Sefunim 8, 10 (Ronen 1984; personal observations), and el-Wad D (Garrod and Bate 1937). Raqefet Levantine Aurignacian's radiocarbon age (*ca* 30 kyear BP) fits the Levantine Aurignacian chronological position (Bar-Yosef 2000).

*Late Kebaran*

Strictly on typological ground, the Raqefet Kebaran industry fits the definition of the Late Kebaran, which is characterized by the frequency of obliquely truncated backed bladelets (Bar-Yosef and Vogel 1987; Goring-Morris 1995; Fellner 1995). Besides this tool type, markers of the early Kebaran, such as micropoints and arch backed bladelets also appear, but their number is particularly low. This industry overlies a Late Upper Palaeolithic deposit and shows similarities to the Late Kebaran of Fazael IIIA (Goring-Morris 1980) and Hayonim Ca (Bar-Yosef 1970).

*Table 2.2. Cultural sequence of area J-M/24-28 by stratigraphic units. Pottery covers unidentified potsherds. Flint covers general lithics without characteristic tools. Capitals mark pits, Roman numerals mark layers.*

| J-M/24-28 | |
|---|---|
| A | Pottery, flint |
| B | Pottery, flint |
| C | ? |
| I | Pottery, flint |
| II | Pottery Neolithic, PPN |
| D | Pottery Neolithic and PPNB |
| E | Pottery, flint |
| F | Pottery, flint, Bronze Age, Roman |
| G | Pottery, flint, Bronze Age-Chalcolithic |
| III | Pottery, flint |
| IV | Pottery, flint, Neolithic |
| V | PPNA, Late Kebaran, Geometric Kebaran, and Late Natufian |
| VI | Geometric Kebaran and Natufian, |
| VII | Geometric Kebaran |
| H | Geometric Kebaran and Late Natufian |
| VIII | ? |
| IX | Late Kebaran? |
| J | Levantine Aurignacian? |
| X | Levantine Aurignacian, Middle Palaeolithic |
| K | Middle and Upper Palaeolithic with traits of Emiren |
| XI | ? |
| XII | Middle Palaeolithic |

From area J-M/24-28 only 4.5% of the assemblages are reliable for lithic technology study. This means only one layer (layer VII) which yielded a Geometric Kebaran assemblage (Table 2.2.). According to the description of the stratigraphy in Raqefet archives, layer VII does not seem to have been disturbed by post-depositional events. However, after studying its assemblage it turns out that part of it (western squares, J-K/24 excavated in 1971) contains a considerable "noise" (2 potsherds and a few dozens of heavily eroded Mousterian artifacts). This part, which most likely was in contact with nearby pits is eliminated, and the larger "clean" part from squares L-M/26-28 is selected for study. The remaining layers in area J-M/24-28 are post-depositionally heavily mixed

except layer IX which contained a lithic assemblage consisting of a few dozens of lithic artifacts probably of Late Kebaran. Layer VIII originally was a clean but it became mixed with the content of Pit D during the excavations in 1971.

*Geometric Kebaran*

This industry from area J-M/24-28 in layer VII overlaid layers containing poor non-geometric microlithic industry. Above this layer a mixture of Natufian and Geometric Kebaran was found.

Typologically the industry is equal to Geometric Kebaran sites lacking large geometric forms. From the Carmel area Neve David (Kaufman 1989; Yaroshevich 2004), from the Galilee Hayonim Terrace (Valla 1989), from the Negev Azariq XVIII and Shunera XIIB (Goring-Moris 1987), and from northern Jordan Wadi Ziqlab 148 (Maher and Banning 2002; L. Maher personal communication 2004) show strict resemblance with Raqefet.

*Table 2.3. Cultural sequence of area A-H/7-17 by stratigraphic units in squares C7-17, D-E/16-17. Pottery covers unidentified potsherds. Flint covers general lithics without characteristic tools. Arabic numerals mark pits, Roman numerals mark layers.*

| Squares C7-17, D-E/16-17 | |
|---|---|
| 1 | Pottery, Kebaran and Natufian |
| 2 | Pottery, Kebaran and Natufian |
| 3 | Pottery, Geometric Kebaran and Natufian |
| 4 | Pottery, Geometric Kebaran and Natufian |
| 5 | Pottery, Geometric Kebaran and Natufian |
| I | Pottery, Levantine Aurignacian, Geometric Kebaran and Natufian |
| II | Pottery, Late Natufian, PPN |
| III | Pottery, flint |
| IV | Kebaran, Geometric Kebaran, and Natufian and Pottery Neolithic |
| V | Early Epipalaeolithic |

*Table 2.4. Cultural sequence of area A-H/7-17 by stratigraphic units in squares D-E/7-13. Pottery covers unidentified potsherds. Flint covers general lithics without characteristic tools. Arabic numerals mark pits, Roman numerals mark layers.*

| D-E/7-13 | |
|---|---|
| 1 | Pottery,Geometric Kebaran and Natufian |
| 2 | Pottery,Geometric Kebaran and Natufian |
| 3 | Pottery, flint |
| 4 | Pottery, flint |
| 5 | Pottery,Geometric Kebaran and Natufian |
| 6 | Pottery,Geometric Kebaran and Natufian |
| I | Roman, Geometric Kebaran, Natufian, Pottery |
| II | Pottery, Natufian, Geometric Kebaran |
| III | Geometric Kebaran, Natufian |
| IV | Natufian |
| V | Natufian |

From area A-H/7-17 only 4% of the entire assemblage is used in the study. On the basis of post-depositional disturbances 85% of the assemblages, on the basis of low artifact number 11% of the assemblages were excluded (Table 2.3-5.). Latter includes Late Natufian assemblages. The sample of area A-H/7-17 in present study is a Natufian assemblage from the 2004 revision field work, from CI-II bedrock mortars.

*Late Natufian*

This assemblage derives from a separate area of the cave, which has no direct stratigraphic connection neither to the Early Upper Palaeolithic-Levantine Aurignacian-Late Kebaran sequence nor the Geometric Kebaran. The Natufian can be classified only on the basis of stone tool typology. The lunates of the sample assemblage are blunt backed. The range of their lengths falls between 12 and 18 mm, with an average of 15.4 mm. The median is at 16 mm. These characteristics and measurements place the assemblage in the Late Natufian, showing close similarities with El-Wad B1 and Nahal Oren VI (15.8 and 15.6 mm lunate length average, respectively) (Valla 1984).

*Table 2.5. Cultural sequence of area A-H/7-17 by stratigraphic units in squares G-H/10-12. Pottery covers unidentified potsherds. Flint covers general lithics without characteristic tools. Arabic numerals mark pits, Roman numerals mark layers.*

| G-H/10-12 | |
| --- | --- |
| 1 | Roman, Geometric Kebaran, Natufian, Pottery |
| I | Roman, Geometric Kebaran, Natufian, Pottery |
| II | Roman, Geometric Kebaran, Natufian, Pottery |
| III | Pottery, Kebaran |
| IV | Geometric Kebaran, Pottery |
| V | Natufian |

## Theoretical background to lithic technology

Any human activity using or processing a material to obtain something can be called technology (Haudricourt 1987). Accordingly, activities connected to stone tool production compose lithic technology (Inizan *et al* 1995). The lithic technology study can show how man approached the issue of stone tool production and what decisions were made to succeed in stone working. The stone tool production is composed of acts built upon sequential steps (Geneste 1991; Lemonnier 1992). The steps in the sequence are enchained with each other. Each step brings the conditions needed to succeed with the next one. It means that without finishing an action successfully, there is no moving along to the next action. Accordingly, the achievement of an action depends on the successful accomplishment of its own and the previous action (Inizan *et al* 1995). This nature of stone tool production process can be studied logically by the appliance of the *chaîne opératoire* (operational sequence).

The concept of the *chaîne opératoire*, first used by ethnologists (Leroi-Gourhan 1965; Lemonnier 1992; Pelegrin *et al* 1988), has been taken up by prehistorians in order to organize their observations in logical manner (Karlin and Julin 1994) from raw material procurement to tool discard (Pelegrin *et al* 1988). The material remains of a *chaîne opératoire* (i.e. the lithic assemblage) are products of series of technical acts (Lemonnier 1992). The acts are driven according to a *schème opératoire* (operational scheme) that guides the realization of the knapping procedure. The operational scheme is based

upon a technical knowledge ("know-how") consisted of an organized memory deriving from preceding experiences (Pelegrin 1985; Pelegrin *et al* 1988). Accordingly, the lithic technology study is a reconstruction of technical processes composed of physical and mental aspects (Pelegrin 1995).

The rough sequence of the *chaîne opératoire* in the exploitation of hard stones can be presented as follows:

1) raw material procurement,
2) preparation of the raw nodule (shaping the core),
3) debitage (making blanks from the cores),
4) management of products as blanks of different types of tools.

Within above sequence there are sub-stages which should be clarified. These are marked by recognizable changes in operation or technique (e.g. blade production, bladelet production). Missing stages are also recognizable (for example ready made blanks were introduced to the site or the blank was taken from the fabrication place) (Pelegrin *et al* 1988).

The *chaîne opératoire* in stone tool production can be reconstructed easily when conjoinable pieces lead to refitting cores and products. In the lack of conjoins "mental refitting" can guide the reconstruction (Pelegrin 1986; 1995). It means that the place of each artifact or group of artifacts can be identified in relation to the others within the technical process, on the basis of that lithic artifacts retain exceptionally well traces of the successive production operations they undergo (Geneste 1991; Inizan *et al* 1995; Perlès 1992). Therefore, in order to accomplish the mental refitting, each lithic element of the *chaîne opératoire*, whether a tool or a waste flake, ought to be studied according to morphology, the presence and position of cortex, features of butt, and the order and aspect of negative removals on their dorsal faces (Pelegrin 1986). These observations can be ordered "chronologically". When the information gained from lithics is in a coherent order, it is possible to recover the *chaîne opératoire* and the operational scheme, from which they sprang (Karlin and Julien 1994).

## Elements of lithic technology

### *Flake*

The term flake is used herein as general denomination to a simple non-laminar removal of the knapping process. Its size can be either microlithic or macrolithic (Inizan *et al* 1995).

### *Blade and bladelet*

Blade or bladelet in general is an elongated "flake" whose length is at least twice the width. The border between blade and bladelet changes from assemblage to assemblage (Kaufman 1986, 1987). Tixier (1963) established the size categories of blades and bladelets for the North African Epipalaeolithic assemblages. After his work, laminar products longer than 5 cm and wider than 1.2 cm are called blades. Bladelets are beneath these limits.

Kaufman (1986) used statistical methods to separate blades and bladelets from each other. His method is based on the size of the microlithic and macrolithic laminar tools and blanks. The method is working perfectly with non-geometric tool based assemblages. At geometric tool based industry this method may give biased results, since the production of geometric tools was usually accomplished by extensive modification of the original blank.

For the PhD thesis (Lengyel 2005) a simple method was sought to distinguishing between blades and bladelets. This made an approximate separation which did not endeavor to set an exact border up by both length and width. Instead, the border was presented only by the length of the laminar product. It was made by two ways. First was the use of histogram that displays length data. When the histogram showed two peaks, the trough of a wave between them may have indicated the border between blades and bladelets (Figure 2.1.). The second was the use of length-width scatterplot. If the scatterplot showed two groups of data, the gap between them may have indicated the border between blade and bladelets (Figure 2.2.). In this case the border appeared the best when the scatterplots showed the data by raw material.

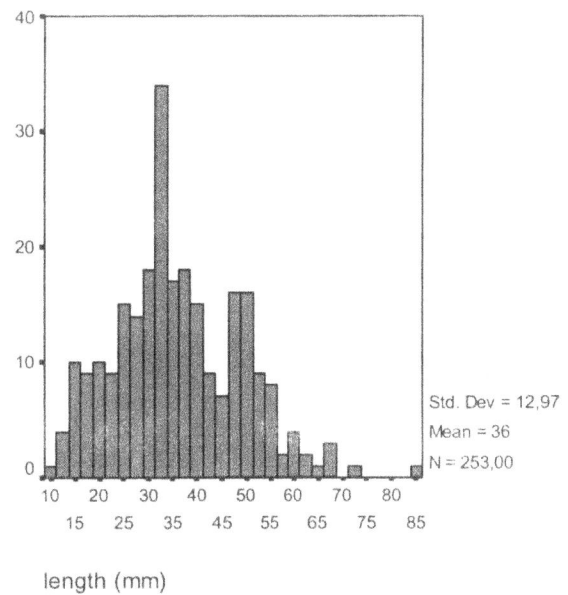

*Figure 2.1.* Length histogram of unretouched laminar blanks in the Geometric Kebaran assemblage.

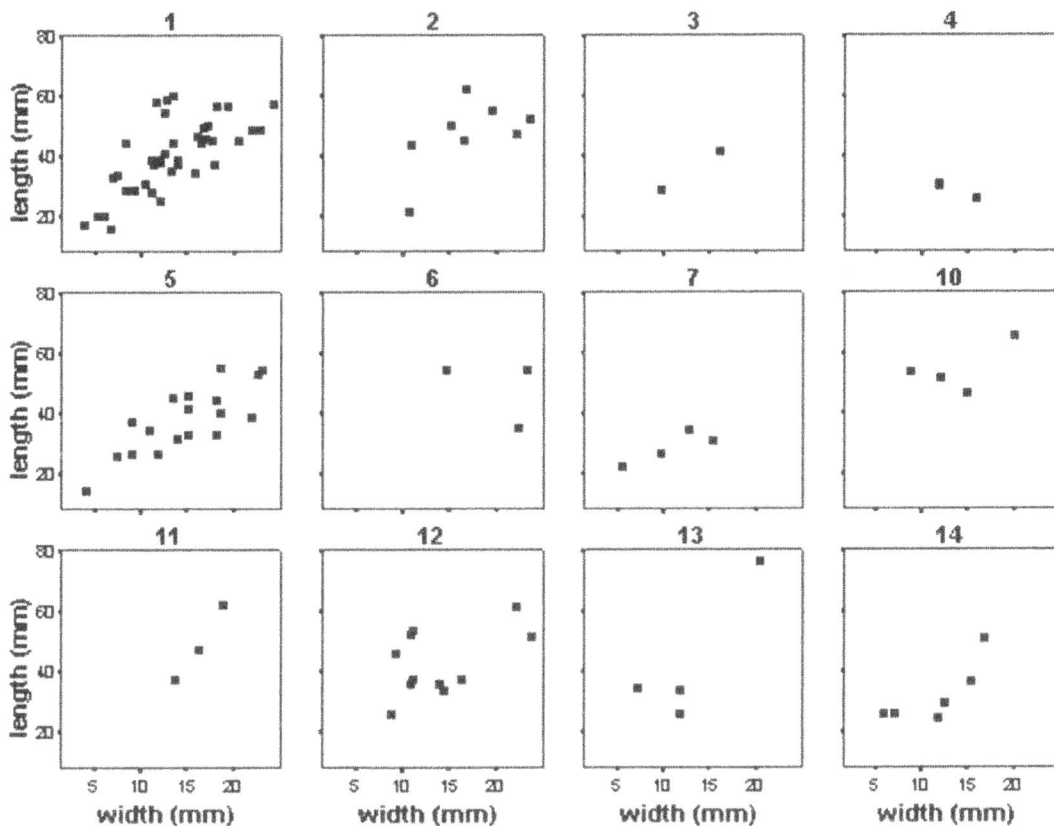

*Figure 2.2.* Scatterplots of laminar blanks by raw material types of the Indeterminate Early Upper Palaeolithic assemblage.

## *The Indeterminate Early Upper Palaeolithic*

In the establishment of the border between blades and bladelets, the histogram displaying the length of the laminar products did not provide solution by itself. Several peaks and dips were displayed. Significant peaks were at 35, 45 and 55 mm. Dips situated at 40 and 50 mm. Thus, these two latter values could have marked the border between blades and bladelets. Further on, examining the size of the laminar products by raw material, there were two groups: items longer and shorter than 40 mm. Therefore, the dip on the histogram at 40 mm was considered as the border between blades and bladelets.

## *Levantine Aurignacian*

On the length histogram of the laminar products, the data distribution displayed peaks between 45 and 55 mm, but significant dip. However, the length-width scattergrams of laminar products by raw material displayed a break at 40 mm in the distribution of length data almost at every type raw material. On the basis of these observations the separating border between blades and bladelets was established at 40 mm.

## *Late Kebaran*

The length histogram of laminar blanks showed the majority fell between 20 and 40 mm. On the histogram, two significant peaks (47.5 and 27.5 mm) and one dip (42.5 mm) was visible. Based upon these observations, the border between blades and bladelets was established at 42 mm.

## *Geometric Kebaran*

The length histogram of laminar blanks showed the majority fell between 20 and 40 mm. On the histogram, two significant peaks (at 32 mm and 50 mm) and one dip (at 45 mm) was visible. Based upon these observations, the border between blades and bladelets is established at 45 mm.

## *Late Natufian*

The length histogram of laminar products showed that near 45 mm the quantity of data suddenly decreases creating a dip in the distribution. Studying the size of the blade/lets on length-width scattergrams by raw material, this break also became visible. Two raw materials (RM1 and RM5) displayed a break in the length distribution near 40 mm. At the remainder raw materials the 45 mm break was clear (at three raw materials, RM7, RM8 and RM15 no larger products than 45 mm appear). Accordingly, the separating border between blades and bladelets was established at 45 mm.

## *Waste*

These are fragmented items from several sides, lacking clear features of flake or laminar fragments. In addition, this group includes waste material from the tool production such as microburin and burin spalls.

## *Core*

A core is a raw material block, from which flakes, blades or bladelets were removed in order to produce blanks (Inizan *et al* 1995).

## *Core trimming elements (CTE)*

This category contains such elements of the knapping procedure as were removed after certain preparations and are products of core rejuvenation. Five categories of CTEs are used:

Crest blade: on the dorsal face perpendicular removals situate with contra-bulbs at the center of the blade (Inizan *et al* 1995).

Sub-crest blade: it is the next removal after the crested blade; longitudinal blade negative scars cutting the scars of the cresting can be seen (Inizan *et al* 1995). The sub-crest blade is not a real core trimming element. It bears only the remains of cresting.

Neo-crest blade: it has scars from the main debitage, and perpendicular removals with the presence of contra-bulb often on one side of the item; these items are removed after re-shaping or correcting of the carination or irregularity of the core's debitage surface (Inizan *et al* 1995; Pelegrin 1995).

Core tablet: it is a flake which detaches the entire surface of the striking platform of a laminar core; its contour has the remains of the debitage surface (Inizan *et al* 1995).

Core rejuvenating flake: it is a flake which removes only a fragment of the striking platform of the core; its butt generally bears the remains of the debitage surface (Inizan *et al* 1995).

## *Accidents*

Although it is the product of a human action, the accident is unintended and unintentional. Accidents are products made by unexpected circumstances as against the ordinary events (Roche and Tixier 1982).

Following Roche and Tixier 1982, the next categories are used herein. One of the types of accidents is the breakage. Breakage can be classified into four types. The first type is the *clear* breakage, which is characterized by flat perpendicular or sub-perpendicular breakage surface to the ventral and dorsal faces. The second type is the *languette*, which has a shape of tong that protrudes from the broken artifact. This type leaves very characteristic negative as well. The third type is the *nacelle* which fragment breaks out from the ventral face of the blade during its detachment. The fourth type is the *siret*. It characteristically happen during hard stone hammer percussion. This accident breaks the product in longitudinal axis starting from the impact point.

The second type of accident is the *plunging* which is caused by an over-proportioned force of percussion. In this case the splintering waves remove more than it was intended.

The third type of accident is called *hinge*. In this case the percussion force is weaker than the ideal, accordingly the splintering waves run out off the surface earlier than in ideal case.

## Tools

In this study each product that bears retouch or modification on its edge or edges is called tool. Tool can be made on any product of the knapping process: flake, blade, bladelet, core or even a waste.

## Knapping techniques

Knapping techniques leave significant traces on the removed products. Since there are no traces either of indirect and pressure technique in Raqefet, the features of those are not presented here in details.

The knapping technique is a modality of accomplishing removals according to three main parameters (after Pelegrin 1995):

1) The mode of application of the force (direct and indirect percussion, pressing).
2) Nature and morphology of the knapping tool (hard stone, antler, wood, *bequille*, etc.).
3) Action performed by a certain movement and position of the body, the mode of holding the item being knapped.

The knapping techniques can be recognized on the basis of the products' base features (after Pelegrin 2000):

1-impact point
2- state of overhang
3- thickness of butt
4-bulbar scars
5-lipping

The knapping technique classification primarily concerns the motion performed during knapping action and the mode of hammer use. It secondarily concerns the matter of the hammer. It was pointed out earlier that the dimension of the bulb and the thickness of the butt depend on a certain manner of hammer use (Tixier 1982). Thin butts arise when the knapper hits the very edge of the core. This action may be accomplished by either soft or hard direct percussion. Therefore, herein there is no differentiation made between soft organic hammer and soft stone hammer, since both techniques require the same preparation and hammer use.

### Hard hammer technique

During the use of hard stone hammer the trajectory of the knapper's hand targets the striking platform of the core. The hammer contacts the core's striking platform at a single point, therefore one of the characteristic markers of the hard stone hammer use is the presence of impact point. The size of the impact point depends on the volume of the hammer. Rarely more than one impact points may appear. This evidences the use of hammer with uneven surface. Further features of the hard stone hammer use are the incipient cone of percussion, wrinkles, usually thick butts of products, unprepared overhang, the unpronounced lip and usually pronounced bulb.

### Soft hammer technique

The main characteristic of the soft hammer technique use is that the trajectory of the knapper's hand targets the edge of the striking platform. In order to obtain successful removals with soft organic hammer, the core's overhang formed by contra-bulbs must be eliminated and abraded. Since the hammer contacts the edge of the striking platform on a short section, contrary to the hard stone hammer use, the impact point does not occur on the products. The butts of these products are usually thin, according to Pelegrin's experiments (1986) 0-4 mm.

**Table 2.6.** Record categories of the artifacts.

| A. Product | B. Fragments |
|---|---|
| flake | distal |
| blade | mesial |
| bladelet | proximal |
| waste | siret |
| | nacelle |
| | |
| C. Cortex | D. Butt type |
| cortical | cortical |
| non-cortical | plain |
| | dihedral |
| | facetted |
| | linear |
| | punctiform |
| | |
| E. Bulb extension | F. Impact point |
| diffused | small |
| convex | big |
| | |
| G. Lip | H. Overhang |
| short | unprepared |
| protruding | abraded |
| | |
| I. Dorsal scars | J. Edges |
| unidirectional | parallel |
| opposite | converging |
| perpendicular | expanding |
| multiple | |
| | |
| K. Profile | L. Distal termination |
| straight | ordinary |
| curved | hinge |
| twisted | plunging |
| | languette |
| | |
| M. Measurements | N. Additions |
| length | unretouched |
| width | tool |
| thickness | CTE |
| butt thickness | janus item |

## Records of the blanks

Each artifact was recorded according to 14 categories of technological features (Table 2.6.). The categories were made uniform to each assemblage.

Within category C (cortex) further division was made, in order to record the extension of the cortex. Five groups are created:

Group 1: 100% cortex coverage; these items are *first flakes* (Inizan *et al* 1995) which are fully covered by cortex even on their butts.

Group 2: 76-99% cortex coverage; included among these are fully cortical items with uncortical butts, as well.

Group 3: 51-75% cortex coverage.

Group 4: 26-50% cortex coverage.

Group 5: 1-25% cortex coverage.

Broken artifacts are recorded with restrictions in the database. Distal and mesial fragments are recorded by categories A and B, and proximal fragments are recorded within categories A, B, D, E, F, G, and H. Artifact fragments bearing cortex are simply recorded as cortical fragments.

Size recording of the artifacts has been performed on unbroken, unretouched and retouched flakes, blades and bladelets:

Length: measured between the butt and the distal end along the technological axis of the item.

Width: measured between the two edges at the largest width of the item.

Thickness: measured between the dorsal and the ventral face at the thickest part of the item.

The thickness of the butt: measured between the dorsal and the ventral face at the thickest part of the butt.

## Records of the cores

Besides the blanks the characteristics of the cores are also recorded. The basic records of the cores are as follows:

Length: distance between the striking platform and the distal end of the core

Width: distance between the two sides.

Depth: distance between the front (debitage surface) and the back of the core.

Cores are not identified according to their shape. They are analytically grouped according to three parameters:

The first presents the type of the last debitage performed on the core; accordingly there are blade, bladelet and flake cores, plus the pre-cores that bear sings only of the initialization of the core.

The second presents the shape of the front of the core: narrow, semi-circular and wide.

The third presents the sides of the debitage surface viewed from the face of the core: this can be parallel or converging.

Additional features are recorded from the cores as follows:

1) Number of striking platforms: single, double (opposite), or multiple.
2) Orientation of knapping (Figure 2.3.):
   a) Unidirectional: a single striking platform and single debitage surface exploited from the direction of the striking platform.
   b) Opposite: it exhibits two opposite striking platforms and one debitage surface; the first debitage surface is not used after the use of the second one.
   c) Multiple: it exhibits more than two striking platforms and debitage surfaces.

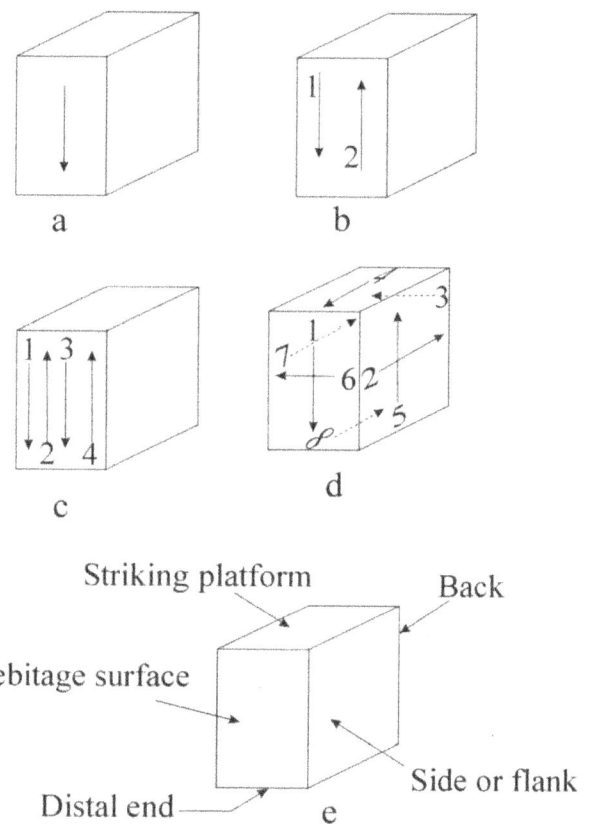

*Figure 2.3. Diagram of the three basic knapping orientation: a, unidirectional; b, c, opposite; d, multiple. Denomination of core parts (e).*

3) State of overhangs of the core (with the distinction of pre and post last removal):
   a) Unprepared: the overhangs are untouched.
   b) Abraded: the overhangs bear scars of removals and heavy abrasion on the margin.
4) Previously performed debitage type of the core on the basis of the shape of scars: flake, blade, bladelet. Type of the last removal:
   a) ordinary
   b) hinge
   c) irregular
5) Remains of debitage surface preparation

a) Cresting: perpendicular scars removed alternating along the longitudinal axis of the core.

b) Remains of cresting: cut cresting negative scars, the contra-bulb is removed by the crest blade.

6) Maintenance remains (with the distinction of pre and post last removal).

a) Core tablet removal.

b) Rejuvenating flake removal.

c) Neo-cresting.

d) Small flake removal at the distal end with the function of keeping the shape of the debitage surface.

7) Blank of the core

a) Small nodule (*ca* 5 cm).

b) Large nodule (*ca* 10 cm or larger).

c) Tabular flint.

d) Flake.

e) Uncharacteristic angular fragment of raw material.

## Records of the tools

For recording tool types besides the record categories of blanks, a uniform list for Levantine Upper Palaeolithic and Epipalaeolithic industries with explicit illustrations was sought. Such typology does not exist. Goring-Morris' typology (Goring-Morris 1987) is provided by illustrations, it is well built up, but the Upper Palaeolithic tool types are not enough explicit. Hours' typology (Hours 1974) lacks illustrations, but his Upper Palaeolithic types for example such as endscrapers are better classified. Therefore, the incorporation of the advantages of these two typologies is used herein. Subsequently, the major tool type groups are ordered according to Goring-Morris 1987, the typological identification of the Upper Palaeolithic types is based on Hours 1974, and the Epipalaeolithic tool types are from Goring-Morris 1987.

A few changes were made in the type lists. Types are presented according to the blanks of tools, in order to assemble typological and technological observations (after Demars 1992). Accordingly, retouched flakes, flake endscrapers and endscraper on retouched blade do not appear as separate types in the list. This approach in studies on the Levant has already appeared (Bar-Yosef and Belfer-Cohen 2004).

Non-geometric microliths are not listed as a separated group in the type list, since the blanks are presented. For instance, the retouched items group contains the Dufour bladelets.

The description of retouched tools contains the localization, distribution, and morphology of the retouch. This follows the categories of Inizan *et al* 1995. The localization of the retouch has five categories: direct, inverse, alternate, alternating and bipolar. The categories

of the retouch distribution are: continuous, discontinuous, partial. The retouch morphology can be: scaled, stepped, sub-parallel, parallel, marginal.

## Lithic technology study presentation

Evidences for certain elements of the given *chaîne opératoire* can derive from several sources. For instance: the shape of the core tablets can shed light upon the front shape of the cores in the debitage; cores abandoned at the beginning of the debitage bring information to the core configuration. Subsequently, a certain type of lithic product may appear at more than one part of the presentation of the *chaînes opératoires*.

### Raw materials

Applying the approach of *chaîne opératoire*, first the raw materials are presented in every assemblage by source, type and quality and in accordance with the distance between Raqefet Cave and the source.

### Blank productions

Each blank production is separately presented in the study. It presents the methods of core configuration, including the issue of decortication, debitage surface preparation, striking platform preparation, and core shaping. This is followed by the presentation of the given debitage process. It deals with the striking platform preparation before removals, the knapping technique, the knapping orientation, and the size and shape of the products.

### Accidents

Breakages are presented first. It is taken into account that clear breaks might have been caused by post-knapping physical impacts (i.e. trampling). Secondly, hinge and plunging accidents are presented.

### Core maintenance

The next step is the presentation of the core maintenance. This deals with the methods of debitage rejuvenations on striking platforms and debitage surfaces.

### Core discard

This presents stages of debitage at which cores were discarded, with special regard to the reason of discard and last actions performed in the core exploitation.

### Tool blank selection and tools

This part discusses generally the blanks used for making tools. It includes the raw material-blank relation, tool type-blank relation, tool type-size relation, and tool type-raw material relation. In addition, there is a breakdown by tool type in order to present the tool kit.

# CHAPTER 3: STONE RAW MATERIALS IN THE UPPER PALAEOLITHIC AND EPIPALAEOLITHIC OF RAQEFET

Raqefet Cave is situated within a Turonian Bina formation that consists of limestone, marl and dolomite (Map of Israeli Geological Survey: MIGS) (Figure 3.1.). This formation contains very rarely flint (Olami 1984; Delage 2001). In the vicinity of Raqefet Cave (*ca* in 500 m radius) flints were not observed.

The stone raw materials (RM) of the assemblages have been grouped according to their visible features: texture and color. In addition their quality is classified on a threefold scale: low, mediocre, good (Table 3.1.). The quality classes are based upon the texture of the flint.

The observations distinguished 19 groups of raw materials. They are grouped together according to their sources. The location of the sources is presented on Fig. 5.1. An additional group was made in order to separate the unrecognizably burnt stones. The term flint is used as general denomination of siliceous stone raw materials.

## Ramat Menashe (RAM)

Ramat Menashe is the closest flint source to the cave, situating south of Raqefet about 1.5-2 km away in Adulam Lower-Middle Eocene geological formation consisting of chalk and chert (MIGS).

This formation is abundant of flint. Among the stone raw materials RM1, can be found in large, even 50 cm large massive blocks on surface in oval or irregular shape, while RM2 and RM3 occurs in the size of 20-40 cm oval nodules. Within geological layers RM1 and RM2 appear in lamina as tabular flint.

### RM1

This flint group is characterized by grey, grayish-brown color which encloses white patches and rarely dark-grey almost black parts. The flint is fine grained, although calcareous inclusions are relative frequently present in its inner part. Sometimes small white dots and under the cortex a dark colored band appear in the material. In some cases cracks and *diaclase* surfaces interrupt the homogeneity of the flint. Its quality is mediocre.

### RM2

It is white, typically coarse grained chalky flint with grayish, brownish hue. Its texture is homogeneous. Its quality is low.

### RM3

It is a semi-fine grained brown, light brown flint with concentric lines. The lines are thin and thick, as well. Its texture is homogeneous. Its quality is low.

### RM4

It is a brown, light-brown fine grained flint. Its texture is homogeneous. Its quality is low.

## Deir Hannah Formation (DH)

Deir Hannah formation is situated about 2-2.5 km from Raqefet. It is Cenomanian of age and consists of limestone, dolomite, marl, chalk and chert (MIGS). It is rich in flints (Delage 2001). RM5, RM7, RM8 and RM11 can be found in small 5-8 cm oval nodules, while RM6 in larger 10-15 cm oval or cube shaped nodules.

### RM5

It is a brown, yellowish brown fine grained flint, which extremely rarely has up to 1 cm large circular inclusions that are, in texture, a bit less fine grained. Frequently small white dots are observed in the raw material, which might be the feature of patination. The flint rarely appears slightly translucent, and the translucent and non-translucent composition can be observed even within one piece of block. Its quality is good.

### RM6

It is a yellow, yellowish-brown coarse grained flint, homogeneous in texture. Rarely, large lighter spots appear in the material. Sometimes orange lines appear in the material close to the surface. Its quality is low.

### RM7

It is a yellowish-brown fine grained flint, its appearance is a bit glossy. Its texture is homogeneous. Its quality is good.

### RM8

It is a yellow, yellowish-brown flint with purple hue. It is fine grained, its surface is shiny. Its texture is homogeneous. Its quality is good.

### RM9

This is a dominantly yellow flint with white bands. It is semi-fine grained. Its texture is varied. Its quality is good.

### RM10

It is a brown, grayish-brown fine grained flint. In a few cases, the color becomes lighter in spots, rarely glossy and translucent. Its texture is homogeneous. Its quality is good.

### RM11

It is a brown, yellowish-brown semi-fine grained flint which has a velvety shine on its knapped surface. Its texture is homogeneous. Its quality is mediocre.

## Daliya ha Carmel (DC)

The source is situated about 4 km from Raqefet in Turonian Bina formation. The raw material of this formation can be found in 10-20 cm large oval nodules at Galilee sources (Delage 2001).

### *RM12*

It is a grey, grayish-brown coarse grained flint. Its texture is homogeneous. It has a very thick cortex in comparison to other raw materials. Its quality is low.

### *RM13*

It is coarse grained chert-like raw material. Its color is grey. Its texture is homogeneous. Its quality is low.

## Nahal Mearot (NM)

*RM14* belongs to this source situating in the north bank of Nahal Mearot (Weinstein-Evron *et al* 2003) about 7-8 km from Raqefet. This part of the Carmel belongs to the Cenomanian Deir Hannah formation, as well. The source yields flints in different size, even in 30 cm large nodules (A. Ronen, personal communication).

This raw material is a light-grey colored fine grained flint with blue and purple hue. It is a bit translucent and contains small deep purple or dark fossils scattered in the material. Its texture is homogeneous. Its quality is good.

## Shamir Formation (SH)

A characteristic flint type, *RM15,* can be found in the Shamir formation of Nahal Galim and in the Mount Oren area. This source is situated about 13 km from Raqefet. At Nahal Galim source, flints can be found in a variety of shapes and sizes of high quality. The Mount Oren Shamir formation flint has finer texture than that of the Nahal Galim (Weistein-Evron *et al* 2003). In present study it was not exactly possible to differentiate between the types of these two sources. The flint found at Raqefet is a fine grained brown flint with homogeneous texture. Its quality is good.

## Ohalo II (OII)

There is a group of flints without exact location of source. This consists of *RM16*. This flint is characteristic at the Late Upper Palaeolithic/Early Epipalaeolithic site of Ohalo II (D. Nadel, personal communication), accordingly its source might be at the area situating close to that site, south to Lake Kineret. Accordingly the distance between Raqefet and the source can be about 45 km. Similar flint occurrence was mentioned in this region (Delage 2001).

The raw material itself is a light grey coarse grained flint with brownish hue. It has black dots and white parallel strips. Its texture is homogeneous. Its quality is mediocre.

## Raw materials from unknown sources

The following flints were not able to be identified according to their sources. They might be either Carmel or non-Carmel Origin. Among them RM17 might be similar to flints reported from the Galilee (Delage 2001).

### *RM17*

It is a dark grey, very fine grained flint. Its texture is homogeneous. Its quality is good.

### *RM18*

It is a light brown fine grained translucent flint with white dots, spots and fossils. Its texture is homogeneous. Its quality is good.

### *RM19*

It is a translucent shiny yellowish-white very fine grained homogeneous translucent flint. Its quality is good.

**Table 3.1.** *The quality of the different raw materials by source.*

| type | RAM | DH | DC | NM | SH | OII | Unknown |
|------|-----|-----|-----|-----|-----|-----|---------|
| 1 | Mediocre | | | | | | |
| 2 | Low | | | | | | |
| 3 | Low | | | | | | |
| 4 | Low | | | | | | |
| 5 | | Good | | | | | |
| 6 | | Low | | | | | |
| 7 | | Good | | | | | |
| 8 | | Good | | | | | |
| 9 | | Good | | | | | |
| 10 | | Good | | | | | |
| 11 | | Mediocre | | | | | |
| 12 | | | Low | | | | |
| 13 | | | Low | | | | |
| 14 | | | | Good | | | |
| 15 | | | | | Good | | |
| 16 | | | | | | Mediocre | |
| 17 | | | | | | | Good |
| 18 | | | | | | | Good |
| 19 | | | | | | | Good |

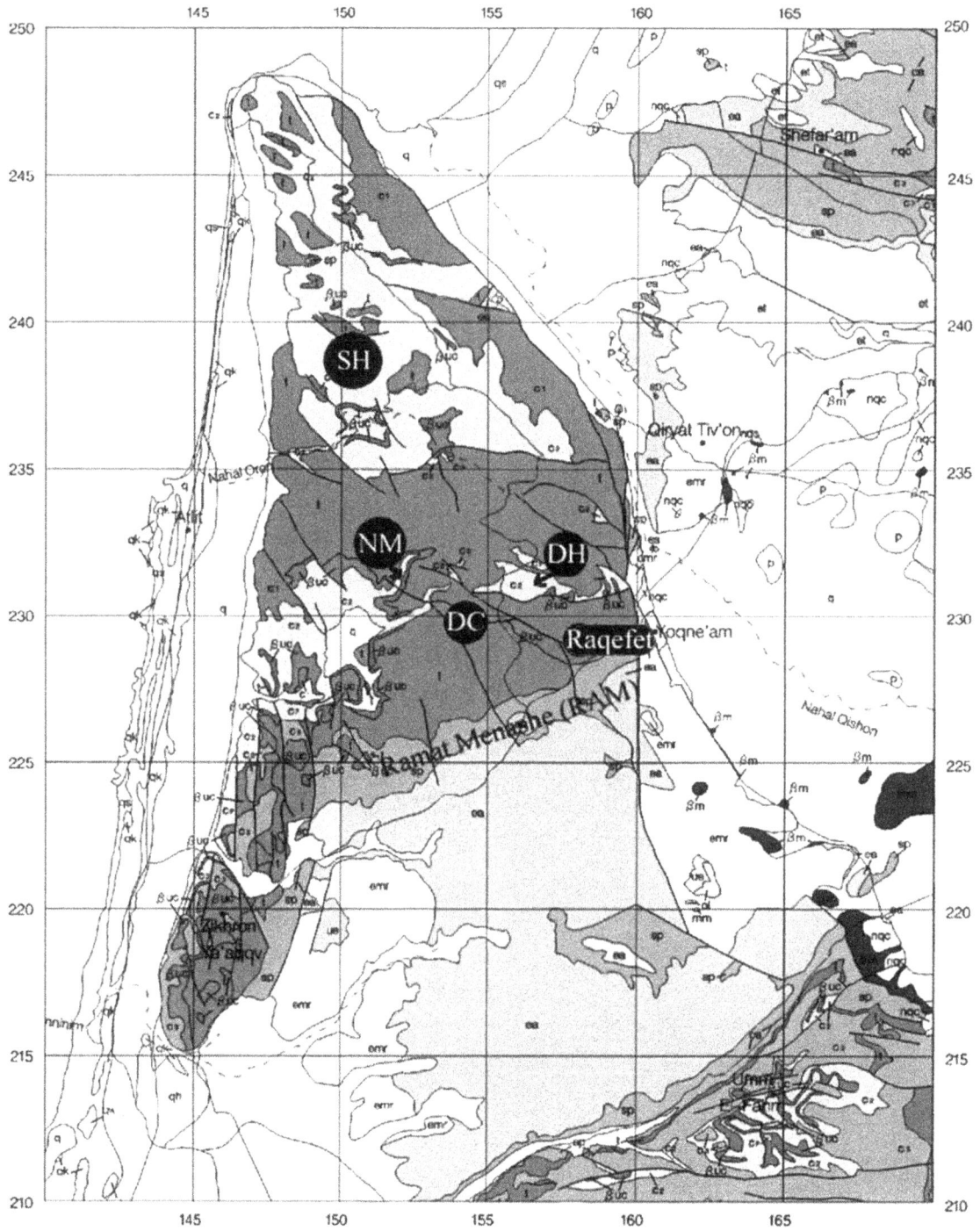

**Figure 3.1.** *The geological map of the Carmel (modified after the Map of Israeli Geological Survey: MIGS). βm, Miocene basalt; βuc, Upper Cretaceous volcanic rock units, basalt, gabro, ultramafics/pyroclastics and flows; c1, Albian-Cenomanian Yagur and Kammon formation; c2, Cenomenian Deir Hannah formation; ea, Lower-Middle Eocen Adulam formation; emr, Middle Eocene chalk, Maresha formation; et, Lower-Middle Eocene limestone chalk and chert, Timra formation; p, Pliocene Bira and Gesher formations; q, Quaternary alluvium; qh, Qaternary red sand and loam (hamra);qk, Quaternary sandstone (kurkar); sp, Senonian-Paleocene chalk, Mount Scopus group; t, Turonian Bina formation.*

## Raw Material

The raw materials of the assemblage derive from four flint sources (Table 4.1). Ramat Menashe (RAM), the closest source to Raqefet, yielded the majority of the raw materials, among which the mediocre quality RM1 is dominant. In addition, this raw material is the most abundant in the whole assemblage.

Deir Hannah formation flints (DH) make up the next largest group of raw material, within which the good quality RM5 is dominant, but the low quality RM6 also appears in significant amount. RM5 constitutes the second most abundant raw material type in the assemblage.

Daliyat ha Carmel low quality raw materials (DC) are present with low frequency. RM12 and RM13 appear almost in the same amount.

Nahal Mearot raw materials (NM) make up the smallest part of the assemblage.

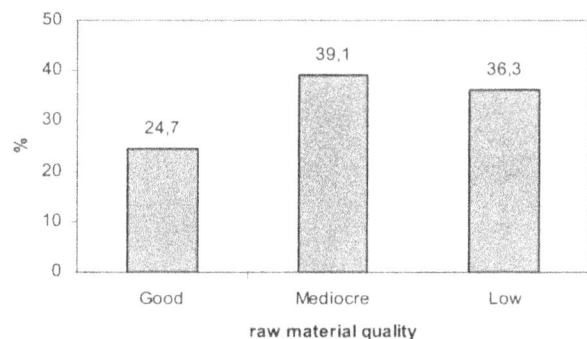

**Figure 4.1.** Frequency of raw materials by quality.

Based on the presence of first flakes in the assemblage, RM1 and RM5 were brought to the site as fully cortical nodules. The remainder raw materials were roughed-out in various extents off-site.

In sum, the raw material acquisition focused on mediocre quality locally available raw materials, while good quality flints make up the smallest part of the assemblage (Figure 4.1).

## Blade production

### *Blade core configuration*
The blade production is connected to mediocre quality flints. Within the mediocre quality flint group RM1 is dominant (Table 4.2.), which is the one raw material that has the whole sequence of blade production. Two flint types, RM4 of low quality and RM8 of good quality were not used in blade production.

Cores, such as one of RM5 and RM10 respectively, illustrate that preforming was accomplished by flake

removals on lateral sides from the proximal part. One of the cores bears (Figure 4.3:5) removals that start from the core back and extend over the lateral side.

Although there are signs of cortex peeling off prior to the debitage on the cores (65.2% of the cortical items are flakes), the cortex was not totally removed from the flint nodules eventually. A total of 31.2% of the blades are cortical. The cortex coverage on the blades in 74% of the cases extends up to 25% of the dorsal face. In the rest of the cases the cortex covers between 50 and 99% of the dorsal face. The cortex on the blades is most often located on one of the edges.

The narrow part of the raw material nodule is frequently the core front.

There are only two crest blades in the assemblage from RM1 and RM6. One core of RM5 has unilateral cresting (Figure 4.3:1). Sub-crest blades are not found. These vestiges show that the core front cresting was occasionally applied to begin removing blades.

The cores' striking platforms were created by the removal of a single or a few flakes. These were rarely cortical, as indicated by the low number of cortical blade butts.

**Table 4.1.** Frequency of raw material types by source.

| Raw material | | Raw material source | | | | Total |
|---|---|---|---|---|---|---|
| quality | type | RAM | DH | DC | NM | |
| Mediocre | RM1 | 227 64,1% | | | | 227 37,1% |
| Low | RM2 | 77 21,8% | | | | 77 12,6% |
| Low | RM3 | 18 5,1% | | | | 18 2,9% |
| Low | RM4 | 32 9% | | | | 32 5,2% |
| Good | RM5 | | 100 62,5% | | | 100 16,3% |
| Low | RM6 | | 21 13,1% | | | 21 3,4% |
| Good | RM7 | | 8 5% | | | 8 1,3% |
| Good | RM8 | | 4 2,5% | | | 4 0,7% |
| Good | RM10 | | 15 9,4% | | | 15 2,5% |
| Mediocre | RM11 | | 12 7,5% | | | 12 2% |
| Low | RM12 | | | 33 43,4% | | 33 5,4% |
| Low | RM13 | | | 41 53,9% | | 41 6,7% |
| Good | RM14 | | | | 24 100% | 24 3,9% |
| Total | | 354 57,8% | 160 26,1% | 74 12,1% | 24 3,9% | 612 100% |

*Table 4.2.* Frequency of lithic products by raw material.

| Raw material source | type | flake | blade | bladelet | waste | CTE | tool | Core flake | blade | bladelet | pre- | Total |
|---|---|---|---|---|---|---|---|---|---|---|---|---|
| RAM | RM1 | 54 23,8% | 40 17,6% | 31 13,7% | 58 25,6% | 10 4,4% | 14 6,2% | 4 1,8% | 4 1,8% | 7 3,1% | 5 2,2% | 227 100,0% |
| | RM2 | 34 44,2% | 10 13% | 4 5,2% | 16 20,8% | 4 5,2% | 9 11,7% | | | | | 77 100% |
| | RM3 | 8 44,4% | 2 11,1% | | 2 11,1% | 4 22,2% | 1 5,6% | | 1 5,6% | | | 18 100% |
| | RM4 | 12 37,5% | | 5 15,6% | 8 25% | 1 3,1% | 6 18,8% | | | | | 32 100% |
| DH | RM5 | 28 28% | 14 14% | 21 21% | 17 17% | 2 2% | 11 11% | | | 5 5% | 2 2% | 100 100% |
| | RM6 | 7 33,3% | 3 14,3% | 2 9,5% | 5 23,8% | 2 9,5% | 2 9,5% | | | | | 21 100% |
| | RM7 | 1 12,5% | 1 12,5% | 4 50% | | | 1 12,5% | 1 12,5% | | | | 8 100% |
| | RM8 | 2 50% | | 1 25% | | | 1 25% | | | | | 4 100% |
| | RM10 | 2 13,3% | 6 40% | 1 6,7% | 2 13,3% | 2 13,3% | | | 1 6,7% | 1 6,7% | | 15 100% |
| | RM11 | 7 58,3% | 2 16,7% | 1 8,3% | | 1 8,3% | 1 8,3% | | | | | 12 100% |
| DC | RM12 | 11 33,3% | 6 18,2% | 8 24,2% | 7 21,2% | | 1 3% | | | | | 33 100% |
| | RM13 | 13 31,7% | 8 19,5% | 5 12,2% | 8 19,5% | 2 4,9% | 5 12,2% | | | | | 41 100% |
| NM | RM14 | 7 29,2% | 3 12,5% | 6 25% | 3 12,5% | 1 4,2% | 3 12,5% | | | | 1 4,2% | 24 100% |
| Total | | 186 30,4% | 95 15,5% | 89 14,5% | 126 20,6% | 29 4,7% | 55 9% | 5 0,8% | 6 1% | 13 2,1% | 8 1,3% | 612 100% |

## Blade debitage

The striking platform of the blade cores remained plain during the debitage as indicated by the high frequency of plain butts (Figure 4.2.). Abraded overhangs characterize 62% of the blades. In the case of RM7 and RM3 it is absent. The butts are dominantly thin (62.3% are thinner than 2 mm). The impact point is visible on 13% of the blades. In a total of 76% of these cases the impact point is minor. A total of 27.3% of the blades have no bulb. The bulb appears as diffused on 52% of the blades. The rest of the blades, 20.7%, have convex bulbs. Lipping is characteristic to 50.6% of the blades. These evidence the use of soft hammer technique. Blades of the best quality raw materials (RM7 and RM9) solely bear characteristics of soft hammer technique.

The length of the blades ranges up to 91 mm. The largest items were made of RM1, RM10 and RM13, with the dominance of mediocre quality flints, while blades of RM5, RM6, and RM14 with good quality dominance are never larger than 55 mm.

*Table 4.3.* Blade edge-profile crosstabulation.

| Edges | Profile straight | curved | twisted | Total |
|---|---|---|---|---|
| parallel | 10 | 14 | 2 | 26 |
| converging | 7 | 5 | 2 | 14 |
| expanding | 6 | 9 | 2 | 17 |
| rhomboid | 2 | 1 | | 3 |
| Total | 25 | 29 | 6 | 60 |

The preponderance of blades with parallel and expanding edges (Table 4.3.) indicates that the cores had debitage surfaces with parallel sides during most part of the blade debitage. In profile, the blades are dominantly curved. Twisted blades are uncommon. The core fronts, according to the shape of the core tablets, were semi-circular or narrows (Figure 4.4: 14).

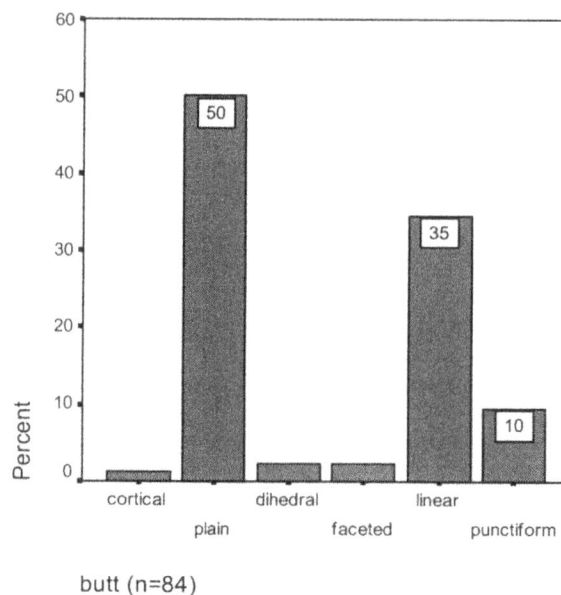

butt (n=84)

*Figure 4.2.* Butt types of blades.

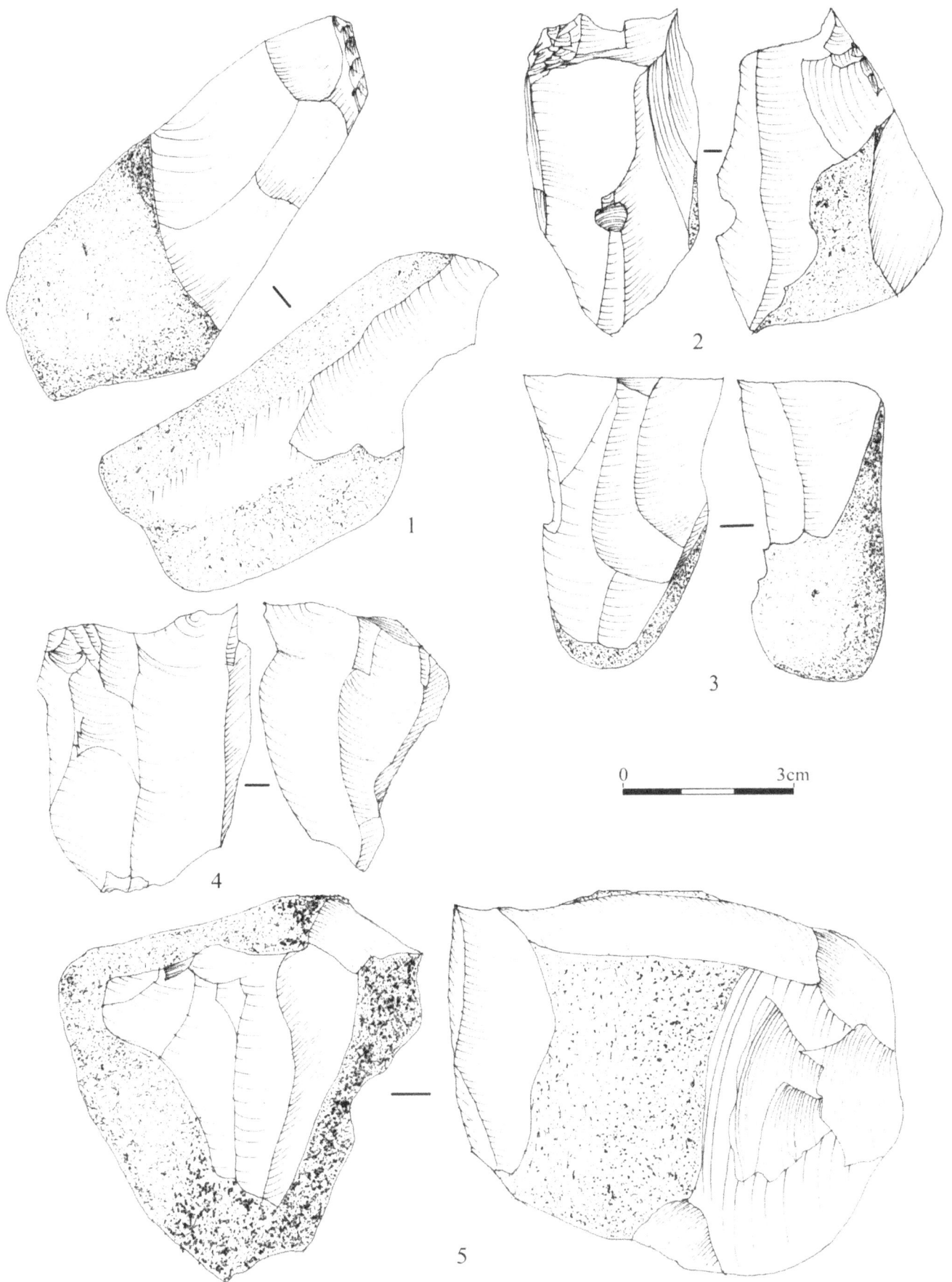

**Figure 4.3.** Blade cores.

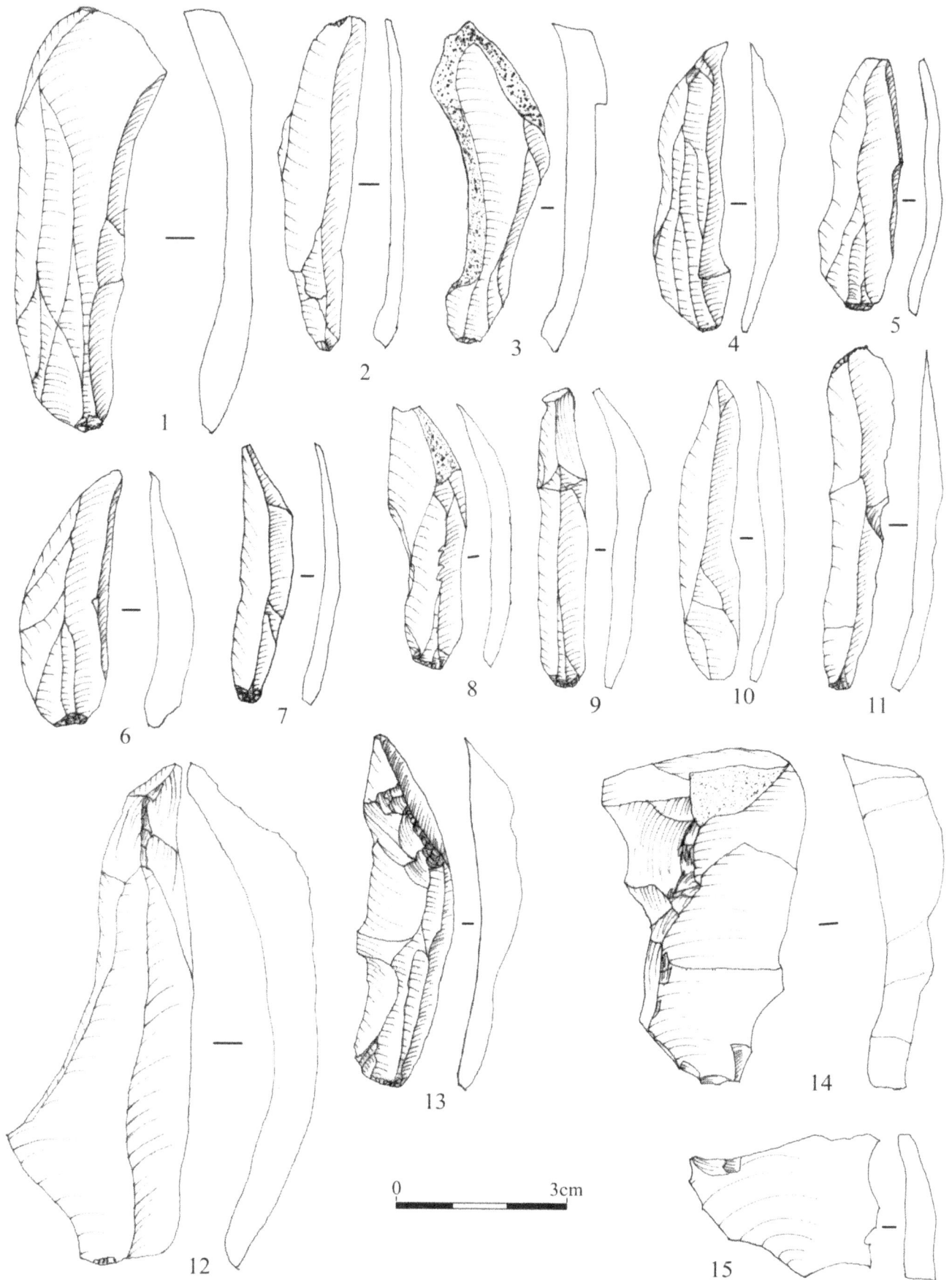

**Figure 4.4.** Blades (1-11), neo-crest blades (12, 13), blade core tablet (14), and blade core platform rejuvenating flake (15).

All cores have a single striking platform and 71% of the blades bear unidirectional dorsal scars (Figure 4.5.). These vestiges indicate that the orientation of the blade debitage was primarily unidirectional. A very few of the opposite removals are definitely in connection with opposite debitage. However, this core exploitation is uncommon, and the presence of non-unidirectional scars on blades may mostly be remnants of cores' side and debitage surface shaping or reshaping.

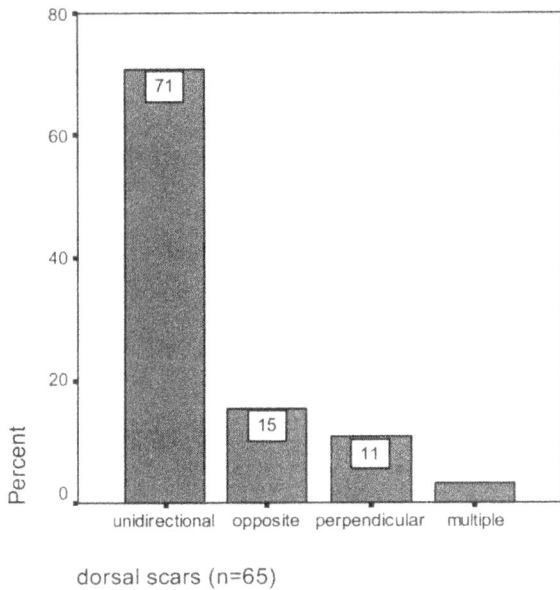

*Figure 4.5.* Direction of dorsal scars on blades.

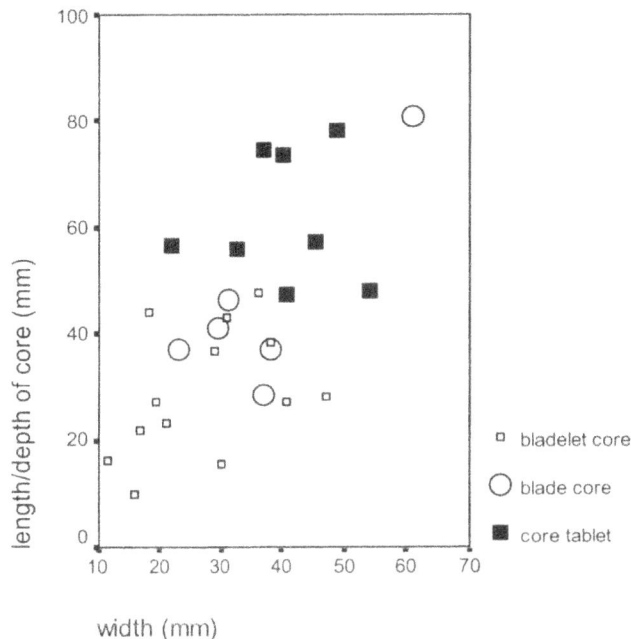

*Figure 4.6.* The size of the laminar cores' striking platform and that of the core tablets.

## Accidents during blade debitage

There are 46.7% broken blades. Most fragments are distal (47.4%), while mesials are 22.8% and proximals are 28%. It is of interest that the number of breaks is higher among the mediocre quality RM1 blades (44.9% of RM1 blades are broken) than among RM5 good quality blades (33.3% of RM5 good quality flint blades are broken). All breaks are "clear", thus it is impossible to distinguish between knapping and post-knapping breaks. Plunging items make up 5.2% while hinged ones are 4.2% of the blade assemblage.

## Blade core maintenance

During blade production, the cores' striking platforms were rejuvenated by rejuvenating flake removals (n=2) (Figure 4.4: 15.), and core tablet removals (n=5) (Figure 4.4: 14.). The core tablets from blade cores are larger than the area of the striking platform of most of the blade cores (Figure 4.6.). This means that the cores had been rejuvenated on striking platform before they reached the present state.

The debitage surface convexity was maintained by neo-cresting (9 neo-crest blades) (Figure 4.4:12, 13.). The neo-cresting was habitually made at the distal part of the cores and only in rare cases performed along the entire length of the debitage surface.

## Blade core discard

Four cores have semi-circular fronts, two of which have parallel sides, while two others have converging sides. Narrow and wide-surfaced cores have converging sides. These are present by a single item, respectively.

Six cores are cortical. One of the cores with significant cortex coverage (51-75%) was discarded at the beginning of the blade debitage (Figure 4.3: 5.). Only two cores were discarded after hinge accidents. The striking platform of one of these was rejuvenated before discard. Other cores discarded have no ultimate knapping accidents.

## Bladelet production

### Bladelet core configuration

The bladelet production is dominated by mediocre quality flints. Within mediocre quality flint group RM1 is dominant (Table 4.1.). One flint type, RM3 of low quality was not used in bladelet production.

From RM1, no blade cores are left behind, while a considerable amount of blades and blade core tablets are present (Table 4.2.). This means the bladelet debitage took place in a joint sequence with the blade debitage in the exploitation of RM1.

According to the preserved original surfaces of the flint nodules, also there was a tendency to collect small nodules for making cores to the bladelet production. These were small, *ca* 5 cm sized flint nodules (Figure 4.9:4, 6.). Besides original nodules, in two cases thick flakes of RM1 and RM10 were used as blanks of bladelet cores (Figure 4.9: 5.).

Vestiges of bladelet core configuration methods are scarce. A few cores show that the lateral sides were shaped from the back and the proximal core part (Figure 4.9: 1, 3.). The configuration removals, since only a total of 16.8% of the entire bladelet assemblage are cortical, were restricted to clean the core front and its environment. The cortex on the bladelets usually appears at the distal part and on one of the dorsal halves along the total length. The cortex coverage on the bladelets in 91% of the cases extends up to 25% of the dorsal face. In the rest of the cases the cortex covers between 50 and 75% of the dorsal face. Since no cortical bladelets among tools in the assemblage, those probably were to remove cortex around the debitage surface.

The cores' striking platforms were created by the removal of a single flake. It rarely remained cortical, as indicated by the low number of cortical blade butts (Figure 4.7.). No vestiges of cresting can be found in bladelet core configuration.

## Bladelet debitage

Most bladelets have linear butts (Figure 4.7.). The butt thickness is less than 1mm in 69.6% of the cases. Of the bladelets, the butt type is linear at 52%, the overhangs are abraded at 71.6%, and the impact point is present at 13.5%. These indicate that soft hammer technique was used for the most part in the debitage.

debitage. The core tablets refer to the use of narrow debitage surfaced cores in bladelet debitage.

All cores have a single striking platform and 85% of the bladelets bear unidirectional dorsal scars (Figure 4.8.). These vestiges indicate that the orientation of the debitage was primarily unidirectional. A very few of the opposite removals may mostly be remnants of cores' side and debitage surface shaping.

## Accidents during bladelet debitage

A total of 32.5% of the bladelets are broken. Distal fragments make up 41.4%, mesial ones make up 31% and proximal ones make up 27.6%. All breaks are "clear", thus it is impossible to distinguish between knapping and post-knapping breaks. Hinge accidents make up 6.7 % of the bladelets while plunging accident is present with a single piece.

**Table 4.4.** Bladelet profile-edge shape crosstabulation.

| Profile | Edges | | | | Total |
|---|---|---|---|---|---|
| | parallel | converging | expanding | irregular | |
| straight | 9 | 6 | 8 | | 23 |
| curved | 5 | 10 | 5 | | 20 |
| twisted | 6 | 5 | 4 | 1 | 16 |
| *Total* | 20 | 21 | 17 | 1 | 59 |

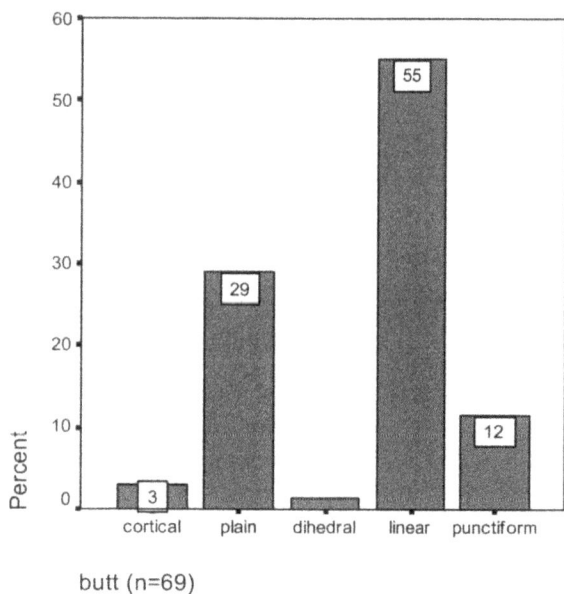

butt (n=69)

**Figure 4.7.** Butt types of bladelets.

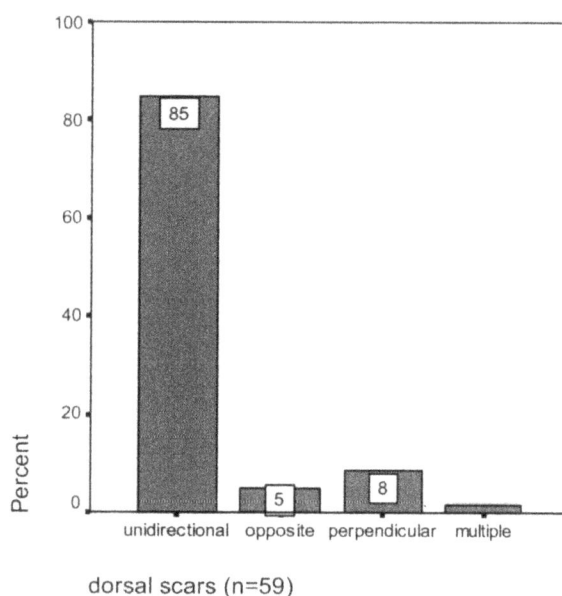

dorsal scars (n=59)

**Figure 4.8.** Directions of dorsal scars on bladelets.

The profile of the bladelets is dominantly straight, in lesser cases curved. Items with twisted profile account for almost the one-third part of the bladelets. The straight bladelets have mostly parallel edges and the curved bladelets have dominantly converging edges (Table 4.4.). The preponderance of bladelets with parallel and expanding edges indicates that the cores had debitage surfaces with parallel sides during most part of the

## Bladelet core maintenance

During bladelet production, the cores' striking platforms were rejuvenated by rejuvenating flake removals (n=3) and core tablet removals (n=3) (Figure 4.10.).

The debitage surface convexity was maintained by neo-cresting (3 neo-crest bladelets). Neo-cresting remains are visible on bladelet cores, too (n=2). The neo-cresting was made at the distal part of the cores.

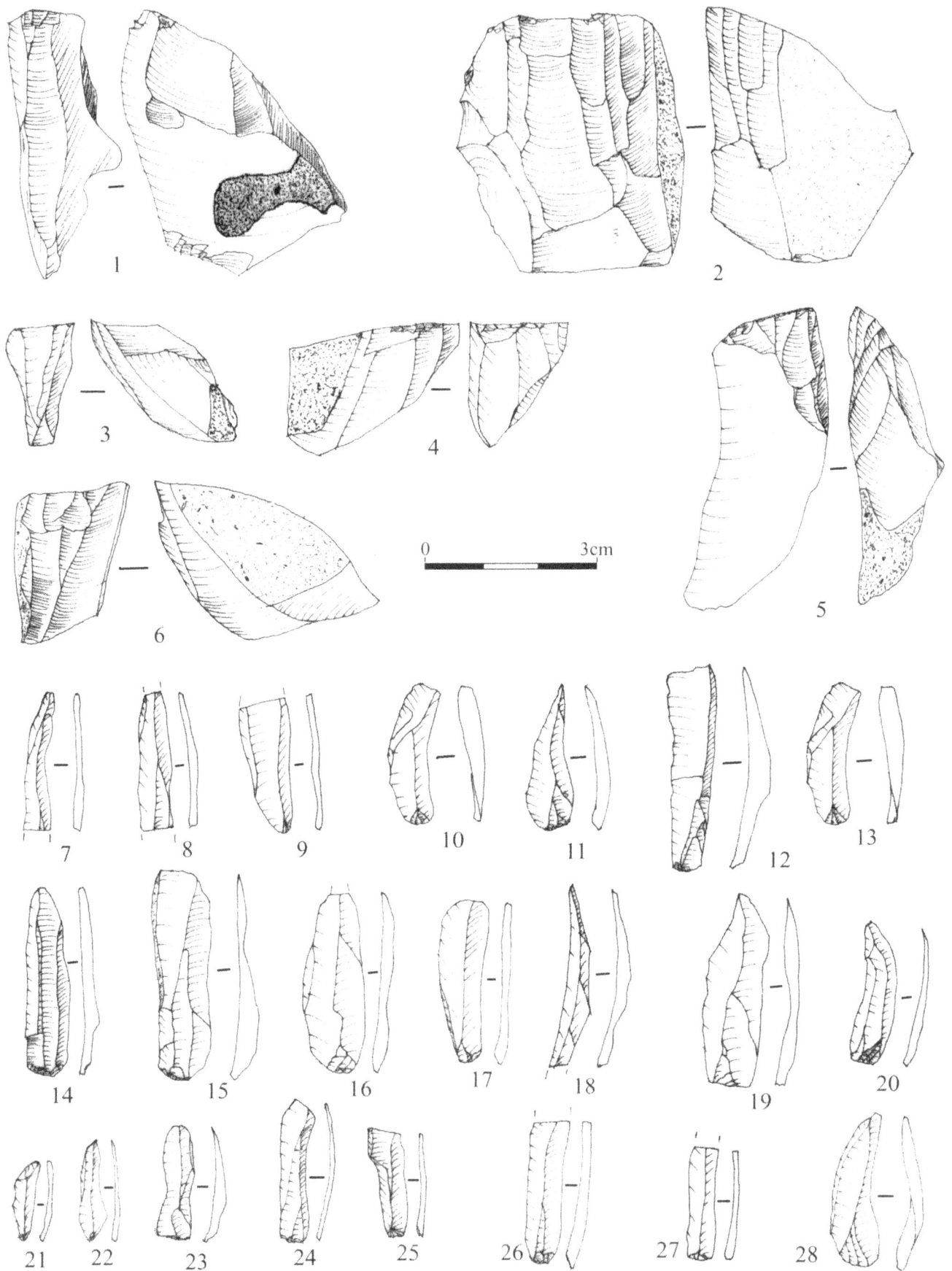

**Figure 4.9**. *Bladelet cores (1-5) and bladelets (7-28).*

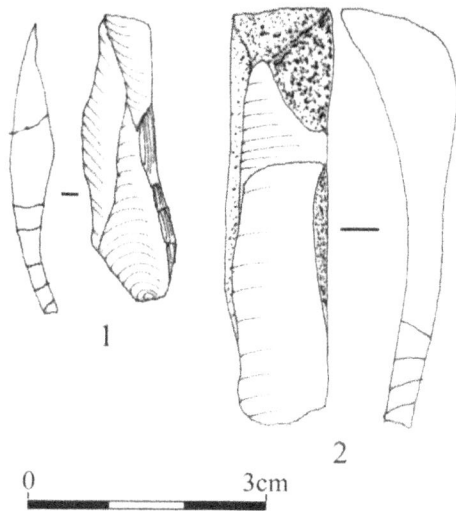

**Figure 4.10.** *Core tablets of the bladelet production.*

always regarded crucial accidents leading directly to discard as evidenced by the presence of hinge scars on the dorsal faces of 10 bladelets.

Five bladelet cores were discarded after hinge removals. Other cores bear no crucial accident. These are the smallest specimens (n=4) whose size is under 30 mm, while all the hinge scar bearer cores are larger (30-51 mm). Therefore, the smallest cores bearing no accidents might have been discarded on the reason of critical diminishing of the size of exploitable surface.

**Table 4.5.** *Crosstabulation of the front shape and sides of the bladelet cores.*

| Front | Sides | | Total |
|---|---|---|---|
| | converging | parallel | |
| narrow | 4 | 1 | 5 |
| semi-circular | 2 | 1 | 3 |
| wide | 4 | 1 | 5 |
| Total | 10 | 3 | 13 |

## *Bladelet core discard*

Two types of bladelet cores are frequent, the narrow and the wide fronted. Semi-circular fronted-cores appear in lesser amount. The lateral sides of the debitage surfaces are dominantly converging (Table 4.5.). Ten cores are cortical.

The cores were discarded in different stages of debitage. Two cores were rejuvenated by flake removals on their striking platforms prior to discard. Seven cores' overhangs were abraded before discard. This preparation for further removals also occurred following hinge accidents, since hinges were not

## Flake production

Flakes are present from every raw material. Their number is especially high of RM1, RM2 and RM5. The number of flakes is extremely high in comparison to that of the flake cores. Three cores, two of RM1 and one of RM7, show scars of flake debitage. Two other cores, of RM1, originally belonged to blade production and only a few flakes were removed from them by debitage. Three of the cores were used with unidirectional and two with multiple orientation of debitage.

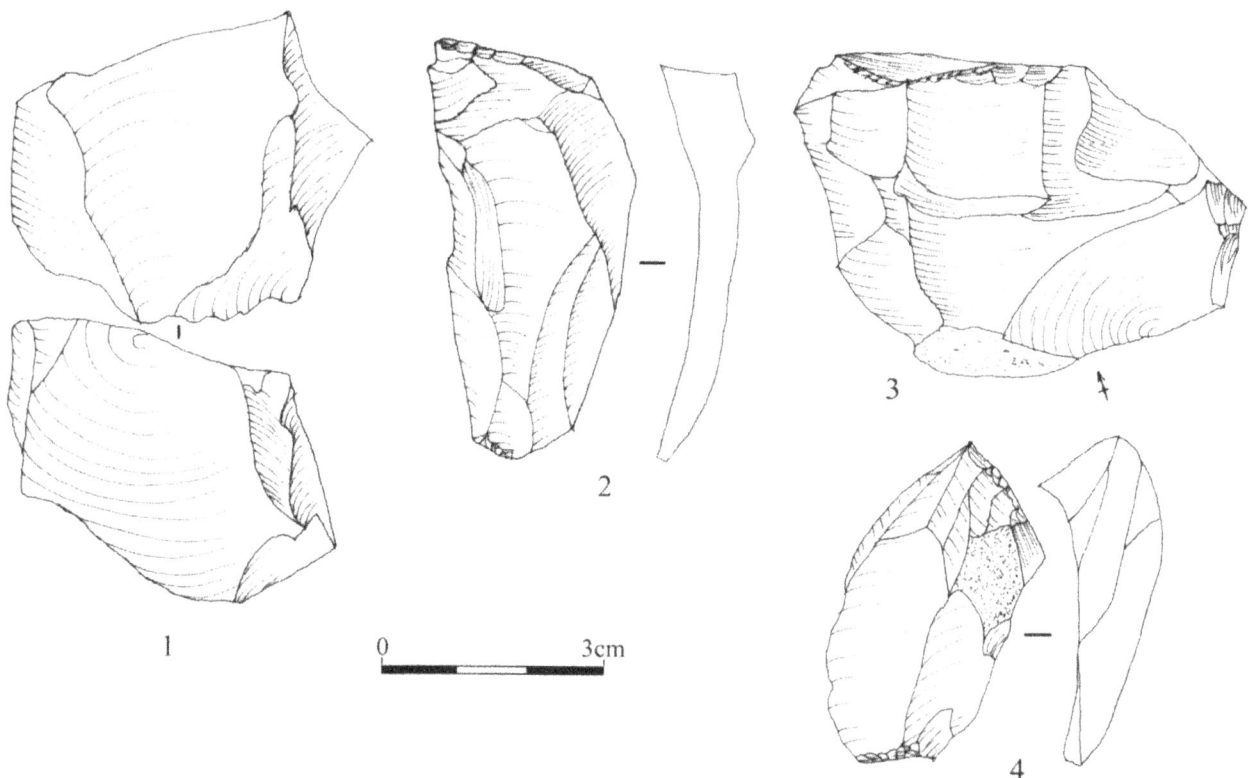

**Figure 4.11.** *Flake core (1) and flakes (2-4).*

Flakes also derive from laminar cores' debitage surfaces, as evidenced by the presence of unidirectional scar bearer flakes with parallel ridges (36% of the flakes) (Figure 4.11: 4.).

Abraded overhangs characterize 22% of the flakes. The butts are dominantly, 75.3%, are thicker than 2 mm. The impact point is visible on 49.2% of the flakes. In half of these cases the impact point is large. A total of 23.6% of the flakes have no bulb. The bulb appears as diffused on 50% of the flakes. The rest of the flakes, 26.4%, have convex bulbs. Lipping is characteristic to 47.3% of the flakes. These evidence the use of both soft and hard hammer technique. The butt of the flakes is predominantly plain.

The fragmentation ratio is very low among flakes. Only 19.9% are broken. Distal fragments make up 72.3%, mesial fragments make up 4.3%, and proximal fragments make up 23.4%. There is a relative high frequency of hinges among flakes (12.4%), while that among plungings is low (1.1%).

## Tool blank selection and tools

### Blade tool blanks
A total of 15.6% of the blades are tools. Most blade tool blanks are of RM1, RM2, and RM5 (Table. 4.12.). More than half of the specimens are cortical (55%). The blank shape is frequently curved in profile with converging lateral edges as against blades with curved profile and parallel edges among unretouched blanks.

*Table 4.12. Tool blanks by raw material*

| Raw material | | Tool blank | | | Total |
|---|---|---|---|---|---|
| source | type | flake | blade | bladelet | |
| RAM | RM1 | 8 | 5 | 1 | *14* |
| | RM2 | 3 | 6 | | *9* |
| | RM3 | 1 | | | *1* |
| | RM4 | 4 | 1 | 1 | *6* |
| DH | RM5 | 7 | 4 | | *11* |
| | RM6 | 1 | 1 | | *2* |
| | RM7 | | 1 | | *1* |
| | RM8 | 1 | | | *1* |
| | RM11 | | 1 | | *1* |
| DC | RM12 | | 1 | | *1* |
| | RM13 | 5 | | | *5* |
| NM | RM14 | 3 | | | *3* |
| Total | | 33 | 20 | 2 | *55* |

### Blade tools
Blades make up 36.3% of the tool kit. They were selected for making endscrapers, retouched items (Figure 4.12: 5, 6.), burins and truncations. Blades are sole blanks for a borer and a composite tool and were not used for notches, sidescrapers, and raclettes (Table 4.13.).

Endscrapers on blades are atypical and simple with converging retouch. Burins are mostly transversal. The retouched items are typically with partial scaled retouch. The single composite tool is composed of end-scraper and burin. The endscraper part is worked out by scaled retouch and the burin part is angled on break.

### Bladelet tool blanks
Only 2.1% of the bladelets are tools. Although most bladelets were produced in high frequency from RM5, the tool blanks were selected from RM1 and RM4 (Table 4.12.). Of the two bladelet tool blanks one is cortical.

### Bladelet tools
Bladelets make up 3.7% of the tool kit. Bladelet blanks were used for making a retouched (Figure 4.12: 7) and a notched item. The retouch is marginal and continuous on one edge.

### Flake tool blanks
A total of 13.1% of the flakes are tools. The majority of them are of RM1 and RM5 (Table 4.12.). Flake tool blanks are frequently cortical, making up 48.5% of the flakes. Included among flake tool blanks are 3 core tablets (Figure 4.12: 3, 9.) and one core platform rejuvenating flake.

### Flake tools
Most of the tools were made on flakes, accounting for 60% of the tool kit. Frequent flake tools are endscrapers (Figure 4.12: 1-4) and retouched items. Flakes are sole blanks of side scrapers and raclettes. Simple retouching techniques are associated with flake tools: endscrapers are mostly with semi-converging retouch, while nosed, thick nosed and atypical endscrapes are uncommon; the single burin is angled on break; retouches on the edges are scaled and marginal with various extents; the truncation is oblique; notches are single; denticulates are with deep scaled retouch; side scrapers are double, convex and converging with scaled and continuous retouch; raclettes are with abrupt retouch.

*Table 4.13.* Tool type list of the Early Upper Palaeolithic assemblage.

| Tool types | | Blank | | | Total | |
|---|---|---|---|---|---|---|
| | | flake | blade | bladelet | # | % |
| Endscrapers | simple | 6 | 2 | | 8 | 14,5 |
| | on retouched blank | 1 | | | 1 | 1,8 |
| | nosed | 1 | | | 1 | 1,8 |
| | thick nosed | 1 | | | 1 | 1,8 |
| | atypical | 1 | 3 | | 4 | 7,3 |
| | *Sub-total* | *10* | *5* | | *15* | *27,3* |
| Burins | dihedral | | 1 | | 1 | 1,8 |
| | on break | 1 | | | 1 | 1,8 |
| | transversal | | 2 | | 2 | 3,6 |
| | *Sub-total* | *1* | *3* | | *4* | *7,3* |
| Retouched items | continuous scaled | 2 | | | 2 | 3,6 |
| | continuous marginal | 1 | | 1 | 2 | 3,6 |
| | discontinuous marginal | 2 | | | 2 | 3,6 |
| | partially scaled | 2 | 5 | | 7 | 12,7 |
| | partially marginal | 1 | 1 | | 2 | 3,6 |
| | continuously alternating scaled | 1 | | | 1 | 1,8 |
| | *Sub-total* | *9* | *6* | *1* | *16* | *29,1* |
| Truncations | straight | | 2 | | 2 | 3,6 |
| | oblique | 1 | 1 | | 2 | 3,6 |
| | *Sub-total* | *1* | *3* | | *4* | *7,3* |
| Borers | | | 1 | | 1 | 1,8 |
| | *Sub-total* | | *1* | | *1* | *1,8* |
| Notches | single | 3 | | 1 | 4 | 7,3 |
| | *Sub-total* | *3* | | *1* | *4* | *7,3* |
| Denticulates | | 4 | 1 | | 5 | 9,1 |
| | *Sub-total* | *4* | *1* | | *5* | *9,1* |
| Side scrapers | double | 1 | | | 1 | 1,8 |
| | convex | 1 | | | 1 | 1,8 |
| | converging | 1 | | | 1 | 1,8 |
| | *Sub-total* | *3* | | | *3* | *5,4* |
| Raclette | | 2 | | | 2 | 3,6 |
| | *Sub-total* | *2* | | | *2* | *3,6* |
| Composites | end-scraper/burin | | 1 | | 1 | 1,8 |
| | *Sub-total* | | *1* | | *1* | *1,8* |
| *Total* | | *33* | *20* | *2* | *55* | *100* |

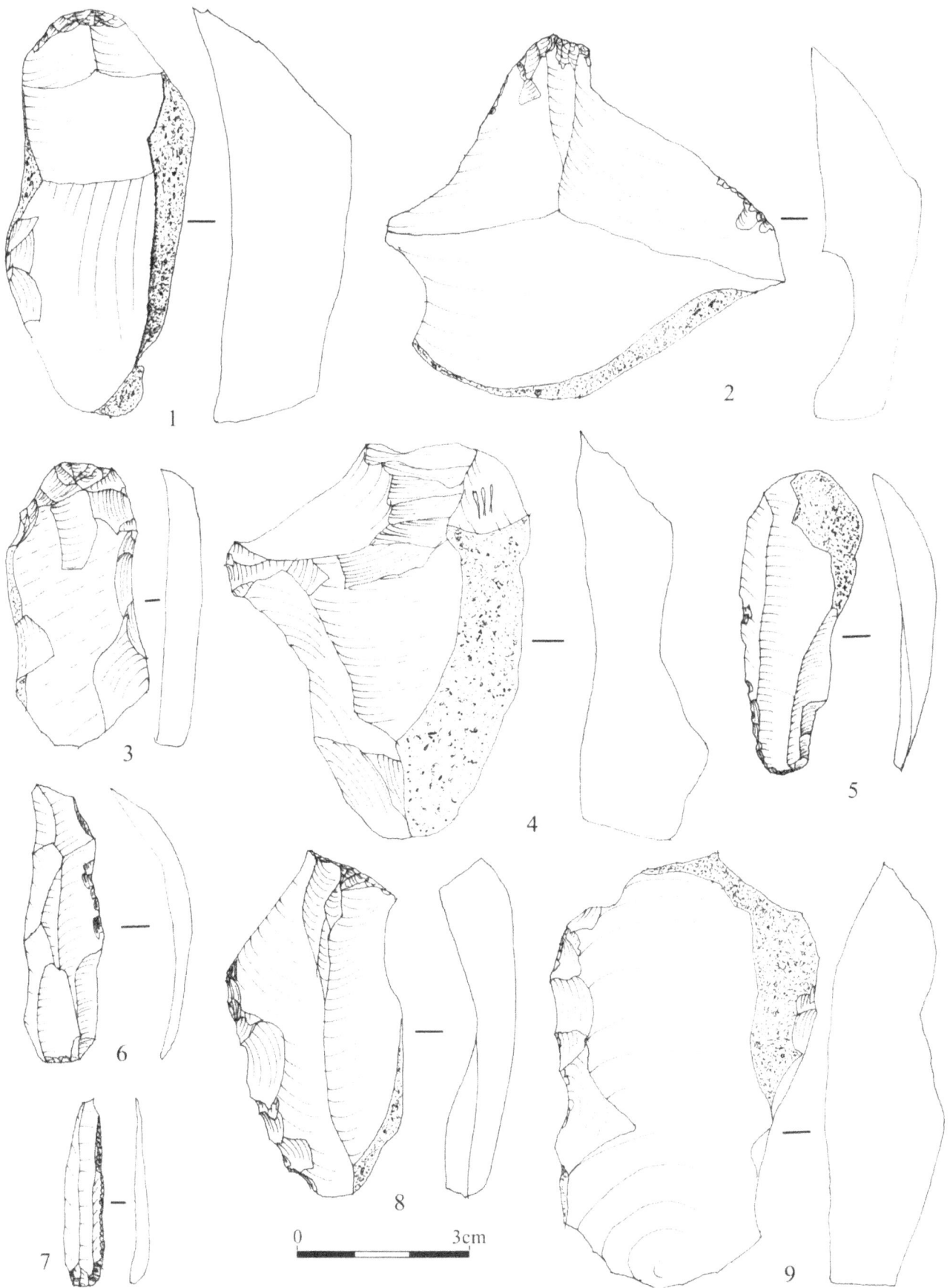

**Figure 4.12.** Endscrapers (1-4), retouched blades (5, 6), retouched bladelet (7), and denticulated flakes (8, 9).

# CHAPTER 5: THE LEVANTINE AURIGNACIAN ASSEMBLAGE
## LAYER III, AREA B-G/18-23

## Raw Material

The raw materials of the assemblage derive from four flint sources (Table 5.1). Ramat Menashe (RAM), the closest raw material source to Raqefet, yielded the majority of the raw materials, among which the mediocre quality RM1 is dominant. In addition, this raw material is the most abundant in the whole assemblage.

*Table 5.1. Frequency of raw materials by source.*

| Raw material quality | type | Raw material source RAM | DH | DC | NM | Total |
|---|---|---|---|---|---|---|
| Mediocre | RM1 | 1091 57,3% | | | | 1091 31,2% |
| Low | RM2 | 470 24,7% | | | | 470 13,4% |
| Low | RM3 | 47 2,5% | | | | 47 1,3% |
| Low | RM4 | 295 15,5% | | | | 295 8,4% |
| Good | RM5 | | 661 60% | | | 661 18,9% |
| Low | RM6 | | 186 16,9% | | | 186 5,3% |
| Good | RM7 | | 90 8,2% | | | 90 2,6% |
| Good | RM8 | | 41 3,7% | | | 41 1,2% |
| Mediocre | RM9 | | 30 2,7% | | | 30 0,9% |
| Good | RM10 | | 30 2,7% | | | 30 0,9% |
| Mediocre | RM11 | | 63 5,7% | | | 63 1,8% |
| Low | RM12 | | | 131 40,7% | | 131 3,7% |
| Low | RM13 | | | 191 59,3% | | 191 5,5% |
| Good | RM14 | | | | 176 100% | 176 5% |
| Total | | 1903 100% | 1101 100% | 322 100% | 176 100% | 3502 100% |

Deir Hannah formation (DH) flints make up the next largest group of raw material, within which the good quality RM5 is dominant, but the low quality RM6 also appears in significant amount. RM5 constitutes the second most abundant raw material type in the whole assemblage.

Daliyat ha Carmel low quality raw materials (DC) are present with low frequency. Nahal Mearot raw materials (NM) make up the smallest part of the assemblage.

In sum, the raw material acquisition focused on low and mediocre quality flints, while good quality flints make up the smallest part of the assemblage (Figure 5.1). Based on the presence of first flakes in the assemblage, RM1, RM5, RM7, RM11, RM13, RM14, raw materials from each source, were brought to the site as fully cortical nodules. The remainder raw materials were roughed-out in various extents off-site.

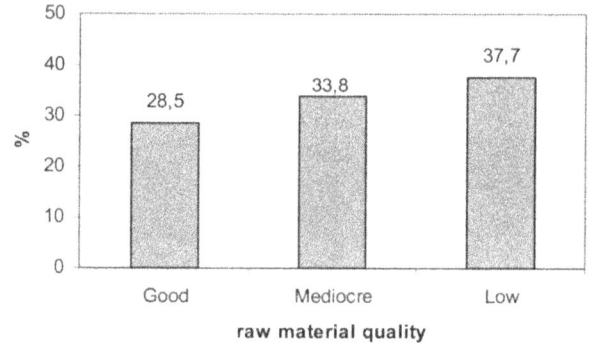

*Figure 5.1. Frequency of raw materials by quality.*

## Blade production

### Blade core configuration

Blades were made of all raw materials. Their production is connected to low quality flints, but the most frequently used individual raw material is RM1 of mediocre quality (Table 5.2.). Except RM2, RM7, RM8, RM10, RM14, all raw materials have the whole sequence of bladelet production, from cores to tools. Of the 42 blade cores, 32 preserved a considerable part of the original shape of the raw material nodule. These illustrate that large nodular and tabular flints with longitudinal natural ridges were collected for blade production (Figures 5.3: 1, 3.). This shape was ideal for blade production without front cresting. The narrow part of the raw material nodule habitually was chosen to be the core front. The striking platforms of the cores were prepared by the removal of a single flake, and rare remained cortical.

Although 83% of the cortical items are flakes, the high percent of cortical blades (53%) and cortical cores (78.6%) shows there is a lack of intensive initial core shaping and decortication. An example for core shaping is a partially refitted core (Figure 5.2.). This shows that the striking platform was created by a large cortical flake removal. Then, a thick flake was detached from the right lateral side from the striking platform. This removal made the flint nodule considerably narrower. All steps of this shaping were carried out by using hard stone hammer technique.

Exploited flake cores (Figure 5.4: 4.) and large flakes (Figure 5.4: 1, 2.) also were used for making blade cores. In the case of using large flakes, the striking platform was set up at the distal end. The front cresting was applied occasionally as the scarce presence of crest blades and cresting on cores evidence (Figure 5.4: 1, 3.). The debitage took place on one of the flake edges. However, there are 10 blades which show that they were removed from the edge of a flake without cresting. Cresting on flake cores turned to blade cores is recorded on a single item (Figure 5.4: 4.), and in the case of cores made of raw flint nodules that is absent.

42

*Figure 5.2. First flake-blade core refit (RM6).Scale 5 cm.*

*Table 5.2. Frequency of lithic products by raw material.*

| Raw material | | Lithic product | | | | | | Core | | | | Total |
|---|---|---|---|---|---|---|---|---|---|---|---|---|
| sources | types | flake | blade | bladelet | waste | CTE | tool | flake | blade | bladelet | pre-core | |
| RAM | RM1 | 378 | 72 | 39 | 234 | 16 | 279 | 36 | 10 | 21 | 6 | 1091 |
| | | 34,6% | 6,6% | 3,6% | 21,4% | 1,5% | 25,6% | 3,3% | 0,9% | 1,9% | 0,5% | 100% |
| | RM2 | 159 | 35 | 11 | 88 | 12 | 148 | 8 | | 7 | 2 | 470 |
| | | 33,8% | 7,4% | 2,3% | 18,7% | 2,6% | 31,5% | 1,7% | | 1,5% | 0,4% | 100% |
| | RM3 | 10 | 13 | 1 | 1 | 1 | 19 | 1 | 1 | | | 47 |
| | | 21,3% | 27,7% | 2,1% | 2,1% | 2,1% | 40,4% | 2,1% | 2,1% | | | 100% |
| | RM4 | 99 | 13 | 12 | 77 | 3 | 84 | 1 | 2 | 3 | 1 | 295 |
| | | 33,6% | 4,4% | 4,1% | 26,1% | 1% | 28,5% | 0,3% | 0,7% | 1% | 0,3% | 100% |
| DH | RM5 | 224 | 28 | 46 | 164 | 14 | 127 | 24 | 12 | 20 | 2 | 661 |
| | | 33,9% | 4,2% | 7% | 24,8% | 2,1% | 19,2% | 3,6% | 1,8% | 3% | 0,3% | 100% |
| | RM6 | 69 | 14 | 4 | 21 | 2 | 60 | 5 | 8 | 2 | 1 | 186 |
| | | 37,1% | 7,5% | 2,2% | 11,3% | 1,1% | 32,3% | 2,7% | 4,3% | 1,1% | 0,5% | 100% |
| | RM7 | 35 | 6 | 9 | 11 | 2 | 23 | 3 | | | 1 | 90 |
| | | 38,9% | 6,7% | 10% | 12,2% | 2,2% | 25,6% | 3,3% | | | 1,1% | 100% |
| | RM8 | 14 | 4 | 1 | 5 | | 10 | 6 | | | 1 | 41 |
| | | 34,1% | 9,8% | 2,4% | 12,2% | | 24,4% | 14,6% | | | 2,4% | 100% |
| | RM9 | 14 | 3 | | 1 | | 4 | 3 | 3 | 2 | | 30 |
| | | 46,7% | 10% | | 3,3% | | 13,3% | 10% | 10% | 6,7% | | 100% |
| | RM10 | 7 | 5 | 2 | 1 | 1 | 12 | 1 | | 1 | | 30 |
| | | 23,3% | 16,7% | 6,7% | 3,3% | 3,3% | 40% | 3,3% | | 3,3% | | 100% |
| | RM11 | 27 | 3 | 3 | 9 | 1 | 15 | 3 | 1 | 1 | | 63 |
| | | 42,9% | 4,8% | 4,8% | 14,3% | 1,6% | 23,8% | 4,8% | 1,6% | 1,6% | | 100% |
| DC | RM12 | 55 | 6 | 8 | 10 | 4 | 42 | 2 | 2 | 2 | | 131 |
| | | 42% | 4,6% | 6,1% | 7,6% | 3,1% | 32,1% | 1,5% | 1,5% | 1,5% | | 100% |
| | RM13 | 80 | 17 | 8 | 18 | 4 | 53 | 3 | 3 | 4 | 1 | 191 |
| | | 41,9% | 8,9% | 4,2% | 9,4% | 2,1% | 27,7% | 1,6% | 1,6% | 2,1% | 0,5% | 100% |
| NM | RM14 | 62 | 8 | 11 | 41 | 4 | 44 | 4 | | 2 | | 176 |
| | | 35,2% | 4,5% | 6,3% | 23,3% | 2,3% | 25% | 2,3% | | 1,1% | | 100% |
| Total | | 1233 | 227 | 155 | 681 | 64 | 920 | 100 | 42 | 65 | 15 | 3502 |
| | | 35,2% | 6,5% | 4,4% | 19,4% | 1,8% | 26,3% | 2,9% | 1,2% | 1,9% | ,4% | 100% |

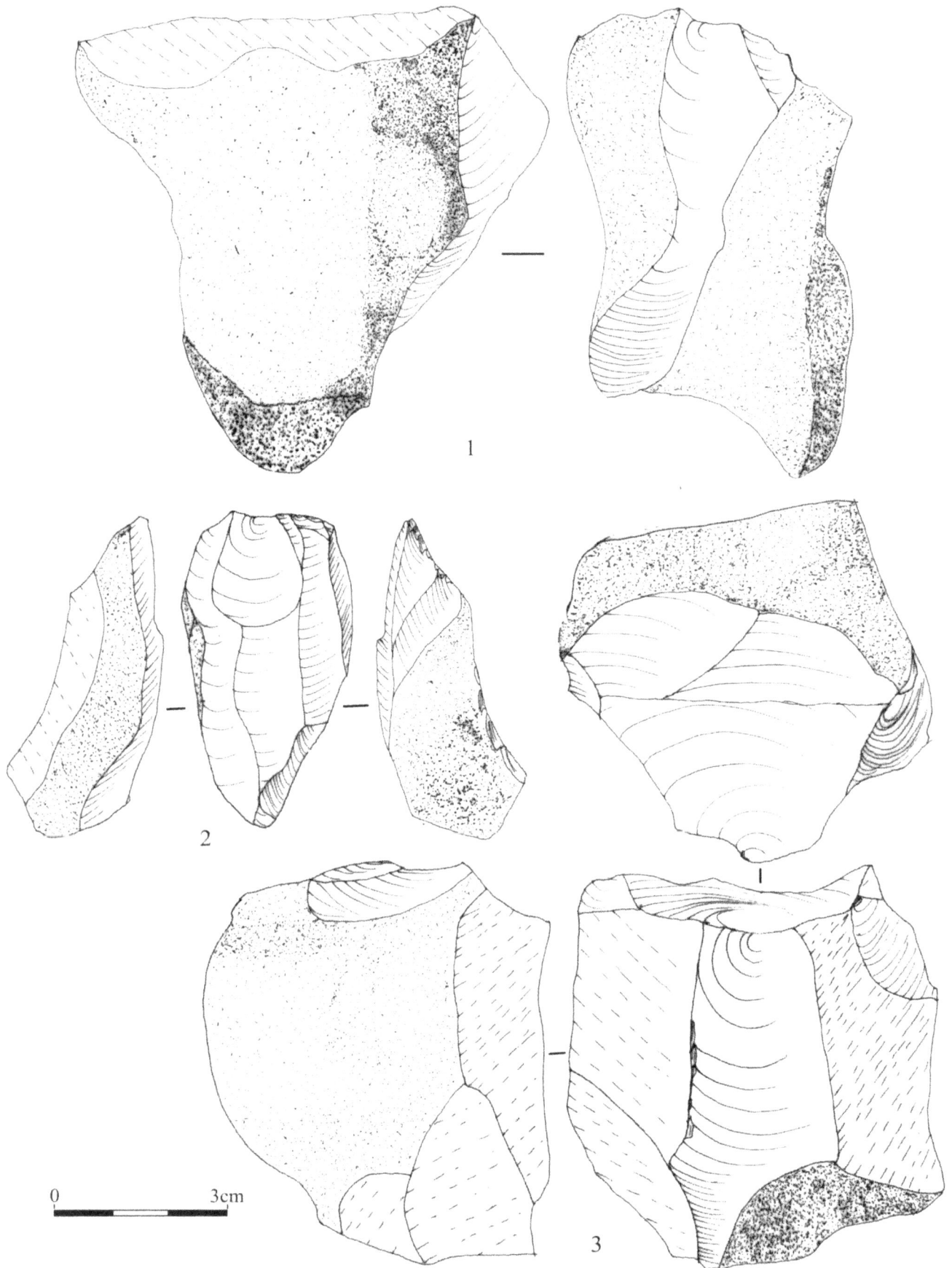

1

2

3

0          3cm

**Figure 5.3.** Blade cores.

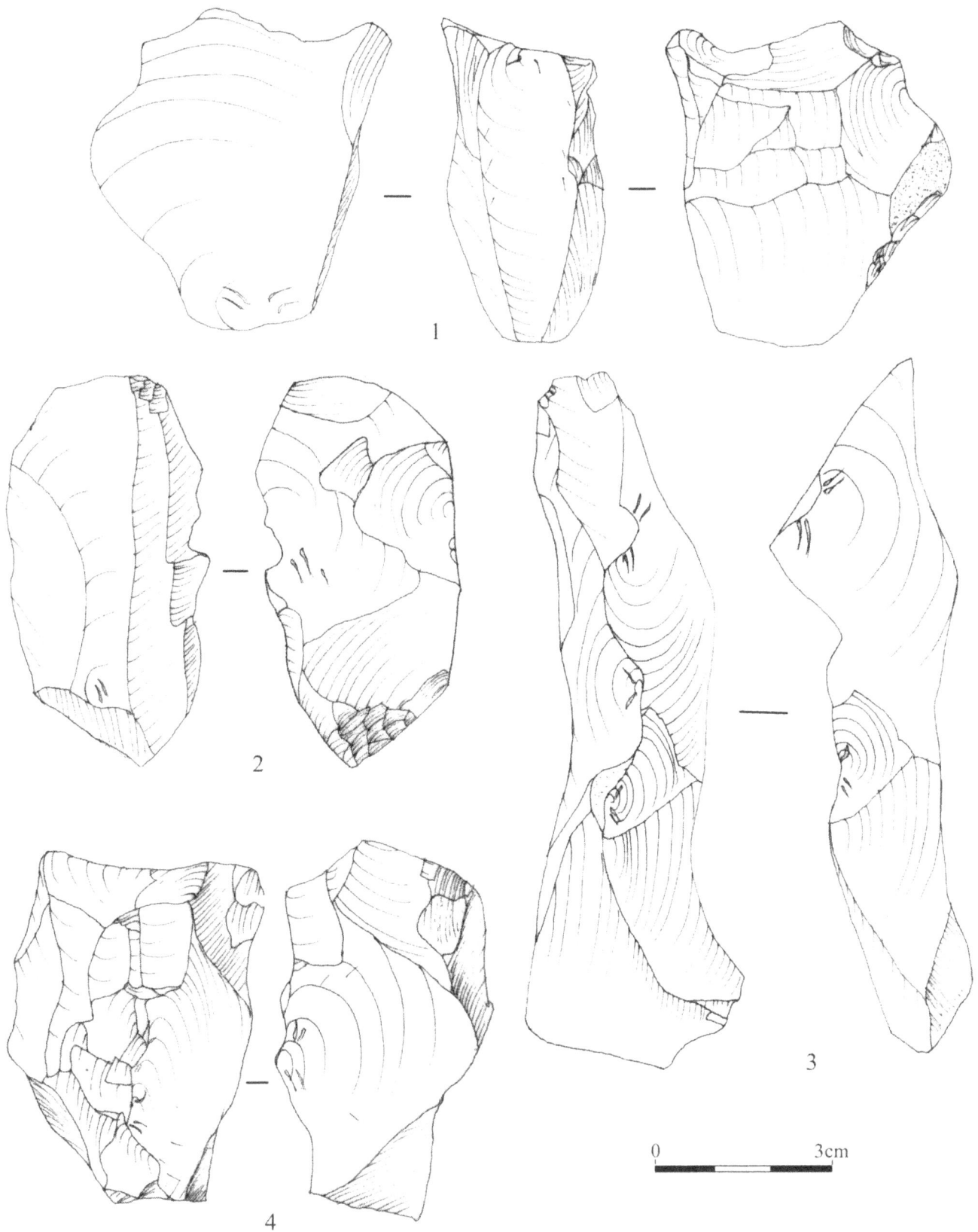

**Figure 5.4.** *Blade cores on flake (1, 2); crest blade (3); flake core with crest preparation for blade debitage (4).*

## Blade debitage

The striking platform of the blade cores remained plain during the debitage as indicated by the high frequency of plain butts (Figure 5.6.). Dihedral and faceted butts make up only 15%.

Abraded overhangs characterize only 24.9% of the blades. The 25.6% of the butts are thinner than 2 mm. The impact point is visible on 25.8% of the blades. In a total of 60.6% of these cases the impact point is minor. A total of 52.5% of the blades have no bulb. The bulb appears as diffused on 24.5% of the blades. The rest of the blades, 23%, have convex bulbs. Lipping is characteristic to 20.5% of the blades. These evidence the use of both hard and soft hammer techniques.

The exploitation of RM1 and RM5 blade cores was prevalently made with hard stone hammer technique. Soft hammer use appears in the highest percentage at the blades of RM4, RM13, and RM14 good quality flint (50-54.5%).

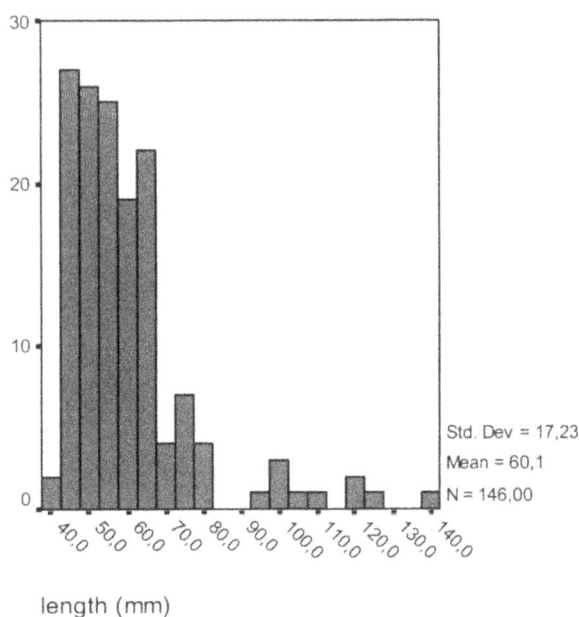

length (mm)

***Figure 5.5.*** *Length histogramm of blades.*

There is a wide variety of blade size (Figure 5.5., 5.9.). The largest blades (*ca* 90-120 mm) were most often detached by hard hammer technique. These are usually made of RM1 and RM2. Smaller blades (*ca* 60-80 mm) were produced with both hard and soft hammer technique, while the smallest and finest blades (*ca* 40-60 mm) were detached by soft hammer technique with high frequency. This is mirrored by mean values: the mean thickness and length of hard hammer technique detached blades are 11.8 mm and 61.3 mm, while these values for soft hammer technique detached blades are 6.8 mm and 56.9 mm.

The largest blades were produced from narrow-fronted cores, and made often of RM2 low quality flint which can be found in the largest size (*ca* 30-50 cm) on

the field. Contrary to this, the soft hammer technique detached finest blades often derive from wide debitage surfaced cores (only wide fronted cores have abraded overhangs).

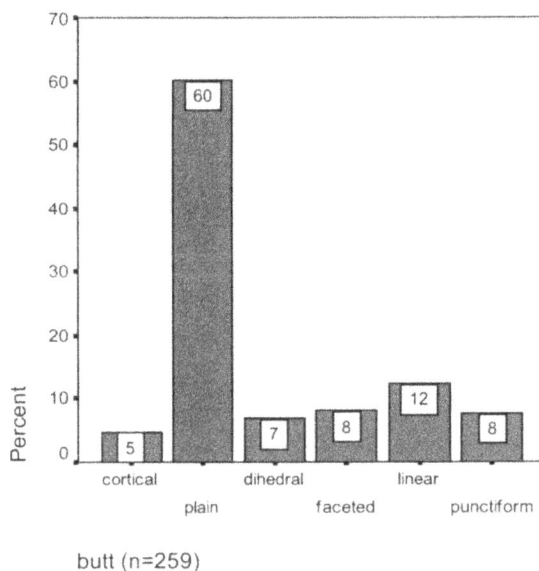

butt (n=259)

***Figure 5.6.*** *Butt types of blades.*

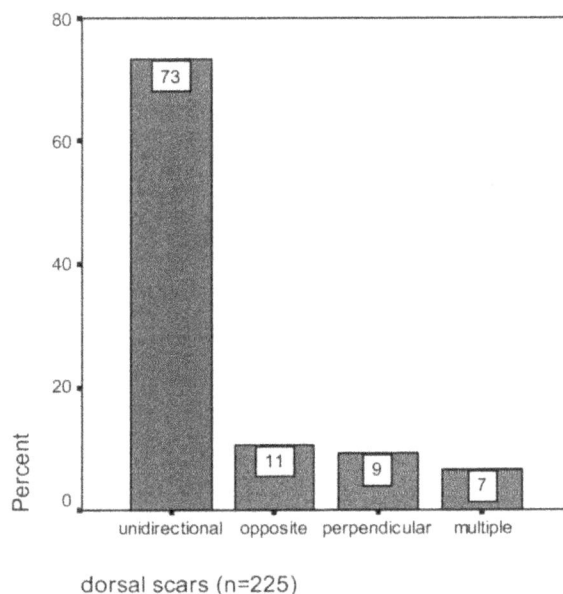

dorsal scars (n=225)

***Figure 5.7.*** *Direction of dorsal scars on blades.*

***Table 5.3.*** *Blade edge-profile crosstabulation.*

| Edges | Profile | | | Total |
|---|---|---|---|---|
| | straight | curved | twisted | |
| parallel | 56 | 32 | 17 | *105* |
| converging | 30 | 24 | 16 | *70* |
| expanding | 17 | 23 | 13 | *53* |
| irregular | 2 | 4 | 3 | *9* |
| *Total* | *105* | *83* | *49* | *237* |

The core front in debitage, according to the shape of the core tablets, was mostly semi-circular (Figure 5.10: 1.). The preponderance of blades with parallel and expanding edges indicates that the cores had debitage surfaces with parallel sides during most part of the blade debitage. In profile, the blades are dominantly straight. Twisted blades are uncommon (Table 5 3.).

A total of 80% of the cores have a single striking platform and 73% of the blades bear unidirectional dorsal scars (Figure 5.7.). These vestiges indicate that the orientation of the blade debitage was primarily unidirectional. The opposite removals on blades and the five cores with opposite striking platforms evidence opposite debitage. However, this core exploitation is uncommon. The multidirectional and perpendicular scars on blades may mostly be remnants of cores' side and debitage surface shaping and the use of multi platform flake cores in the blade debitage (Figure 5.4: 4.).

## Accidents during blade debitage

A total of 46.4% of the blades are broken. Most fragments are distal (79.7%), while mesial and proximal make up 8.2% and 12.1%, respectively. Some breaks definitely are of knapping accident origin.

A typical knapping break, *cassure en languette* (Roche and Tixier 1982), appears rarely in the assemblage, accounting for 7 blades. A very rare and special accident, the *nacelle,* is also present with two specimens from RM1 and RM6.

Following the breaks, the hinge is the next most common accident (6.5% of the blade assemblage). One core shows that after a series of blade removals hinge flakes were repeatedly produced instead of proper blades (Figure 5.8.). This is a definite hallmark of the action of an unskilled flint knapper.

Plunging items appear in smaller amount than the hinges. They constitute only 4.3% of the blade assemblage.

## Blade core maintenance

During blade production, the cores' striking platforms were rejuvenated by rejuvenating flake removals (n=35) and core tablet removals (n=11) (Figure 5.10: 1-4.).

The debitage surface convexity was maintained by neo-cresting (18 neo-crest blades) (Figure 5.10: 5-6.). The neo-cresting was habitually made at the distal part of the cores and only in rare cases performed along the entire length of the debitage surface.

Hinge accidents on the blade cores' debitage surfaces were remedied by detaching the surface bearing hinge negative scars (n=17).

## Blade core discard

The discarded cores mostly narrow with parallel lateral sides (Table 5.4.). Most of them are also cortical (33 specimens of 49).

The discard took place in different stages of debitage: after unsuccessful blade removal resulting in hinge (n=19), after a few successful blade removals (n=13); and after striking platform rejuvenation (n=1). Although hinge accidents led to core discard in most cases, those did not always constrain the knapper to discard the core. Twenty-six blades were successfully detached from debitage surfaces bearing hinge accident negatives.

In rare cases, the blade cores were secondarily exploited for producing flakes. There are three blade cores that bear definite vestiges of subsequent flake production.

*Table 5.4*. Crosstabulation of the front shape and sides of the blade cores.

| Front | Sides | | Total |
|---|---|---|---|
| | converging | parallel | |
| narrow | 5 | 11 | 16 |
| semi-circular | 4 | 4 | 8 |
| wide | 5 | 3 | 8 |
| Total | 14 | 18 | 32 |

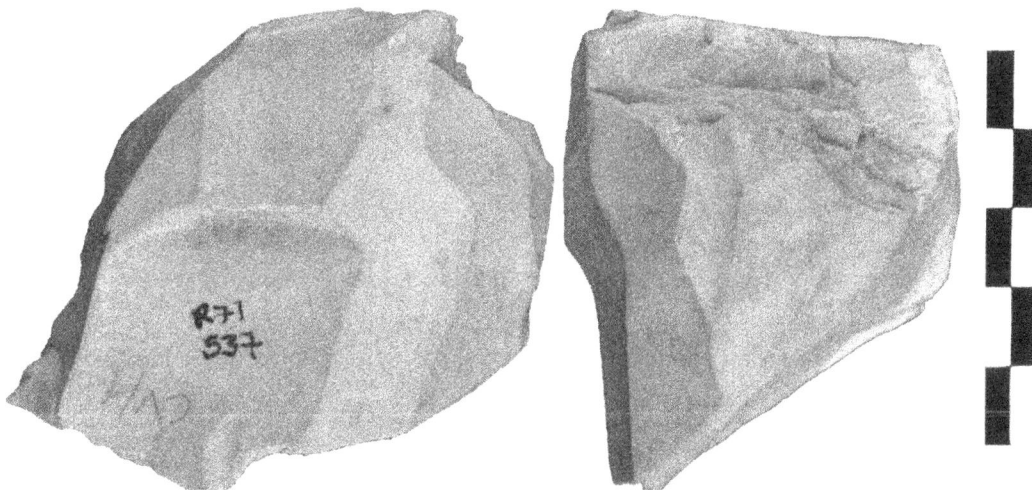

*Figure 5.8. Secondarily used blade core with repeated hinge removals. Scale 5 cm.*

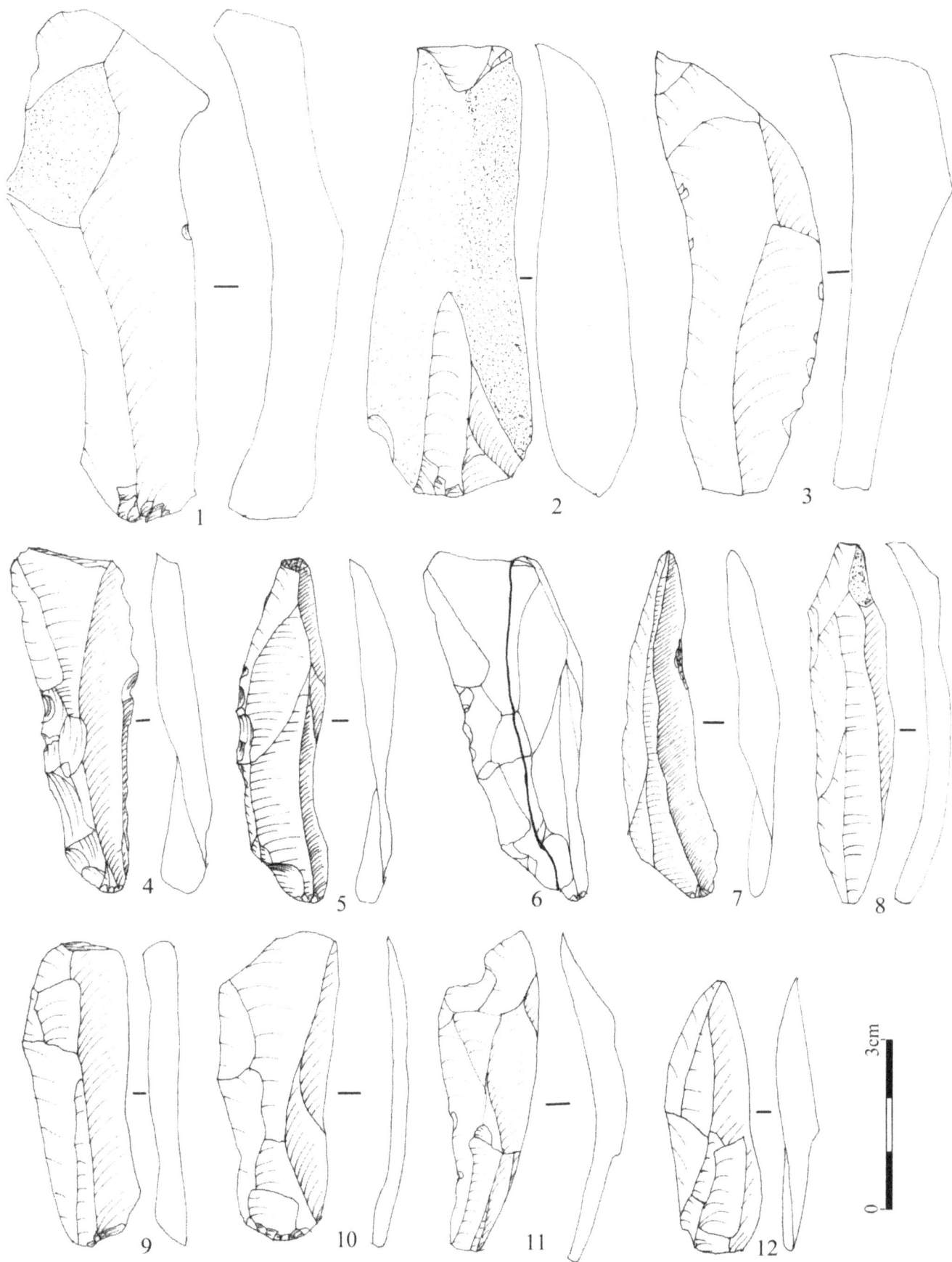

*Figure 5.9. Blades. No. 6 is the refit of 4 and 5.*

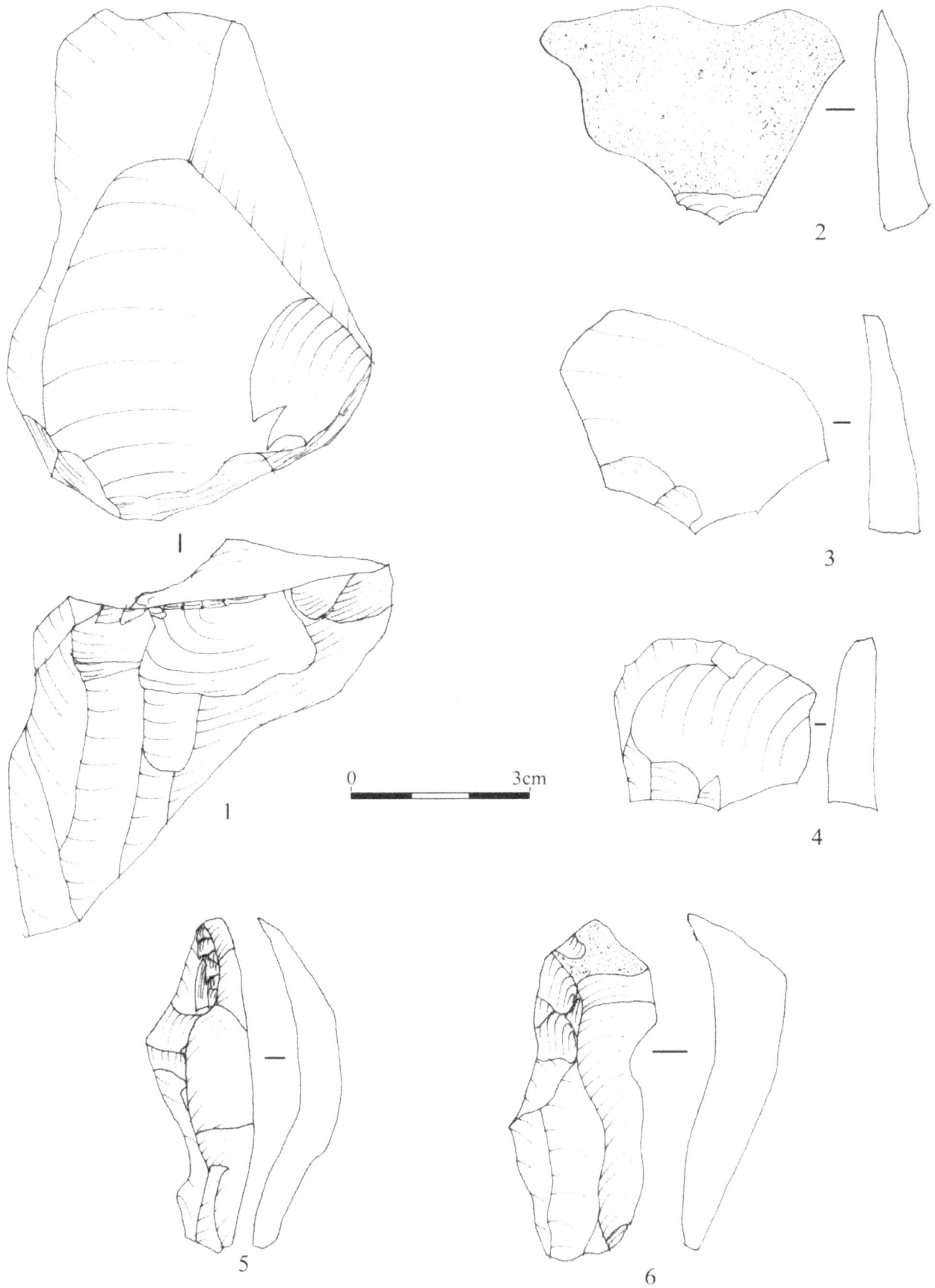

**Figure 5.10.** Core trimming elements of the blade production: core tablet (1); cortical rejuvenating flake (2); rejuvenating flakes (3, 4); neo-crest blades (5, 6).

## Bladelet production

### Bladelet core configuration

The bladelet production was based on good quality flints. Among good quality flints RM5 is dominant (Table 5.1.). One flint type, RM3 of low quality was not used in bladelet production.

Three types of bladelet core blanks are distinguished here:

1) Small flint nodule (Figure 5.13: 1, 2, 4.). According to the preserved original surfaces on cores (8 specimens), these were small *ca* 5 cm oval nodules. The striking platform is created by the removal of a single flake. After the striking platform, the lateral sides were flaked from the striking platform in order to create the debitage surface. The debitage surface was not crested. The first bladelet removals were made along the ridges formed by flake removals. In rare cases, fully cortical bladelets were removed. The front of these cores is wide and semi-circular, never narrow.

2) Thick flakes (n=21) (Figure 5.13: 3, 5, 6.), between 14 mm and 37 mm of thickness. These are frequently cortical (n=14). The debitage surfaces of these cores were set up at the distal end or at one of the edges of the flake. The set up of striking platform was made by a small flake removal. No front cresting is evidenced. The removal of bladelets commenced on the unprepared flake edge (n=5). The core front is solely narrow.

3) Exhausted blade core. Only three bladelet cores have vestiges of prior blade production.

The cortex, similarly to those of blades, was not entirely removed from the cores of bladelets (20.5% of the entire bladelet assemblage are cortical). The cortex on the bladelets usually appears at the distal part and on one of the dorsal halves along the total length. Since no cortical bladelet tools are found in the assemblage, those probably were to clean the debitage surface area from cortex.

**Table 5.5.** *Crosstabulation of bladelet profile, length and the shape of the edges.*

|  | Edges | Profile | | | Total |
|---|---|---|---|---|---|
|  |  | straight | curved | twisted |  |
| 1-20 mm | parallel | 3 | 6 | 2 | *11* |
|  | converging |  | 5 | 2 | *7* |
|  | expanding | 2 | 3 | 1 | *4* |
| 20-40 mm | parallel | 14 | 11 | 5 | *30* |
|  | converging | 13 | 11 | 9 | *33* |
|  | expanding | 5 | 7 | 9 | *9* |
| Total |  | *37* | *43* | *28* | *84* |

### Bladelet debitage

Most bladelets have linear butts (Figure 5.11.). The butt thickness is less than 1 mm at 49.5% of the cases. The overhangs are abraded at 45.8% of the bladelets and the impact points are present at 8.5%. These indicate the use of soft hammer technique for the most part in the debitage.

The profile of the bladelets is dominantly curved (Table 5.5.). Items with twisted profile account for almost the one-third part of the bladelets. The preponderance of bladelets with parallel and converging edges indicates that the cores had debitage surfaces with parallel sides, to lesser extent converging during most part of the debitage. The bladelets smaller than 20 mm (Figure 5.13: 13-20.) are most likely the by-products of carinated and thick nosed and shouldered endscraper retouching. Their profile is commonly curved.

A total of 97.1% of the cores have a single striking platform and 86.1% of the bladelets bear unidirectional dorsal scars (Figure 5.12.). These vestiges indicate that the orientation of the bladelet debitage was primarily unidirectional. A very few of the opposite removals may mostly be remnants of cores' side and debitage surface shaping.

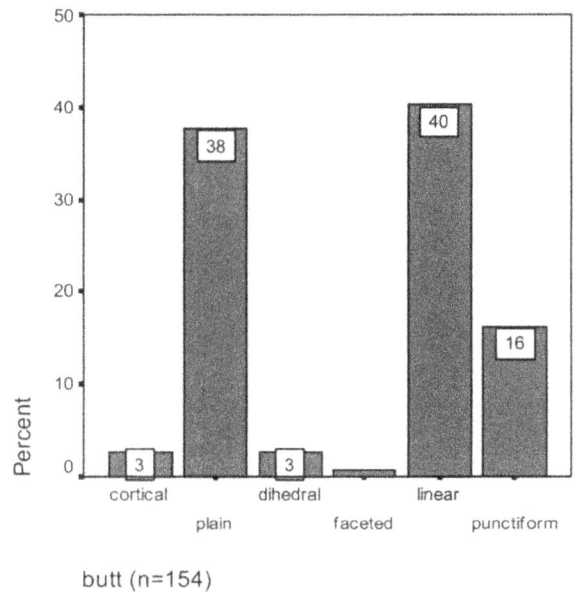

*Figure 5.11.* Butt types of bladelets.

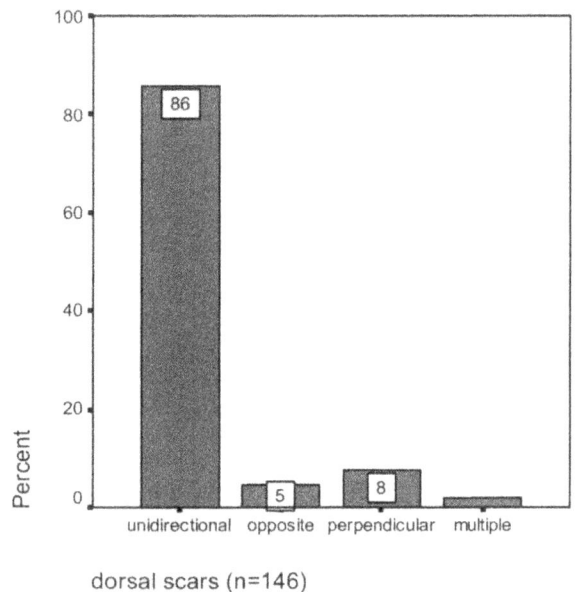

*Figure 5.12.* Direction of dorsal scars on bladelets.

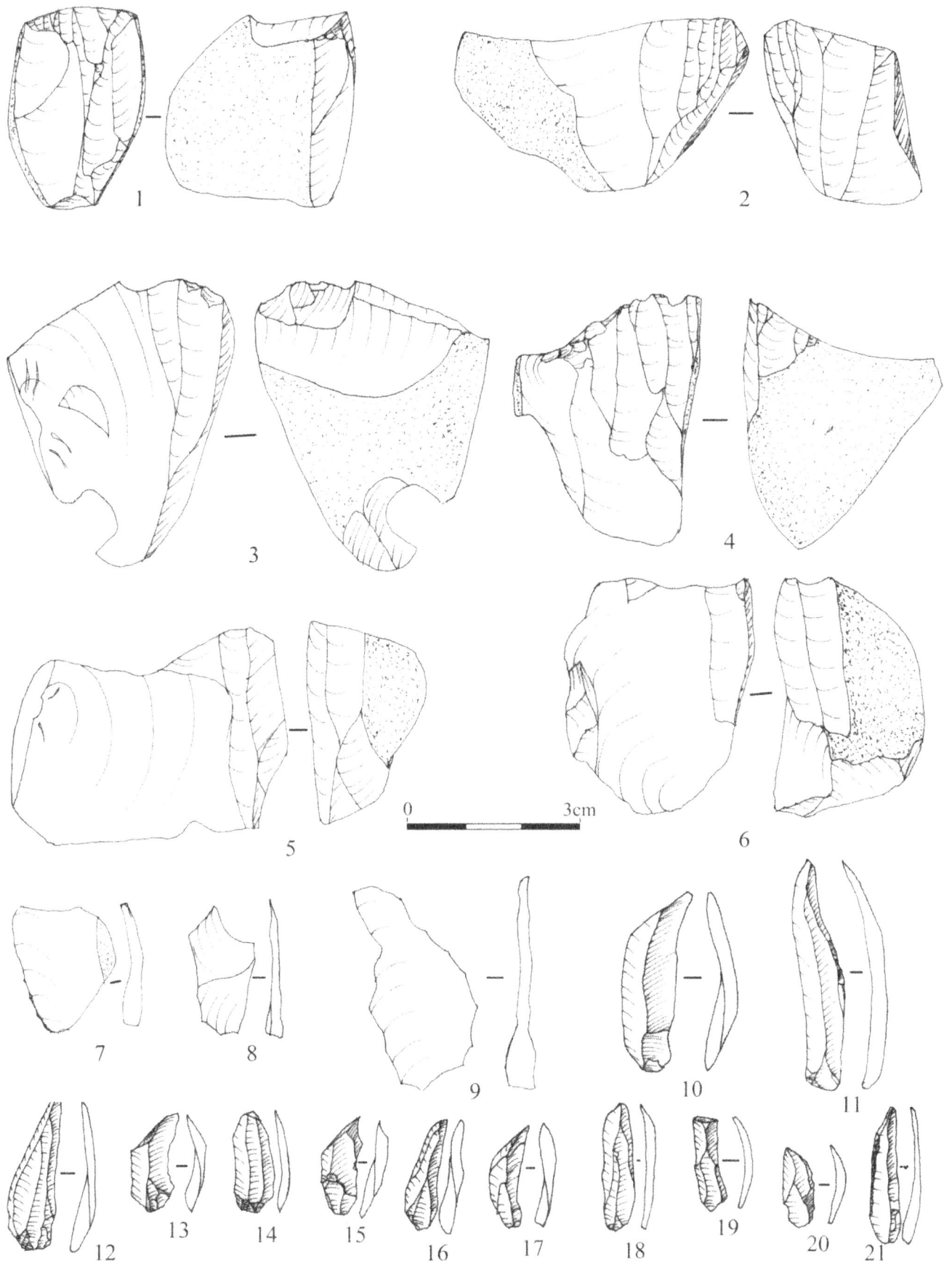

**Figure 5.13.** *cores made on small nodule (1, 2, 4); bladelet cores made on flakes (3, 5, 6,); striking platform rejuvenating flakes (7-9); bladelets (10-21).*

## Accidents during bladelet debitage

A total of 31.7% of the bladelets are broken. Most fragments are proximal (43.1%) while distal make up 41.5% and mesial 15.4%. All breaks are "clear", thus it is impossible to distinguish between knapping and post-knapping breaks. There are 12 hinged bladelets, while there is only one plunging.

## Bladelet core maintenance

During bladelet production, the cores' striking platforms were rejuvenated by rejuvenating flake removals (n=6) and core tablet removals (n=4) (Figure 5.13: 7-9.).

The debitage surface convexity was maintained by neo-cresting (3 neo-crest bladelets). The neo-cresting was made at the distal part of the cores.

## Bladelet core discard

The front of the discarded bladelet cores is mostly narrow. The lateral sides of the cores are dominantly converging (Table 5.6.). Of the 65 cores 51 items have cortex, especially the cores made on flakes.

The discard often happened after a few ordinary removals. Hinge accident led to core discard only in 32.9% of the cases.

*Table 5.6. Crosstabulation of the front shape and sides of the bladelet cores.*

| Profile | Edges | | Total |
|---|---|---|---|
| | converging | parallel | |
| narrow | 16 | 13 | 29 |
| semi-circular | 15 | 4 | 19 |
| wide | 14 | 3 | 17 |
| Total | 45 | 20 | 65 |

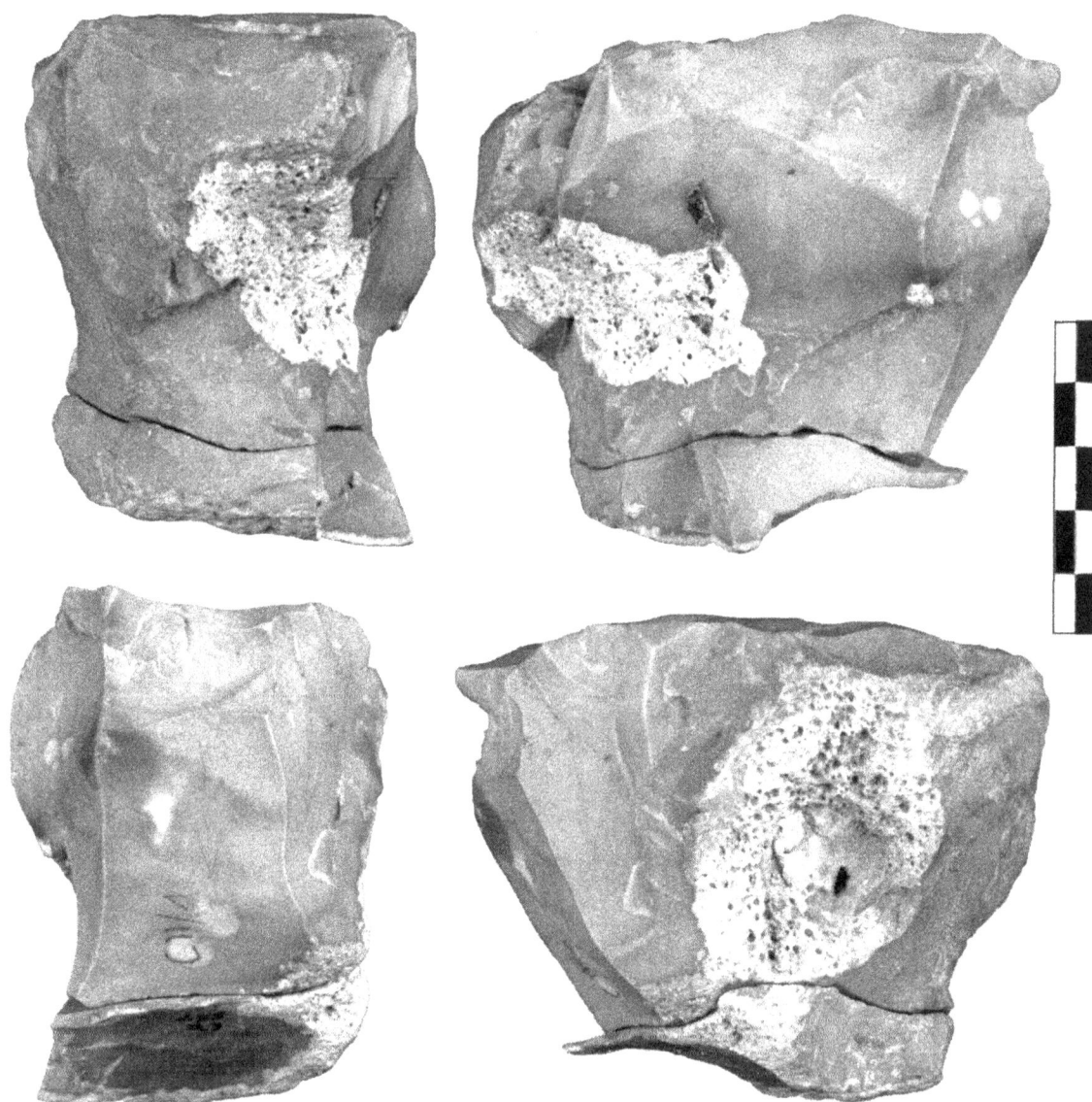

*Figure 5.14. Cube-shaped flake core and a flake refitted. Scale 5 cm.*

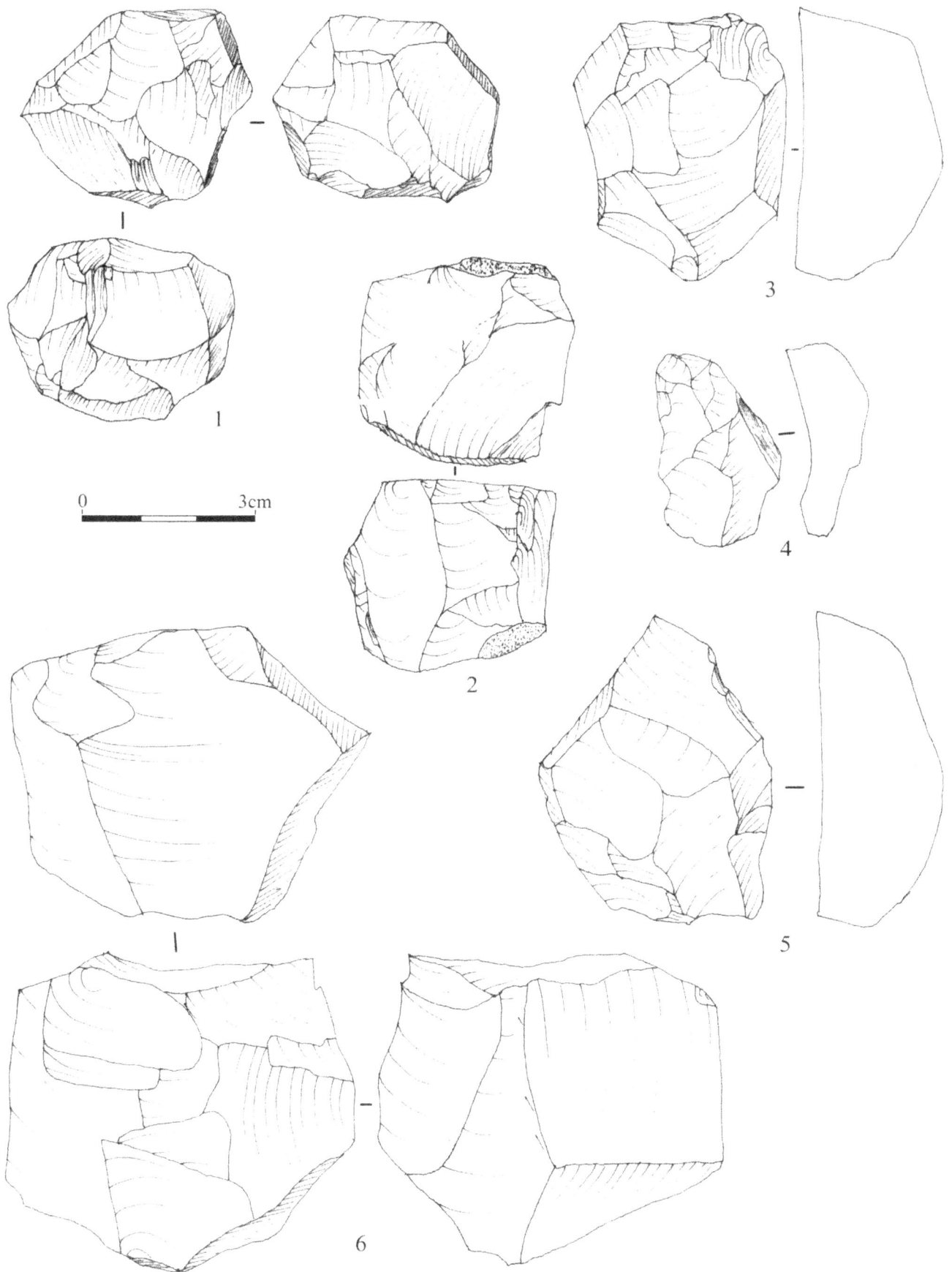

**Figure 5.15.** *flake cores with multiple striking platform (1, 2, 6); thick flakes with multiple orientation of dorsal scars (3-5).*

## Flake production

Each raw material is present with flakes and flake cores, especially RM1 and RM5. Except four cores of RM1, one of RM6, one of RM7, and two of RM14 which originally belonged to blade production, all flake cores are strict vestiges of flake debitage.

Globular or cube-shaped nodules of RM1 and RM5 were collected for flake production.

Although most flakes have unidirectional dorsal sscar pattern, the majority of the flake cores (77%) have multiple striking platforms with multiple orientation of debitage (Table 5.7.). During multidirectional debitage the dimension of the core was intensively reduced from all surfaces. Flakes from these cores were systematically removed in order to keep the core in globular or cube shape (Figure 5.14., 5.15: 1, 2, 6.). These flakes are often thick, bear non-unidirectional dorsal scars, and have steep distal terminations (Figure 5.15: 3-5.). Figure 5.14. shows that non-unidirectional scar bearer flakes outnumber unidirectional scar bearer ones among thick items.

Flakes were produced from single platform cores, as well (n=17 cores). As by-products of blade core re-shaping and rejuvenation, flakes also appear in the assemblage. Of all flakes, 247 have unidirectional scars together with parallel ridges. They were detached from blade core's debitage surface and lateral sides.

**Table 5.7.** *Debitage orientation and the striking platform on flake cores.*

| Debitage | Striking platform | | | | Total |
|---|---|---|---|---|---|
| | single | opposite | double | multiple | |
| unidirectional | 17 | | | | *17* |
| opposite | | 2 | | | *1* |
| bi-directional | | | 4 | | *3* |
| multiple | | | | 77 | *77* |
| *Total* | *18* | *2* | *4* | *76* | *100* |

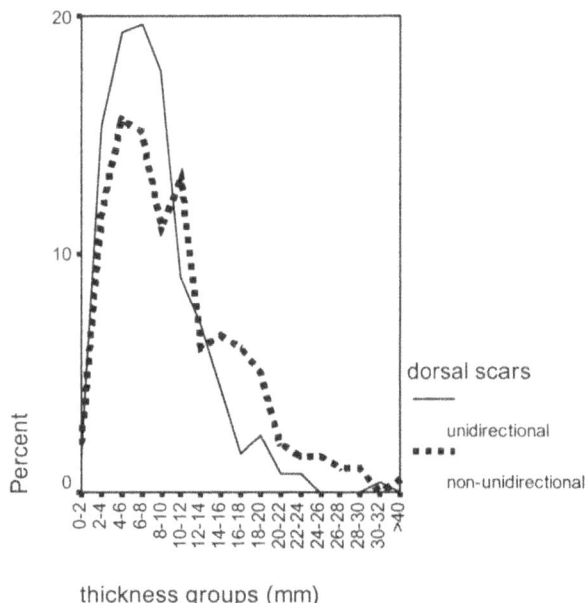

thickness groups (mm)

**Figure 5.16.** *Direction of dorsal scars by the thickness of flakes.*

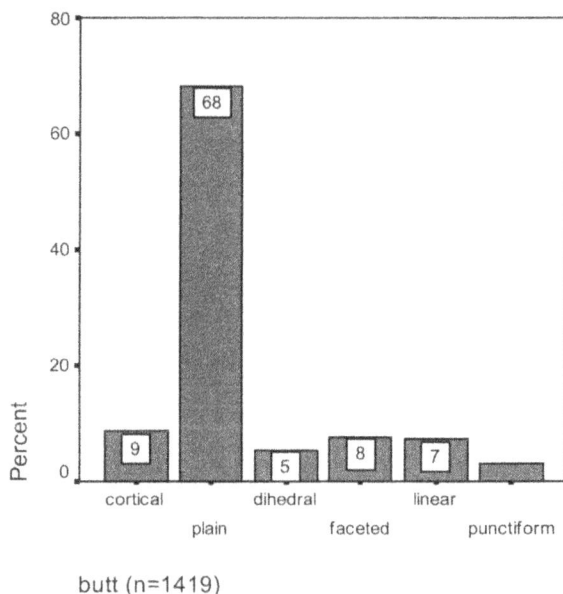

butt (n=1419)

**Figure 5.17.** *Butt types of flakes.*

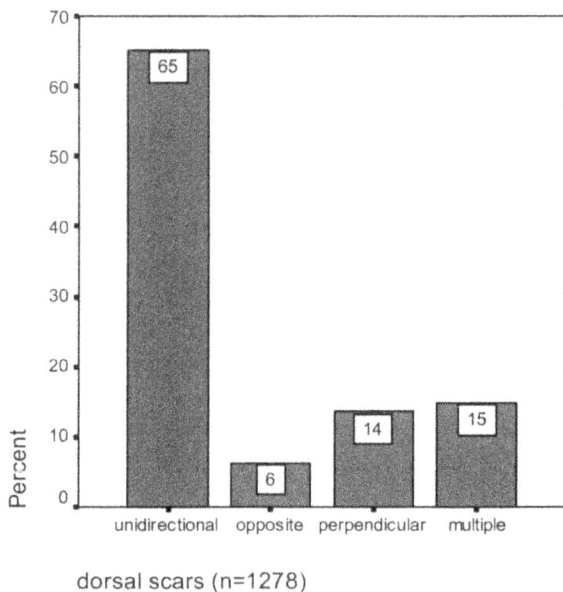

dorsal scars (n=1278)

**Figure 5.18.** *Direction of dorsal scars on flakes.*

There are 42 flakes which were produced from flakes (Figure). A few thick flakes demonstrate that these removals were made close to the bulb by hard stone hammer technique (the impact points can be seen well). This flaking modality is somewhat similar to the Kombewa (Inizan *et al* 1995) or Nahr Ibrahim (Solecki and Solecki 1970) methods which produce flakes with two ventral faces (Janus flakes, Inizan *et al* 1995) (Figure). It is important to note that Janus flakes were not used as blank for tools.

Abraded overhangs characterize 5.2% of the flakes. The butts are dominantly thick (86.8% are thicker than 2 mm) and plain (Figure 5.17.). The impact point is visible on 37.3% of the flakes. At 45.5% of these cases the impact point is large. A total of 43.3% of the flakes have no bulb. The bulb appears as diffused on 30.1% of the flakes. The rest of the flakes, 26.6%, have convex bulbs. Lipping is characteristic to 18.6% of the flakes. These evidence the dominant use of hard hammer technique over soft hammer technique.

Only 12.7% of the flakes are broken. Most fragments are distal (8.1%), while mesial ones make up 1.1%, proximal ones make up 2.6%, and lateral ones account for 0.9%. Of 17 lateral fragments 9 specimens are *siret* breaks, which are typical to hard stone hammer percussion (Inizan *et al* 1995). *Languette* en cassure breaks appear in a very small percentage (0.4%). The number of hinges is relative high (12.2%) while plunging accident (1.2%) hardly occurred.

## Tool blank selection and tools

### Blade tool blanks

A total of 47.6% of the blades are tools. Most blade tool blanks are of RM1 and RM2 (Table 5.8.). More than half of the blade tool blanks are cortical (54.7%). The tool blanks are characterized by straight profile with parallel edges likewise the unretouched blanks. Included among tool blanks are 3 crest and 6 neo-crest blades.

### Blade tools

Although a high percent of the blades are tools, those make up only 23.1% of the tool kit. Commonly, blades are blanks of all tool types and were used most frequently for endscrapers (Table 5.10.). The endscraper blanks are often thick (Figure 5.20.). The endscrapers fronts are retouched by converging removals and their edges by scaled and large scaled removals (Figure 5.23: 3, 4, 8., 5.24: 5, 7.). There are 10 endscraper fronts snapped-off blades and flakes with lateral blow. These might be wastes of endscraper front rejuvenations.

Burins are often dihedral, made angled on break, and truncation (Figure 5.24: 1, 2.).

Among retouched items blades habitually have retouched with scaled retouch continuously or partially on one edge (Figure 5.24: 6.). Special retouched blade forms, such as two strangulated blades (Figure 5.23: 2.) and one blade with two large notches on both edges resembling strangulated blade (Figure 5.23: 1.), are also present. One of the endscrapers also demonstrates the use of strangulating retouch (Figure 5.23: 8.).

Truncations on blades are commonly straight. Thinnest blades are sole blanks of el-Wad points shaped by delicate retouch (Figure 5.23: 5, 6.), while large blades are usual blanks of denticulates shaped by large deep scaled retouch (Figure 5.19., 5.23: 7., 5.24: 4.).

### Bladelet tool blanks

A total of 24% of the bladelets are tools. They primarily are of RM1 and RM5 type flints (Table 5.8.). Only 13.7% of the bladelet tools are cortical. Bladelet blanks are frequently longer than 20 mm. Most bladelet tool blanks are curved in profile with converging edges, while in

slightly smaller number they are straight with converging edges and twisted with parallel edges. These shapes are present with the same frequency among unretouched blanks.

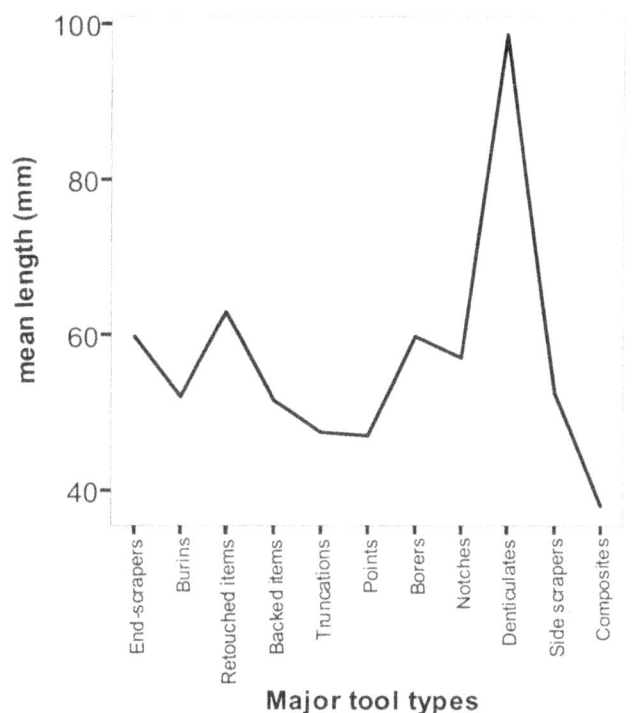

**Figure 5.19.** *Mean length of major blade tool types.*

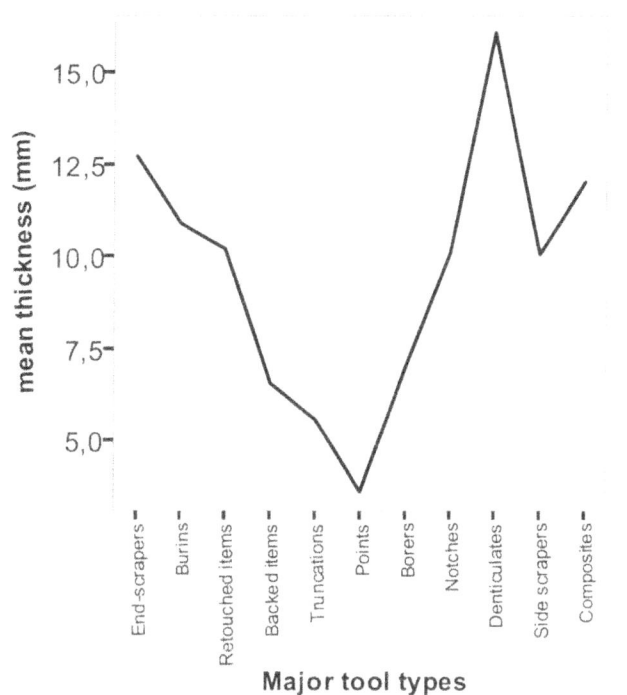

**Figure 5.20.** *Mean thickness of major blade tool types.*

## Bladelet tools

Bladelets make up 5.4% of the tool kit. The majority of the bladelet tools are simply retouched items with one retouched edge, mostly by direct, partial marginal removals (Figure 5.21: 4.). The single both edge retouched item is a typical Dufour bladelet with slightly curved profile (Figure 5.21: 1.). Blanks for shouldered tools are bladelets. The retouch is abrupt and scaled on the left proximal part of the blank. One of these was inversely retouched on its right edge (Figure 5.21: 5.). These tools are not pointed.

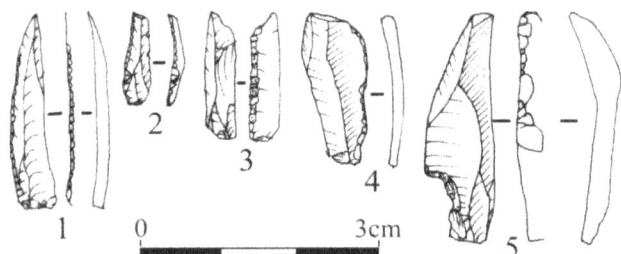

**Figure 5.21.** *Dufour bladelets (1, 3); retouched bladelets (2, 4); shouldered bladelet (5).*

## Flake tool blanks

A total of 31.4% of the flakes are tools. They are frequently cortical, making up 54.6%. Flake tool blanks primarily are of RM1 (Table 5.8.). Included among tool blanks are 2 core tablets and 11 platform rejuvenating flakes.

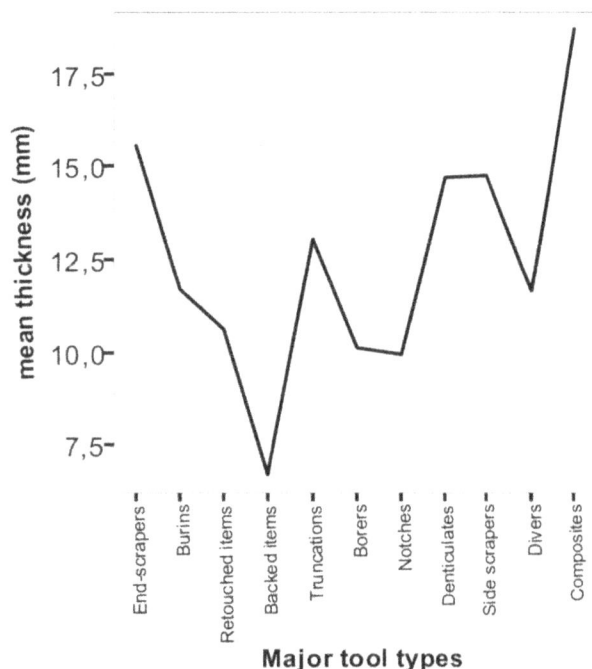

**Figure 5.22.** *Mean thickness of major flake tool types.*

## Flake tools

Most of the tools were made of flakes, accounting for 65.7% of the tool kit (Table 5.10.). Flakes dominate almost every tool type. For endscrapers, habitually thick flakes were used (Figure 5.22.). The most frequent end-scraper type is the thick nosed (Figure 5.25: 1-5., 5.26: 1, 6.). Their nosed fronts were created by two or more lateral notching flake removals. The ridges created by the nosing flakes were used to guide the fine retouching of the front with small tiny laminar or converging laminar removals. The fine retouching appears to have been accomplished by soft hammer technique. The edges of the nosed endscrapers are frequently retouched by scaled removals. Other types, such as simple endscraper with converging or scaled front retouch, endscraper on retouched blank with converging or scaled front retouch and scaled partial edge retouch (Figure 5.25: 10, 11.), shouldered (Figure 5.25: 7, 12.) and carinated types with laminar front retouch (Figure 5.25: 6.) are also abundant.

The burins made of flakes (Figure 5.26: 8, 10.) are mostly on break and in fewer cases they are dihedral and carinated.

Retouched items dominantly have partial scaled retouch.

Denticulates and notches are habitually made by deep scalar removals (Figure 5.26: 3, 9.).

Truncations are straight and side scrapers are mostly single straight.

Most composite tools are of endscraper/burin type (Figure 5.26: 4.). The endscraper part forms either ogival, nosed, shouldered, carinated or simple, while the burin part dihedral, on break, and on straight truncation.

**Table 5.8.** *Tool blanks by raw material.*

| Raw material | | Tool blank | | | | Total |
|---|---|---|---|---|---|---|
| source | type | flake | blade | bladelet | waste | |
| RAM | RM1 | 191 | 58 | 14 | 16 | 279 |
| | RM2 | 99 | 35 | 3 | 11 | 148 |
| | RM3 | 13 | 6 | | | 19 |
| | RM4 | 55 | 18 | 3 | 8 | 84 |
| DH | RM5 | 80 | 27 | 12 | 8 | 127 |
| | RM6 | 39 | 11 | 5 | 5 | 60 |
| | RM7 | 15 | 8 | | | 23 |
| | RM8 | 5 | 3 | 1 | 1 | 10 |
| | RM9 | 3 | | 1 | | 4 |
| | RM10 | 8 | 3 | 1 | | 12 |
| | RM11 | 11 | 2 | 1 | 1 | 15 |
| DC | RM12 | 21 | 15 | 4 | 2 | 42 |
| | RM13 | 31 | 17 | 4 | 1 | 53 |
| NM | RM14 | 29 | 13 | 1 | 1 | 44 |
| | burnt | 19 | 2 | 1 | | 22 |
| Total | | 619 | 218 | 51 | 54 | 942 |

## Wastes as tool blanks

Besides ordinary blanks, multi-fractured wastes of the knapping process also were used as tool blanks. They appear with higher frequency than bladelets, making up 5.7% of the tool blanks. These specimens primarily were used for notches.

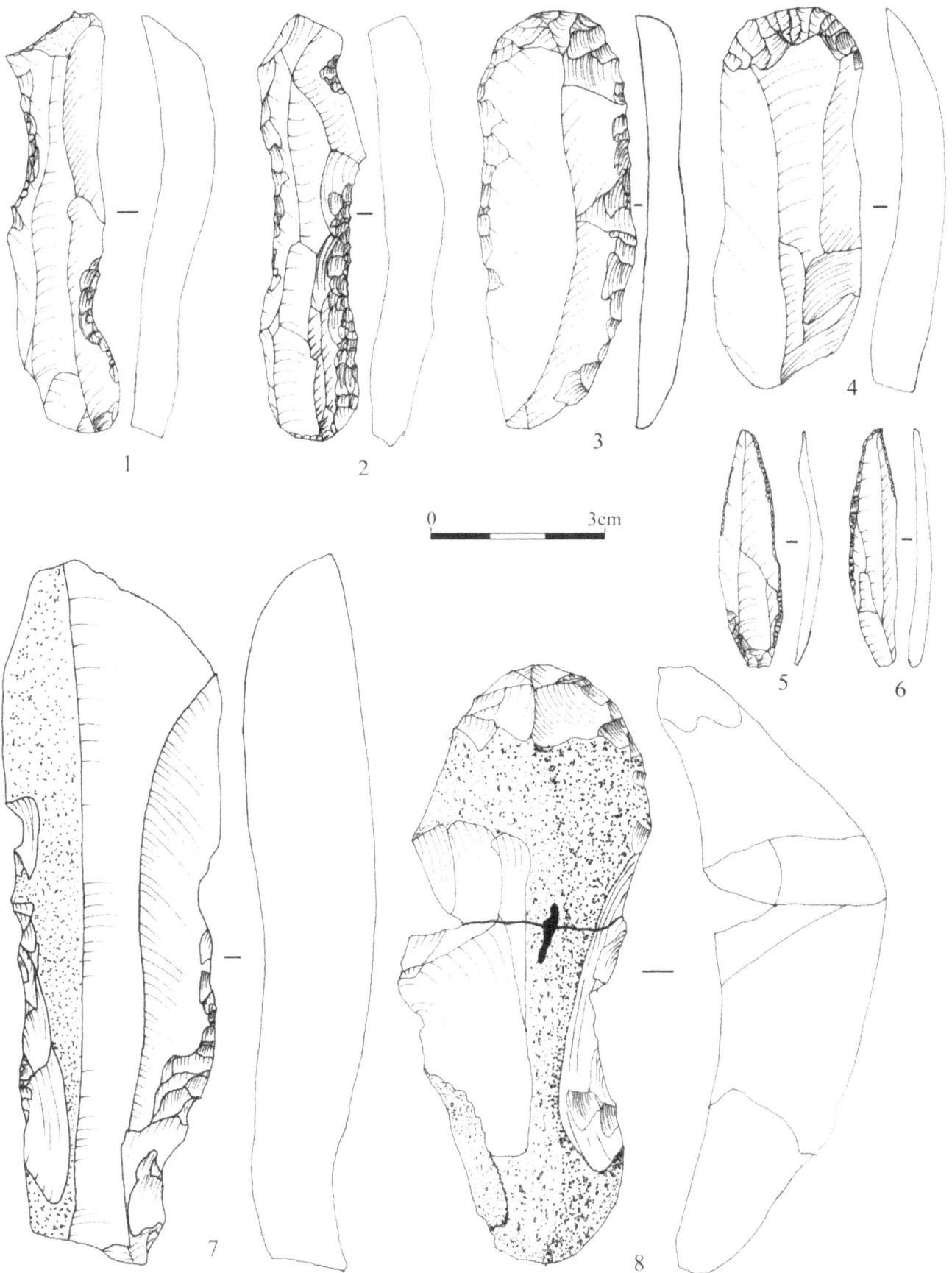

**Figure 5.23.** *Strangulate blades (1, 2); endscraper on retouched blade (3, 8); endscraper on blade (4); el-Wad points (5, 6); denticulate blade (7).*

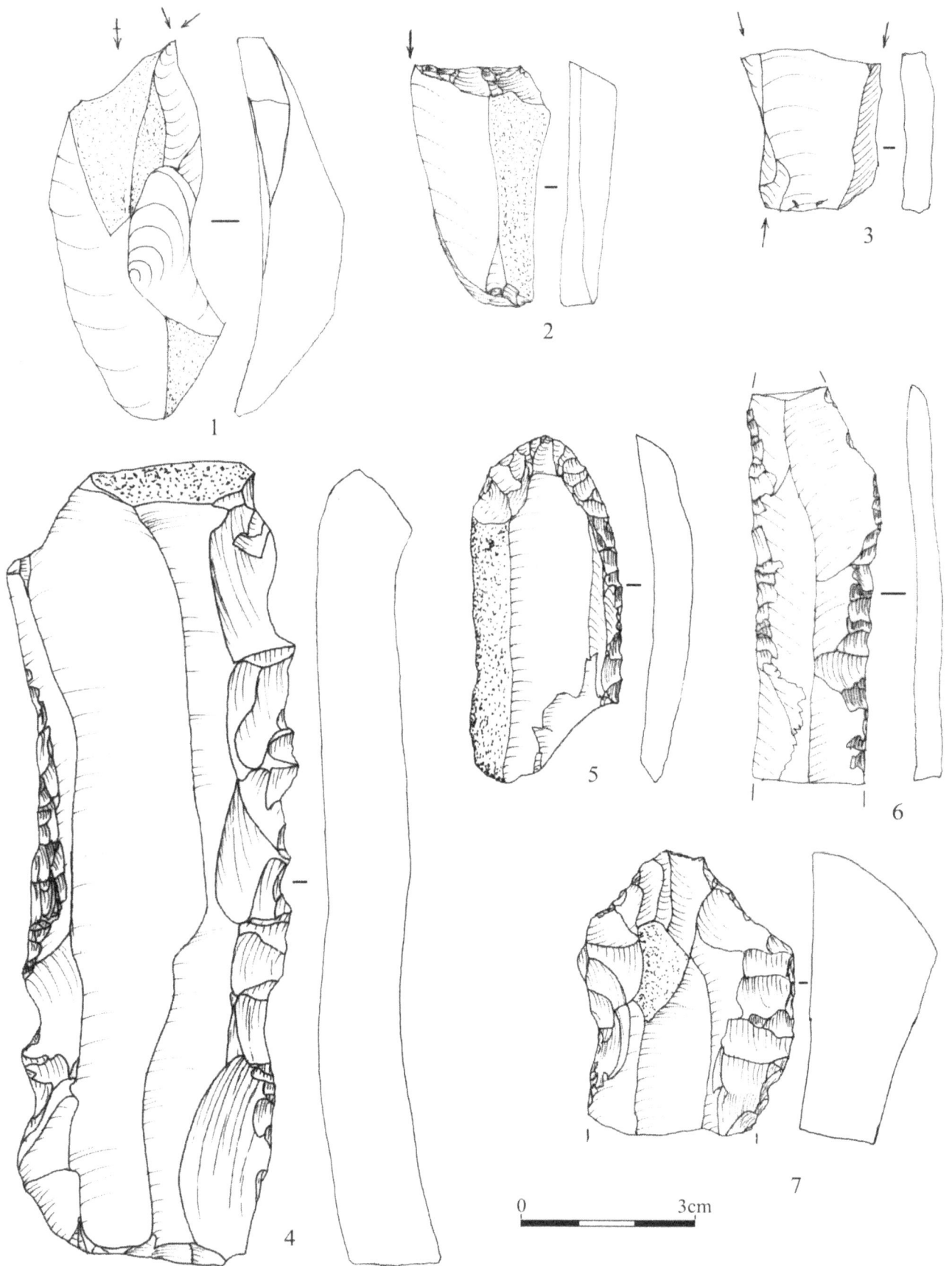

**Figure 5.24.** *Dihedral burin (1); burin on truncation (2); burin angled on break (3); denticulate blade (4); ogival endscraper (5); retouched blade (6); nosed endscraper (7).*

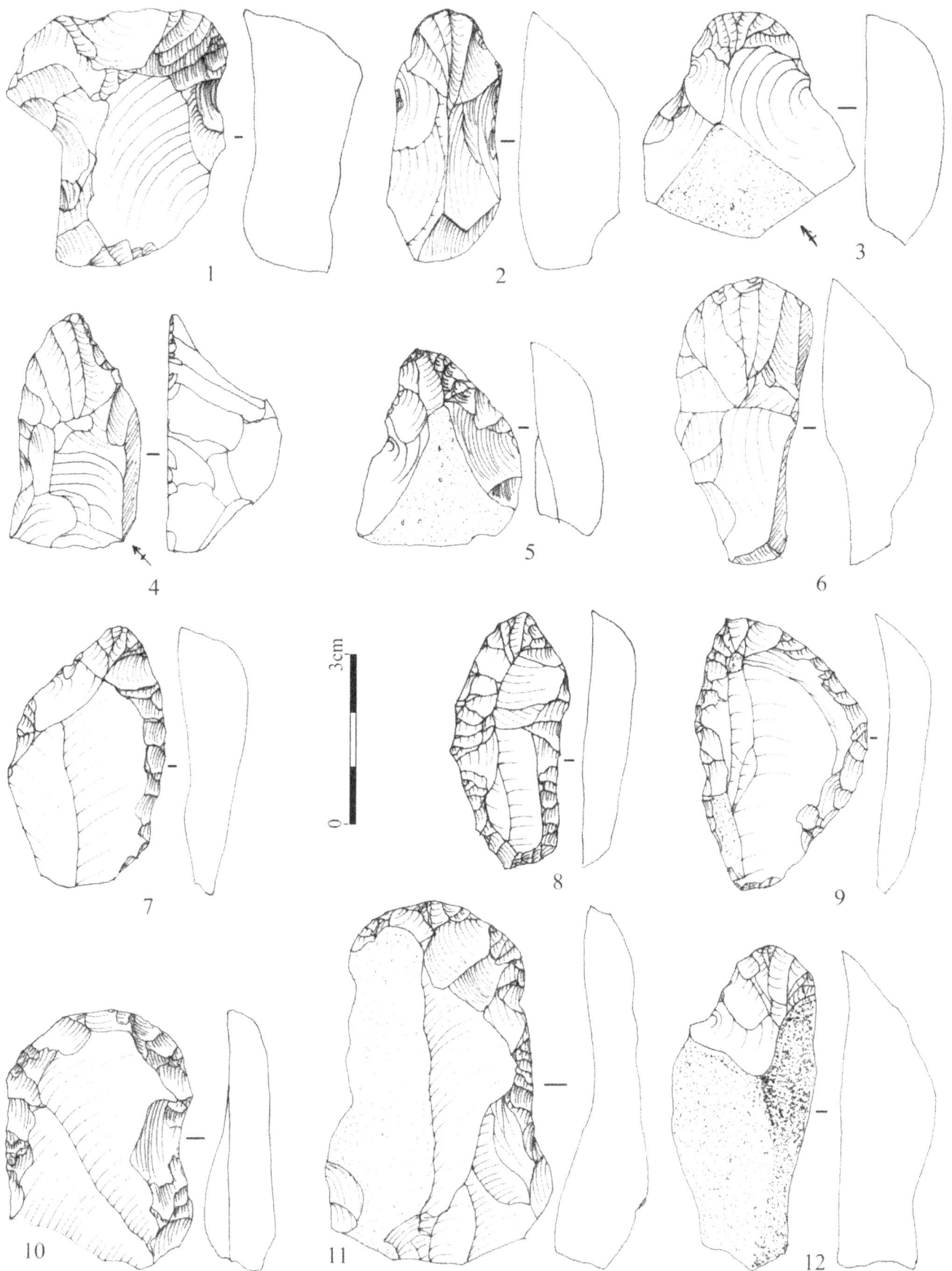

**Figure 5.25.** Nosed endscrapers (1-5); carinated endscraper (6); shouldered endscrapers (7, 12); ogival endscrapers (8, 9); endscraper on retouched flake (10, 11).

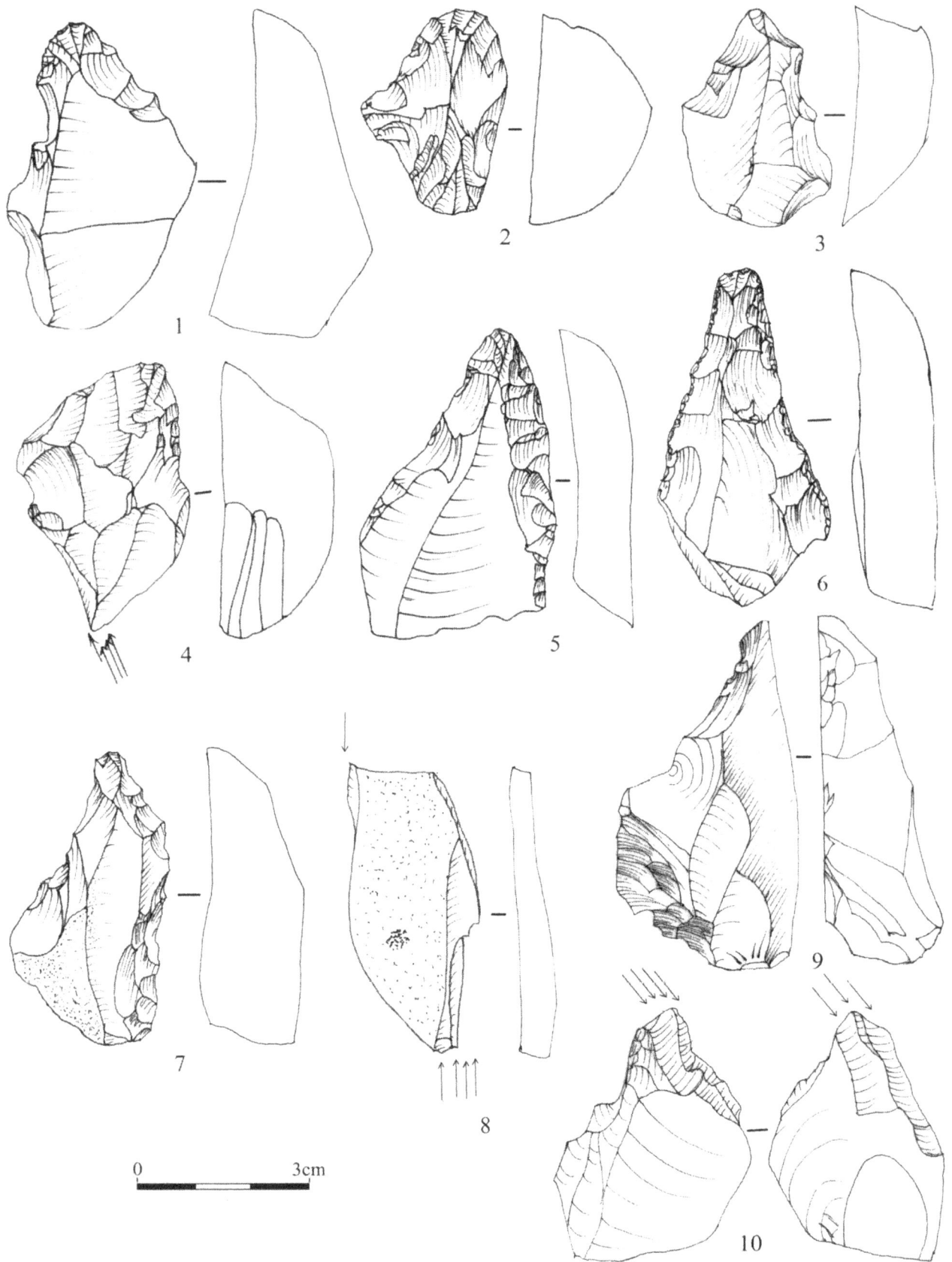

***Figure 5.26.*** *Nosed endscrapers (1, 6); double carinated endscraper (2); denticulate flakes (3, 9); endscraper-burin (4); ogival endscraper (5); borer (5); burin angled on break (8); dihedral burin (10).*

## Tool blanks from Mousterian deposits

In addition to the Aurignacian lithics themselves, heavily patinated Mousterian Levallois and ordinary flakes also were used as tool blanks. The retouch on these specimens cut the patinated surface, indicating deep time gap between the debitage and the retouching. There are 52 tools, mostly end-scrapers, notches and denticulates, which belong to this group (Table 5.9.).

*Table 5.9. Frequency of double patinated Mousterian blanks in the Levantine Aurignacian tool kit.*

| Tool types | Frequency | Percent |
|---|---|---|
| end-scraper | 20 | 38,5 |
| burin | 3 | 5,8 |
| borer | 1 | 1,9 |
| knives and backed items | 3 | 5,8 |
| truncation | 1 | 1 |
| notches and denticulates | 13 | 25 |
| retouched item | 6 | 11,5 |
| divers | 4 | 7,7 |
| side scraper | 1 | 1,9 |
| *Total* | *52* | *100* |

*Table 5.10. Tool type list of the Levantine Aurignacian assemblage.*

| Tool types | | Blank | | | | Total | |
|---|---|---|---|---|---|---|---|
| | | flake | blade | bladelet | waste | # | % |
| **End-scrapers** | simple | 38 | 11 | | 1 | 50 | 5,3 |
| | on retouched blank | 31 | 29 | | | 60 | 6,4 |
| | ogival | 7 | 6 | | | 13 | 1,4 |
| | nosed | 1 | 3 | | | 4 | 0,4 |
| | thick nosed | 41 | 8 | | 4 | 53 | 5,6 |
| | shouldered | 3 | 1 | | | 4 | 0,4 |
| | thick shouldered | 26 | 3 | | | 29 | 3,1 |
| | carinated | 17 | 7 | | 2 | 26 | 2,8 |
| | double carinated | 1 | | | | 1 | 0,1 |
| | circular | 1 | | | | 1 | 0,1 |
| | thumbnail | 1 | | | | 1 | 0,1 |
| | double | 3 | 2 | | | 5 | 0,5 |
| | atypical | 14 | 1 | | 1 | 16 | 1,7 |
| | *Sub-total* | *184* | *71* | | *8* | *263* | *27,9* |
| **Burins** | carinated | 8 | 1 | | 1 | 10 | 1,1 |
| | dihedral | 11 | 6 | | 1 | 18 | 1,9 |
| | on break | 16 | 6 | 1 | 2 | 25 | 2,7 |
| | on straight truncation | 2 | 1 | | 1 | 4 | 0,4 |
| | on oblique truncation | 3 | 4 | | 1 | 8 | 0,8 |
| | on concave truncation | 3 | 2 | | | 5 | 0,5 |
| | transversal | 7 | 3 | | 1 | 11 | 1,2 |
| | flat | 2 | 1 | | | 3 | 0,3 |
| | multiple | 3 | 3 | | | 6 | 0,6 |
| | double angled | 3 | 3 | | | 6 | 0,6 |
| | *Sub-total* | *58* | *30* | *1* | *7* | *96* | *10,2* |
| **Retouched items** | continuous scaled | 13 | 14 | | 1 | 28 | 3,0 |
| | continuous marginal | 5 | 1 | 5 | | 11 | 1,2 |
| | discontinuous scaled | 6 | 6 | | | 12 | 1,3 |
| | discontinuous marginal | 1 | 3 | 2 | | 6 | 0,6 |
| | partially scaled | 54 | 16 | 3 | 8 | 81 | 8,6 |
| | partially marginal | 12 | 6 | 8 | 1 | 27 | 2,9 |
| | inverse continuous marginal | | | 8 | | 8 | 0,8 |
| | continuously alternating scaled | 13 | | | | 13 | 1,4 |
| | continuously alternating marginal | 5 | 1 | 1 | | 7 | 0,7 |
| | discontinuously alternating scaled | 7 | | | | 7 | 0,7 |
| | discontinuously alternating marginal | 2 | | 1 | | 3 | 0,3 |
| | partially alternating scaled | 9 | 1 | | 2 | 12 | 1,3 |
| | partially alternating marginal | 1 | 1 | | | 2 | 0,2 |
| | both edges continuous scaled | 1 | 3 | | | 4 | 0,4 |
| | both edges partial scaled | 3 | 2 | | | 5 | 0,5 |
| | strangulated blade | | 3 | | | 3 | 0,3 |
| | alternate | 2 | | 1 | | 3 | 0,3 |
| | both edges mixed retouches | 1 | 10 | 3 | | 14 | 1,5 |
| | both edges | 2 | | | | 2 | 0,2 |
| | alternating | 1 | | 1 | | 2 | 0,2 |
| | *Sub-total* | *138* | *67* | *33* | *12* | *250* | *26,5* |

*Table 5.10. Continued.*

| Tool types | | Blank | | | | Total | |
|---|---|---|---|---|---|---|---|
| | | flake | blade | bladelet | waste | # | % |
| Backed items | straight partially | 6 | 2 | | | 8 | 0,8 |
| | curved partially | 1 | 1 | | | 2 | 0,2 |
| | irregular | | 1 | | | 1 | 0,1 |
| | *Sub-total* | *7* | *4* | | | *11* | *1,2* |
| Truncations | straight | 17 | 5 | 2 | | 24 | 2,5 |
| | concave | 4 | 1 | 2 | | 7 | 0,7 |
| | *Sub-total* | *21* | *6* | *4* | | *31* | *3,3* |
| Points | el-Wad | | 1 | | | 1 | 0,1 |
| | el-Wad A | | 2 | 1 | | 3 | 0,3 |
| | *Sub-total* | | *3* | *1* | | *4* | *0,4* |
| Borers | atypical | 10 | 1 | 1 | 2 | 14 | 1,5 |
| | typical | 19 | 2 | | 1 | 22 | 2,3 |
| | *Sub-total* | *29* | *3* | *1* | *3* | *36* | *3,8* |
| Notches | simple | 81 | 16 | 4 | 13 | 114 | 12,1 |
| | clactonian | 12 | 1 | | 2 | 15 | 1,6 |
| | two or more simple | 15 | 2 | 1 | 2 | 20 | 2,1 |
| | *Sub-total* | *108* | *19* | *5* | *17* | *146* | *15,8* |
| Denticulates | | 34 | 10 | 3 | 6 | 53 | 5,6 |
| | *Sub-total* | *34* | *10* | *3* | *6* | *53* | *5,6* |
| Side scrapers | simple | 13 | 2 | | | 15 | 1,6 |
| | double | 2 | | | | 2 | 0,2 |
| | transversal | 2 | | | | 2 | 0,2 |
| | concave | 1 | | | | 1 | 0,1 |
| | convex | 2 | 1 | | | 3 | 0,3 |
| | dejete | 3 | | | | 3 | 0,3 |
| | *Sub-total* | *23* | *3* | | | *26* | *2,8* |
| Divers | shouldered | | | 3 | | 3 | 0,3 |
| | splintered tool | 6 | | | 1 | 7 | 0,7 |
| | raclette | 4 | | | | 4 | 0,4 |
| | *Sub-total* | *10* | | *3* | *1* | *14* | *1,4* |
| Composites | end-scraper/burin | 5 | 1 | | | 6 | 0,6 |
| | end-scraper/borer | 1 | | | | 1 | 0,1 |
| | truncation/borer | 1 | | | | 1 | 0,1 |
| | truncation/burin | | 1 | | | 1 | 0,1 |
| | *Sub-total* | *7* | *2* | | | *9* | *0,9* |
| Total | | 619 | 218 | 51 | 54 | 942 | 100 |

# CHAPTER 6: THE LATE KEBARAN ASSEMBLAGE
## LAYER I, AREA B-G/18-23

## Raw material

The raw materials of the assemblage derive from four flint sources (Table 6.1.). Ramat Menashe (RAM), the closest source to Raqefet, yielded the majority of the raw materials, within which the mediocre quality RM1 is dominant. In addition, this raw material is the most abundant in the whole assemblage.

Deir Hannah formation (DH) flints make up the next largest group of raw material, within which the good quality RM5 is dominant. RM5 constitutes the second most abundant raw material type in the assemblage.

*Table 6.1. Frequency of raw material types by sources.*

| Raw material | | Raw material source | | | | | |
|---|---|---|---|---|---|---|---|
| quality | type | RAM | DH | DC | NM | Unk. | *total* |
| Mediocre | RM1 | 503 86,6% | | | | | *503 56,5%* |
| Low | RM2 | 37 6,4% | | | | | *37 4,2%* |
| Low | RM3 | 16 2,8% | | | | | *16 1,8%* |
| Low | RM4 | 25 4,3% | | | | | *25 2,8%* |
| Good | RM5 | | 97 57,4% | | | | *97 10,9%* |
| Low | RM6 | | 17 10,1% | | | | *17 1,9%* |
| Good | RM7 | | 20 11,8% | | | | *20 2,2%* |
| Good | RM8 | | 16 9,5% | | | | *16 1,8%* |
| Mediocre | RM9 | | 1 0,6% | | | | *1 0,1%* |
| Good | RM10 | | 10 5,9% | | | | *10 1,1%* |
| Mediocre | RM11 | | 8 4,7% | | | | *8 0,9%* |
| Low | RM12 | | | 34 53,1% | | | *34 3,8%* |
| Low | RM13 | | | 30 46,9% | | | *30 3,4%* |
| Good | RM14 | | | | 56 100% | | *56 6,3%* |
| Good | RM17 | | | | | 20 100% | *20 2,2%* |
| *Total* | | *575 65,3%* | *169 19%* | *64 7,2%* | *56 6,3%* | *20 2,2%* | *890 100%* |

Daliyat ha Carmel low quality raw materials (DC) are present with low frequency. RM12 and RM13 appear almost in the same amount.

Nahal Mearot raw materials (NM) make up a small part of the assemblage, as well as flints from unknown sources are rare. They all are of good quality.

On the basis of the presence of two first flakes, only RM5 was brought to the site as fully cortical nodule.

Other raw materials were roughed-out in various extents off-site.

In sum, the raw material acquisition focused on mediocre quality raw materials, while good and low quality flints make up the smallest part of the assemblage (Figure 6.1.).

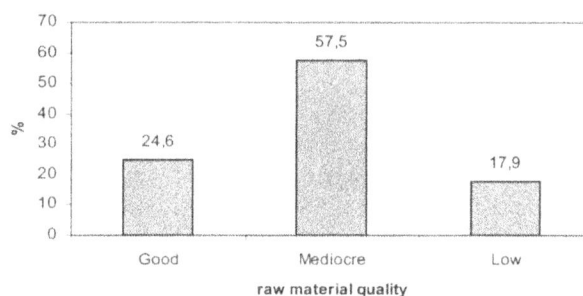

*Figure 6.1. Frequency of raw materials by quality.*

## Blade production

### Blade core configuration

The blade production is connected to mediocre quality flints. Among the mediocre quality flints RM1 is dominant (Table 6.2.). Three raw material types, RM6, RM9 and RM11, are not present in blade production.

No blade cores preserved the original shape of the raw material nodule and the sets of configuration. Although 59% of the cortical items are flakes, the high percent of cortical blades (47%) and cortical cores (66.6%) shows there was a lack of intensive initial core shaping and decortication.

To prepare the blade core front, cresting was applied. It is evidenced by crest blades (n=4) (Figure 6.3: 9.) and sub-crest blades (n=2) (Figure 6.3: 8.). Cores' striking platforms were prepared by single flake removals. These were made before cresting, since none of the flakes bears remains of cresting on butts.

The striking platforms of the cores were prepared by the removal of a single flake. It was rarely cortical, as indicated by the plain blade butts (Figure 6.2.).

### Blade debitage

The striking platform of the blade cores remained plain during the debitage as indicated by the high frequency of plain butts (Figure 6.2.). Abraded overhangs characterize 56.9% of the blades. A total of 44% of the butts are thinner than 2 mm. The impact point is visible on 18.7% of the blades. In a total of 66.6% of these cases the impact point is minor. A total of 30.6% of the blades have no bulb. The bulb appears as diffused on 57.1% of the blades. The rest of the blades, 12.3%, have convex bulbs. Lipping is characteristic to 41.7% of the blades. These evidence the use of soft hammer technique in the blade debitage.

***Table 6.2.*** *Frequency of lithic products by raw material.*

| Raw materials | | Lithic product | | | | | | Core | | | | Total |
| source | types | flake | blade | bladelet | waste | CTE | tool | flake | blade | bladelet | pre- | |
| RAM | RM1 | 138 27,4% | 31 6,2% | 121 24,1% | 103 20,5% | 31 6,2% | 42 8,3% | 4 0,8% | 2 0,4% | 30 6% | 1 0,2% | 503 100% |
| | RM2 | 12 32,4% | 4 10,8% | 1 2,7% | 15 40,5% | | 5 13,5% | | | | | 37 100% |
| | RM3 | 7 43,8% | 2 12,5% | 3 18,8% | 1 6,3% | 2 12,5% | | | | 1 6,3% | | 16 100% |
| | RM4 | 12 48% | 1 4% | 5 20% | 5 20% | | 1 4% | | | 1 4% | | 25 100% |
| DH | RM5 | 18 18,6% | 4 4,1% | 22 22,7% | 33 34% | 5 5,2% | 6 6,2% | | 3 3,1% | 6 6,2% | | 97 100% |
| | RM6 | 6 35,3% | | 6 35,3% | | 1 5,9% | 4 23,5% | | | | | 17 100% |
| | RM7 | 5 25% | 2 10% | 8 40% | | 1 5% | 2 10% | | 1 5% | 1 5% | | 20 100% |
| | RM8 | 6 37,5% | 2 12,5% | 3 18,8% | | 2 12,5% | 1 6,3% | 1 6,3% | | 1 6,3% | | 16 100% |
| | RM9 | 1 100% | | | | | | | | | | 1 100% |
| | RM10 | 2 20% | 3 30% | | | 2 20% | 3 30% | | | | | 10 100% |
| | RM11 | 2 25% | | 1 12,5% | 1 12,5% | | 2 25% | | 1 12,5% | 1 12,5% | | 8 100% |
| DC | RM12 | 7 20,6% | 3 8,8% | 10 29,4% | 3 8,8% | 2 5,9% | 7 20,6% | | 2 5,9% | | | 34 100% |
| | RM13 | 13 43,3% | 1 3,3% | 5 16,7% | 4 13,3% | 2 6,7% | 2 6,7% | 2 6,7% | | 1 3,3% | | 30 100% |
| NM | RM14 | 17 30,4% | 4 7,1% | 25 44,6% | 5 8,9% | 2 3,6% | 2 3,6% | | | 1 1,8% | | 56 100% |
| unknown | RM17 | 8 40% | 1 5% | 5 25% | 1 5% | 4 20% | 1 5% | | | | | 20 100% |
| Total | | 254 28,5% | 58 6,5% | 215 24,2% | 171 19,2% | 54 6,1% | 78 8,8% | 7 0,8% | 9 1% | 43 4,8% | 1 0,1% | 890 100% |

The size of the blades is varied. Most fall between 45 and 60 mm. The preponderance of blades with parallel and expanding edges indicates that the cores had debitage surfaces with parallel sides during most part of the blade debitage (Table 6.3.). In profile, the blades are dominantly curved.

A total of 88.9% of the cores have a single striking platform and 53% of the blades bear unidirectional dorsal scars (Figure 6.4.). These vestiges indicate that the orientation of the blade debitage was primarily unidirectional. The 28% of opposite removals on blades are definitely in connection with opposite bi-directional debitage and there is a single core with opposite striking platforms. However, this core exploitation is uncommon, and the presence of non-unidirectional scars on blades may mostly be remnants of cores' side and debitage surface shaping.

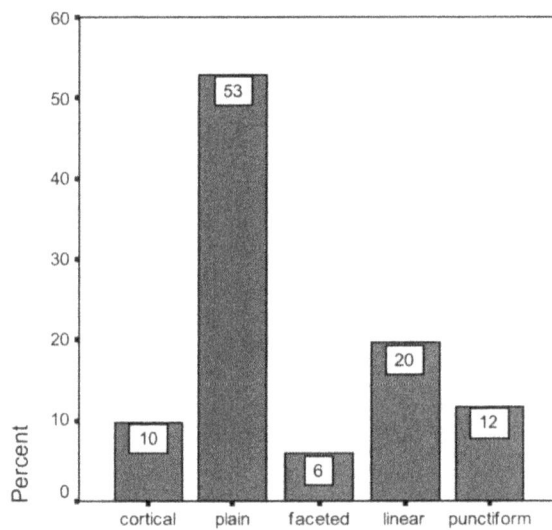

butt (n=51)

***Figure 6.2.*** *Butt types of blades.*

***Table 6.3.*** *Blades edges-profile crosstabulation.*

| Profile | Edges | | | Total |
| | parallel | converging | expanding | |
| straight | 13 | | 4 | 17 |
| curved | 7 | 5 | 8 | 20 |
| twisted | 5 | 2 | 3 | 10 |
| Total | 25 | 7 | 15 | 47 |

## Accidents during blade debitage

A total of 35.2% of the blades are broken. Most fragments are distal (73%), while mesial make up 11.5% and proximal account for 15.5%. All breaks are "clear", thus it is impossible to distinguish between knapping and post-knapping breaks. Hinge and plunging accidents constitute together 16.3% of the blade assemblage.

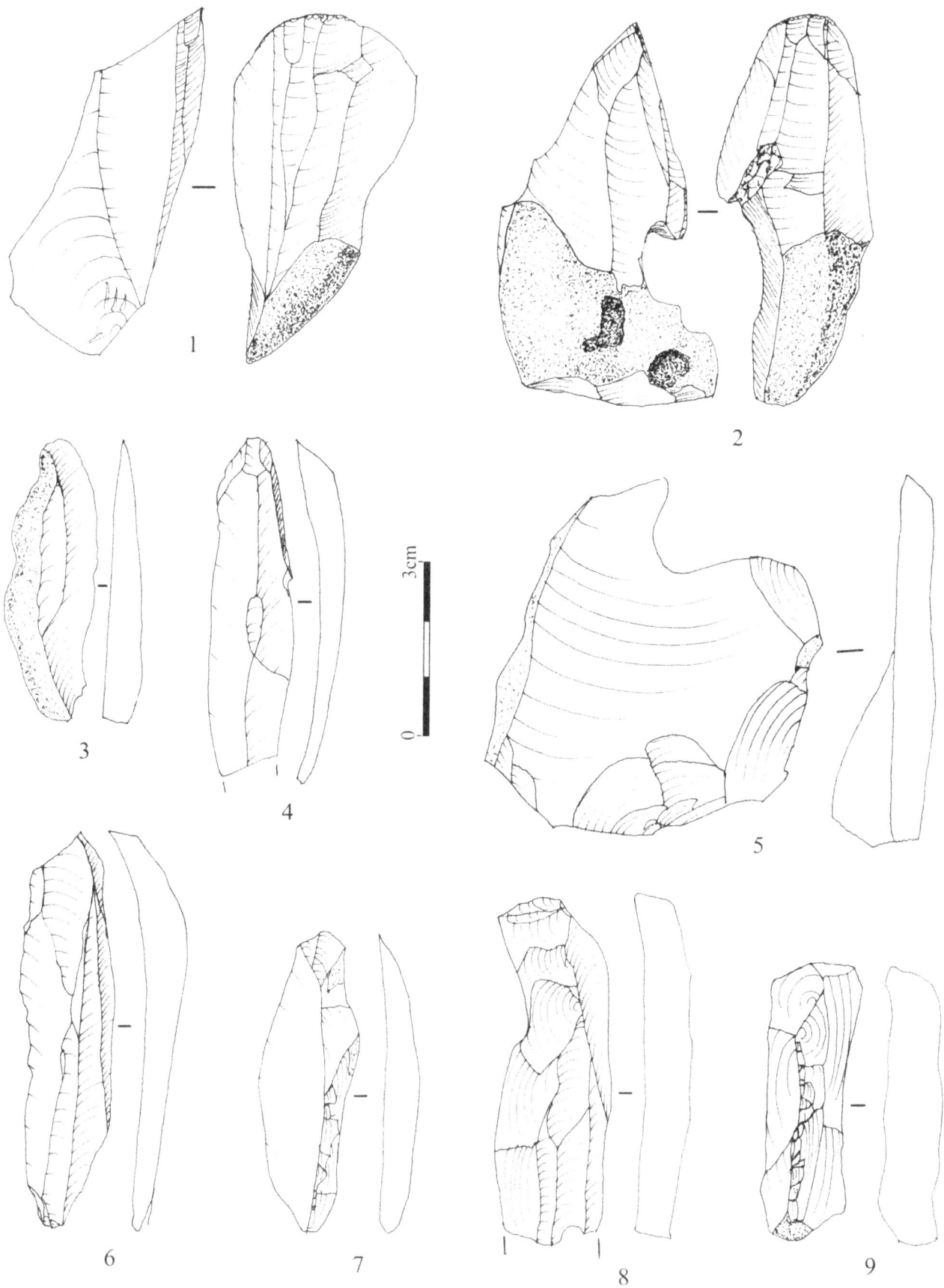

**Figure 6.3.** *Blade cores (1, 2); blades (3, 4, 6); blade core tablet (5); neo-crest blade (7) sub-crest blade (8); crest blade (9).*

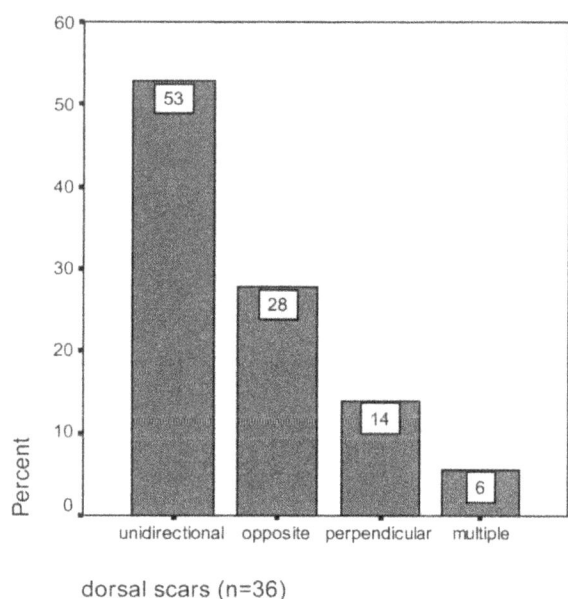

*Figure 6.4.* Direction of dorsal scars on blades.

## Blade core maintenance

During blade production, the cores' striking platforms were rejuvenated by rejuvenating flake removals (n=3) and core tablet removals (n=3) (Figure 6.3: 5.). These, except a single core tablet of RM5, belong to the laminar processing of RM1.

The debitage surface convexity was maintained by neo-cresting (6 neo-crest blades) (Figure 6.3: 7.). The neo-cresting was made at the distal part of the cores and along the entire length of the debitage surface.

## Blade core discard

The fronts of the discarded blade cores are wide (n=4), semi-circular (n=3) and narrow (n=2) almost in equal shares. The sides of the cores are converging in most cases (n=5) and then parallel (n−4). Six of the 9 cores are cortical. A total of 8 cores have a single striking platform while one item has double.

The cores were discarded in different stages of the debitage. Four of the blade cores have laminar hinge negative scars, and the remaining 5 bear negatives of ordinary removals. Two cores with hinge scars were abraded on their overhangs before discard.

## Bladelet production

### Bladelet core configuration

The bladelet production was based on mediocre quality flints. Within mediocre quality flint group RM1 is dominant (Table 6.2.). Two flint types, RM9 of mediocre quality and RM10 of good quality are not present in bladelet production.

The bladelet debitage took place in a joint sequence with the blade debitage in the cases of the exploitation of RM1. From RM1, two blade cores are left behind, while considerable amount of blades are present (Table 6.2.).

According to the preserved original surfaces of the flint nodules, also there was a tendency to collect small nodules for making cores to the bladelet production. Thus, small, *ca* 5 cm sized flint nodules (Figure 6.6: 25.), tabular flints and strongly patinated Middle Palaeolithic thick flakes (n=3) were used for making bladelets

Vestiges of bladelet core configuration methods are scarce. A few cores show that the lateral sides were shaped striking the back and the proximal core part (Figure 6.6: 22.). The configuration removals were restricted to clean the core front and its environment, although the cortex was not entirely removed from the bladelet cores. A total of 17% of the entire bladelet assemblage are cortical. The cortex on the bladelets usually appears at the distal part and on one of the dorsal halves along the total length.

The striking platform of the bladelet cores was created by the removal of a single flake. The debitage surface in a few cases was prepared with cresting. Evidences to this are two crest bladelets (Figure 6.6: 14, 15.).

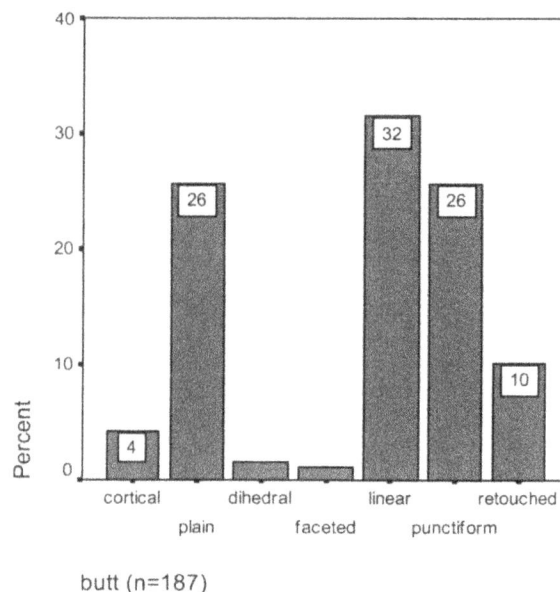

butt (n=187)

*Figure 6.5.* Butt types of bladelets.

### Bladelet debitage

Most bladelets have linear butts (Figure 6.5.). The butt thickness is less than 1mm in 63% of the cases. The overhangs are abraded on 57.8% of the bladelets and impact points are present at 7.4%. These indicate that soft hammer technique was used for the most part in the debitage.

The profile of the bladelets is dominantly curved. Items with twisted profile appear in significantly higher amount than straight ones. The straight and curved bladelets have mostly parallel edges and the bladelets with twisted profile have converging edges (Table 6.3.). The preponderance of bladelets with parallel and converging edges indicates that the cores primarily had parallel lateral sides, to lesser extent converging during most part of the debitage.

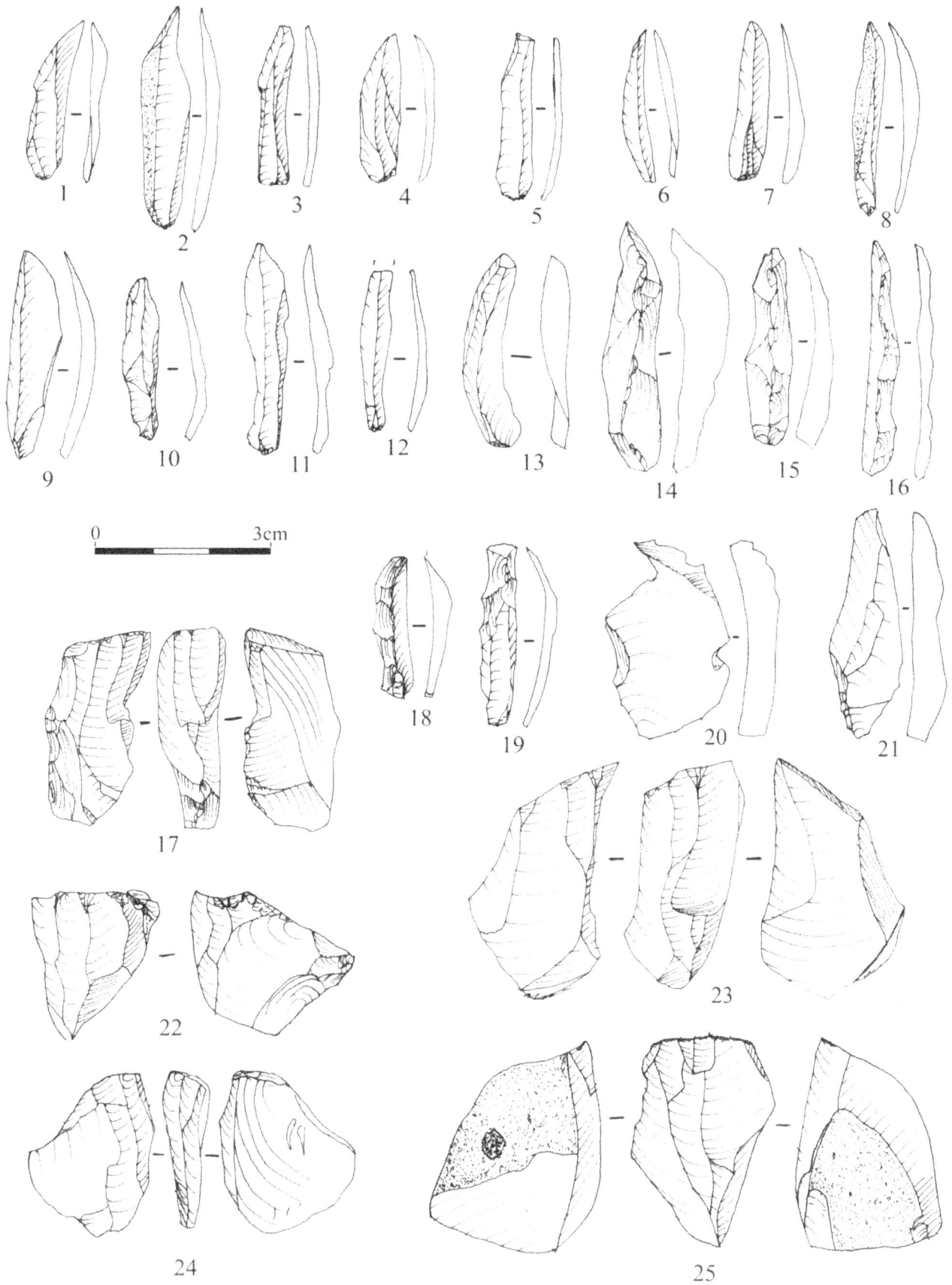

**Figure 6.6.** *Bladelets (1-13); crest bladelets (14, 15); neo-crest bladelets (16, 18, 19); bladelet core tablets (20, 21); bladelet cores (17, 22-25).*

**Table 6.3.** *Bladelet profile-edge shape crosstabulation.*

| Profile | Edges | | | Total |
|---|---|---|---|---|
| | parallel | converging | expanding | |
| straight | 22 | 9 | 6 | *37* |
| curved | 35 | 18 | 13 | *66* |
| twisted | 14 | 23 | 13 | *50* |
| *Total* | *71* | *50* | *32* | *153* |

**Table 6.4.** *Crosstabulation of the shape of the front and the sides of the debitage surface of the bladelet cores.*

| Front | Sides | | | Total |
|---|---|---|---|---|
| | converging | parallel | irregular | |
| narrow | 9 | 12 | 1 | *22* |
| semi-circular | 13 | 4 | 1 | *18* |
| wide | 1 | 1 | 1 | *3* |
| *Total* | *23* | *17* | *3* | *43* |

A total of 86% of the cores have a single striking platform and 76% of the bladelets bear unidirectional dorsal scars (Figure 6.7.). These vestiges indicate that the orientation of the bladelet debitage was unidirectional. The opposite removals may mostly be remnants of cores' side and debitage surface shaping.

### Accidents during bladelet debitage

Fragments make up 48% of the bladelet assemblage. There are 53.5% distal fragments while mesials are 16.1% and proximals are 23.4 %. All breaks are "clear", thus it is impossible to distinguish between knapping and post-knapping breaks. Hinge and plunging accidents number the same amount, accounting for 4.2% and 3.7% of the bladelet assemblage, respectively.

### Bladelet core maintenance

During bladelet production, the cores' striking platforms were rejuvenated by rejuvenating flake removals (n=6) and core tablet removals (n=6) (Figure 6.6: 20, 21.). Three core tablets and all rejuvenating flakes have been removed by hard stone hammer technique. The three other tablets have no clear markers of their detaching techniques.

The debitage surface convexity was maintained by neo-cresting (25 neo-crest bladelets, 10.4% of the bladelet assemblage) (Figure 6.6: 16, 18, 19.). The neo-cresting always was made at the distal part of the cores.

### Bladelet core discard

Most of the discarded bladelet cores have a narrow front. Wide fronted cores are in insignificant amount (Table 6.4.). Of the 43 bladelet cores 31 items are cortical.

The core discard occurred in different debitage stages. One core bears scars of the prior blade debitage. Twenty-six specimens have been discarded after hinge accident. However, five bladelets bear hinge scars on their dorsal face, meaning that the debitage was not always stopped after knapping hinge accident. Among the cores with hinge scars, two were rejuvenated on their striking platforms following the hinge accidents, before discard. It is also noticeable that thirteen cores' overhangs were abraded after the last bladelet removal. This especially characterizes the hinge negative bearer cores (n=9).

The rest of the cores do not have crucial accidents which would have made them useless. Since the smallest bladelet cores do not have hinge accident scars on their debitage surfaces, those were discarded on the reason of reaching a small size inappropriate for continuing the removal of bladelets.

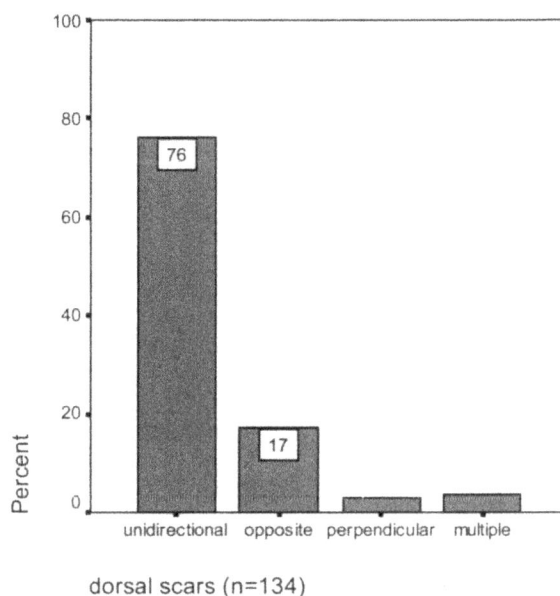

**Figure 6.7.** *Directions of dorsal scars on bladelets.*

## Flake production

Flakes are present from every raw material. Their number is especially high among RM1 products. The number of flakes is extremely high in comparison to that of the flake cores.

Three cores, two of RM13 and one of RM8, show unambiguous scars of flake debitage (Figure 6.8: 1, 2.). Two other cores, both of RM1, originally belonged to blade production and only a few flakes were removed from them by debitage. The core of RM13 has several striking platforms, while all others have single striking platforms.

Flakes also derive from laminar cores' debitage surfaces, as evidenced by the presence of unidirectional scar bearer flakes with parallel ridges (3.1% of the flakes). The butt of the flakes is predominantly plain.

Abraded overhangs characterize 37.1% of the flakes. The butts are dominantly thicker (81.6%) than 2 mm. The impact point is visible on 41% of the flakes. In 27.5% of these cases the impact point is large. A total of 23.6% of the flakes have no bulb. The bulb appears as diffused at 50% of the flakes. The rest, 26.4% have convex bulbs. Lipping is characteristic to 36.5% of the flakes. These evidence the use of both soft and hard hammer technique. A total of 30.4% of the flakes are broken. Distal fragments make up 78.9%, mesials 7%, and proximals 14.1%. Hinge flakes (8.5%), and plungings (2.6%) are present, too.

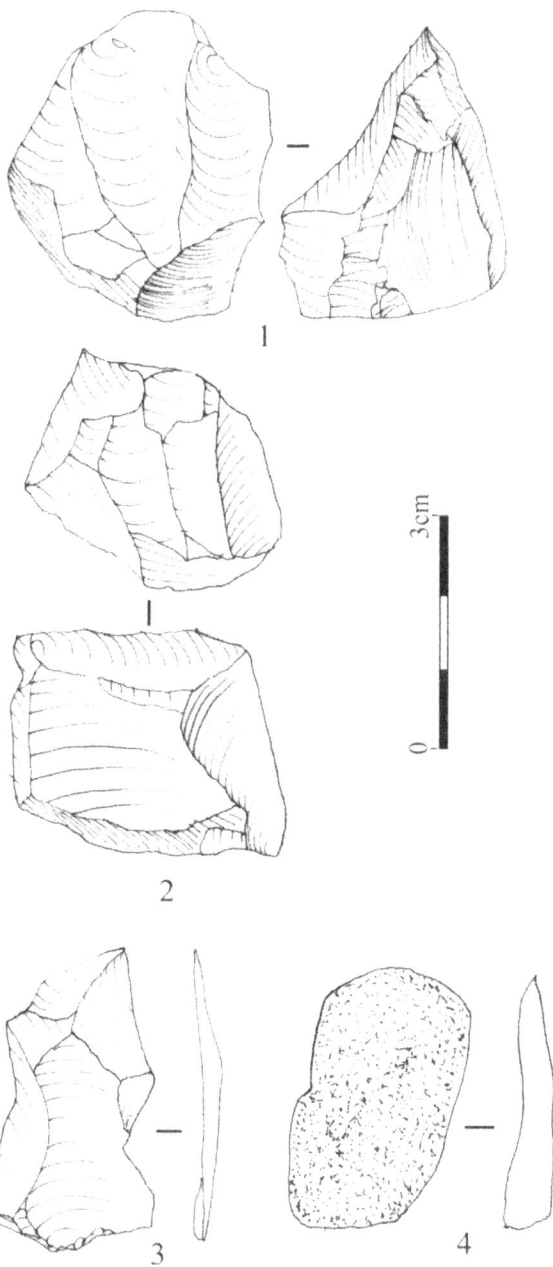

**Figure 6.8.** *Flake cores (1, 2); flake (3); first flake (4).*

## Tool blank selection and tools

### Blade tool blanks

A total of 9.5% of the blades are tools. Blade tool blanks are of RM1, RM6, RM7 and RM10 (Table. 6.5.). This constitutes 26.6% of the raw material spectrum.

The blade tool blanks have straight or twisted profile with parallel or expanding edges likewise most unretouched blanks. Of the 7 blades 3 are cortical and one is a neo-crest item.

### Blade tools

Blades make up 8.2% of the tool kit. Most blade tools are retouched items (Table 6.6.). Their retouch is scaled or fine marginal and never continuous on the edge (Figure

6.9: 26, 27.). Other tools on blades are a simple end-scraper with converging front retouch, a transversal burin and a truncation burin and a notched item.

**Table 6.5.** *Tool blanks by raw material.*

| Raw material | | Tool blank | | | Total |
|---|---|---|---|---|---|
| source | type | flake | blade | bladelet | |
| RAM | RM1 | 15 | 2 | 25 | 42 |
| | RM2 | 4 | | 1 | 5 |
| | RM4 | 1 | | | 1 |
| DH | RM5 | 2 | | 4 | 6 |
| | RM6 | 1 | 1 | 2 | 4 |
| | RM7 | 1 | 1 | | 2 |
| | RM8 | | | 1 | 1 |
| | RM10 | 1 | 2 | | 3 |
| | RM11 | 1 | | 1 | 2 |
| DC | RM12 | 2 | | 5 | 7 |
| | RM13 | | | 2 | 2 |
| NM | RM14 | 2 | | | 2 |
| | RM17 | | | 1 | 1 |
| | burnt | 1 | 2 | 5 | 8 |
| Total | | 31 | 8 | 47 | 86 |

### Bladelet tool blanks

A total of 15.8% of the bladelets are tools. Most bladelet tool blanks are of RM1 (Table 6.5.). Three types of raw materials were not selected for bladelet blanks (Table 6.5.). This means that 80% of the raw materials were used for bladelet tools.

Of the 48 bladelet tools only 6 (12.5%) are cortical. Most bladelet tool blanks are straight in profile (edge shape is out of count because the reason of high percentage of blunting retouch), which is in striking contrast with the high presence of curved and twisted bladelets among unretouched blanks. The use of core trimming elements as tool blanks is uncommon, only a single item of neo-crest bladelet is present among tools.

### Bladelet tools

The vast majority of the tools were made on bladelets, making up 55.8% of the tool kit (Table 6.6.). Bladelets are exclusive blanks of backed (Figure 6.9: 20, 21.), backed-truncated (Figure 6.9: 1-8, 24.), truncated tools (Figure 6.9: 15-19, 28.) and points. Among backed bladelets straight backs are dominant. Arch backed items were often shaped at the proximal end of the bladelets (Figure 6.9: 9-12.). The backing of micropoints was made by very fine abrupt retouch (Figure 6.9: 22, 23.). On backed-truncated bladelets, the backing retouch is consistently direct, and removed only the margin of the blank. The backing is not always very regular and not totally straight. The truncation is oblique, and in most cases made on the proximal end of the blank. Truncated bladelets are of oblique type, and similarly to the truncations on backed-truncated types, frequently made at the blank's proximal end. There are two points made of bladelets. One of them was pointed at the base on both edges, and the distal part of the right edge was also retouched but not pointed. The other point is a distal fragment of a shouldered, unilaterally pointed bladelet (Figure 6.9: 25.). The retouch at the tip and the proximal shouldering are on the same, right edge. Typologically, this form is very similar to the European Late Pleistocene Hamburgian point (Demars and Laurent 1992). Bladelets are also common among simply edge-retouched tools. The retouch is basically marginal, partial and discontinuous on one edge (Figure 6.9: 13.).The presence of bladelets among burins and composite tools is unusual. The burins are with truncation and transversal and the composite tools are endscraper/truncation and endscraper/burin.

## Flake tool blanks

A total of 8.8% of the flakes were used for tools. The majority of the flake tool blanks are of RM1. Three types of raw materials were not selected for blanks (Table 6.5.). This means that 80% of the raw materials were used for

flake tools. It is of interest that the high quality raw material of Nahal Mearot is solely present among flake tools. A large part, 48.4% of the flake tool blanks, is cortical. In addition to ordinary blanks, a core tablet and a platform rejuvenating flake also were used in tool making.

## Flake tools

Flake blanks are relative frequent in the tool kit, they make up 36%. Flakes are common blanks of burins, endscrapers, notches and straight and convex side scrapers. The prevalent type of burin is the dihedral (Figure 6.9: 33.). Other burin types such as transversal, on truncation (Figure 6.9: 32.) and on break are uncommon. Most flake endscrapers are simple with scaled front retouch (Figure 6.9: 29.).

**Table 6.6.** Tool type list of the Late Kebaran assemblage.

| Tool types | | Blank | | | Total | |
|---|---|---|---|---|---|---|
| | | flake | blade | bladelet | # | % |
| **Endscrapers** | simple | 5 | 1 | | 6 | 7,0 |
| | Thin nosed | 1 | | | 1 | 1,2 |
| | circular | 1 | | | 1 | 1,2 |
| | *Sub-total* | *7* | *1* | | *8* | *9,3* |
| **Burins** | on break | 1 | | | 1 | 1,2 |
| | on straight truncation | 2 | | | 2 | 2,3 |
| | on oblique truncation | | 1 | | 1 | 1,2 |
| | on concave truncation | | | 1 | 1 | 1,2 |
| | Dihedral burins | 8 | | | 8 | 9,3 |
| | Transversal burins | 3 | 1 | 1 | 5 | 5,8 |
| | *Sub-total* | *14* | *2* | *2* | *18* | *20,9* |
| **Retouched items** | continuous scaled | | | 1 | 1 | 1,2 |
| | partial scaled | 1 | 1 | 2 | 4 | 4,7 |
| | continuous marginal | 1 | | 1 | 2 | 2,3 |
| | partial marginal | | 2 | 1 | 3 | 3,5 |
| | both edges | | | 1 | 1 | 1,2 |
| | discontinuous scaled | | 1 | | 1 | 1,2 |
| | discontinuous marginal | | | 2 | 2 | 2,3 |
| | *Sub-total* | *2* | *4* | *8* | *14* | *16,3* |
| **Backed items** | straight | | | 4 | 4 | 4,7 |
| | straight partial | | | 2 | 2 | 2,3 |
| | curved partial | | | 1 | 1 | 1,2 |
| | arch | | | 3 | 3 | 3,5 |
| | micropoint | | | 2 | 2 | 2,3 |
| | Curved pointed backed | | | 1 | 1 | 1,2 |
| | *Sub-total* | | | *13* | *13* | *15,1* |
| **Truncations** | oblique | | | 5 | 5 | 5,8 |
| | *Total* | | | *5* | *5* | *5,8* |
| **Points** | simple | | | 1 | 1 | 1,2 |
| | shouldered point | | | 1 | 1 | 1,2 |
| | *Sub-total* | | | *2* | *2* | *2,3* |
| **Backed truncated tool** | | | | 12 | 12 | 13,6 |
| **Notches** | double | 1 | | | 1 | 1,2 |
| | single | 3 | 1 | 3 | 7 | 8,1 |
| | *Sub-total* | *4* | *1* | *3* | *8* | *9,3* |
| **Side scrapers** | straight | 1 | | | 1 | 1,2 |
| | convex | 1 | | | 1 | 1,2 |
| | *Sub-total* | *2* | | | *2* | *2,3* |
| **splintered item** | | 1 | | | 1 | 1,2 |
| **Composites** | end-scraper—truncation | | | 1 | 1 | 1,2 |
| | end-scraper—burin | 1 | | 1 | 2 | 2,3 |
| | *Sub-total* | *1* | | *2* | *3* | *3,5* |
| *Total* | | *31* | *8* | *47* | *86* | *100* |

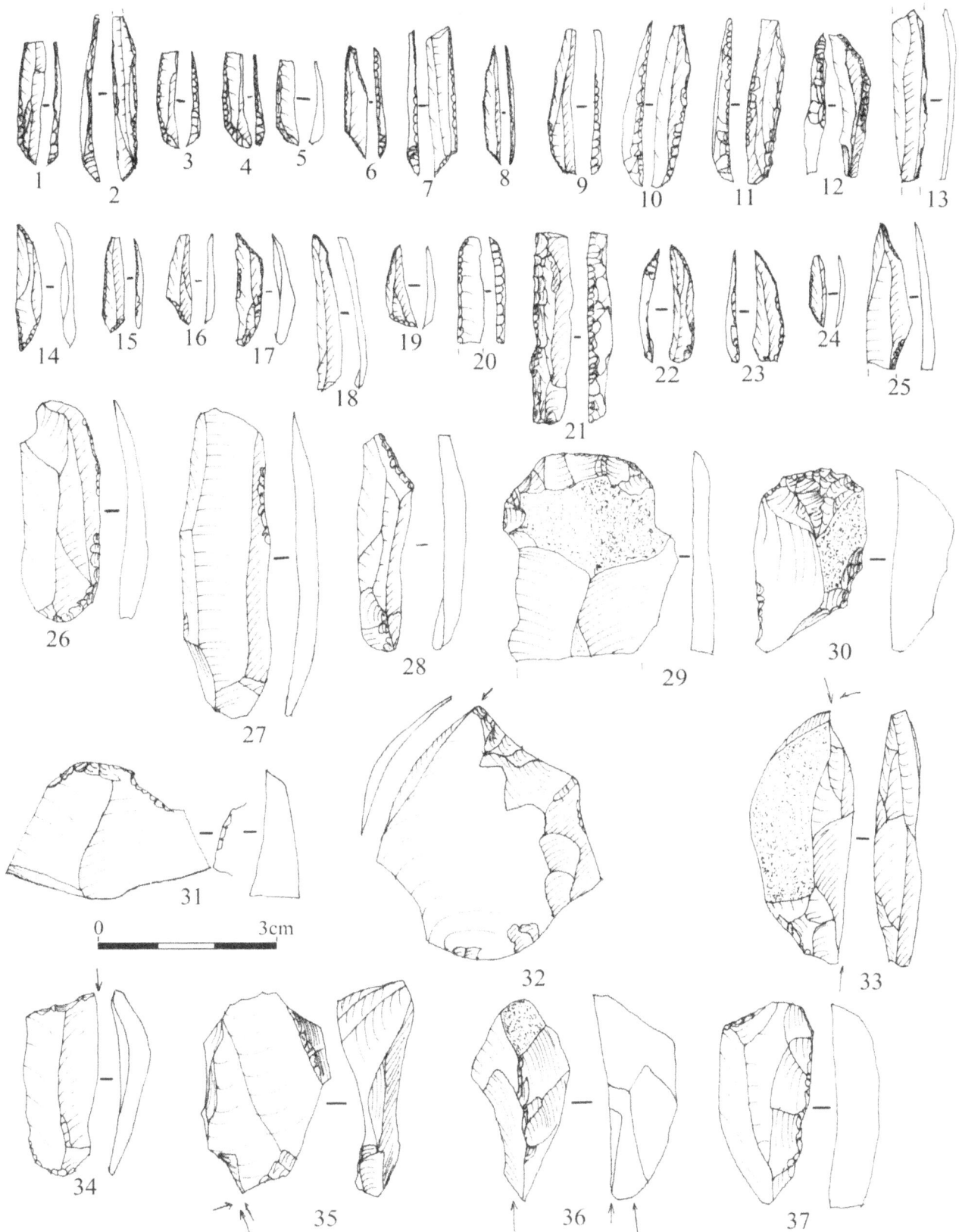

**Figure 6.9.** *Backed truncated bladelets (1-8, 24); arch backed bladelets (9-12); retouched bladelet (13); borer (14); obliquely truncated bladelets (15-19, 28); backed bladelets (20, 21); narrow micropoints (22, 23); Hamburgian point-like tool (25); retouched blades (26-27); endscrapers (29-31); burins (32-36); sidescraper (37).*

# CHAPTER 7: THE GEOMETRIC KEBARAN ASSEMBLAGE
## LAYER VII, AREA J-M/24-28

## Raw material

The raw materials of the assemblage derive from six flint sources (Table 7.1). Deir Hannah formation (DH) yielded the majority of the raw materials, among which the good quality RM5 is dominant. In addition, this raw material is the most abundant in the whole assemblage.

Ramat Menashe (RAM) flints, the closest source to Raqefet, make up the next largest group of raw material. Among them the mediocre quality RM1 is dominant. RM1 constitutes the second most abundant raw material type in the assemblage.

Nahal Mearot good quality raw materials (NM) make up the third largest group of raw material.

Daliyat ha Carmel low quality raw materials (DC) are present with low frequency.

Shamir formation good quality raw materials (SH) derived from the farthest part of the Carmel to Raqefet. They constitute a small portion of the assemblage.

Ohalo II mediocre quality raw material (OII) derives from the greatest distance, *ca* 45km east to Raqefet. This is the smallest group of raw material.

Good quality raw materials of unknown origin make up a quite large portion of the assemblage, larger than DC raw materials.

On the basis of the presence of two first flakes, only RM5 was brought to the site as fully cortical nodule. Other raw materials were roughed-out in various extents off-site.

The artifacts of OII long-distance raw material are present by bladelets and a very few flakes, without cores. These were introduced to the site as ready made products.

In sum, the raw material acquisition focused on good quality raw materials from the closest source, while mediocre and especially low quality flints make up the smallest part of the assemblage (Figure 7.1).

*Table 7.1. Frequency of raw material types by source.*

| Raw material quality | type | Raw material source | | | | | | | | | Total |
|---|---|---|---|---|---|---|---|---|---|---|---|
| | | RAM | DH | DC | NM | SH | OII | unknown | | | |
| Mediocre | RM1 | 464 85,8% | | | | | | | | | 464 24,9% |
| Low | RM2 | 7 1,3% | | | | | | | | | 7 0,4% |
| Low | RM3 | 12 2,2% | | | | | | | | | 12 0,6% |
| Low | RM4 | 58 10,7% | | | | | | | | | 58 3,1% |
| Good | RM5 | | 576 71,9% | | | | | | | | 576 31% |
| Low | RM6 | | 36 4,5% | | | | | | | | 36 1,9% |
| Good | RM7 | | 49 6,1% | | | | | | | | 49 2,6% |
| Good | RM8 | | 28 3,5% | | | | | | | | 28 1,5% |
| Mediocre | RM9 | | 2 0,2% | | | | | | | | 2 0,1% |
| Mediocre | RM11 | | 110 13,7% | | | | | | | | 110 5,9% |
| Low | RM12 | | | 45 63,8% | | | | | | | 45 2,4% |
| Low | RM13 | | | 27 36,2% | | | | | | | 27 1,5% |
| Good | RM14 | | | | 270 100% | | | | | | 270 14,5% |
| Good | RM15 | | | | | 26 100% | | | | | 26 1,4% |
| Mediocre | RM16 | | | | | 6 100% | | | | | 6 0,3% |
| Good | RM17 | | | | | | | 89 100% | | | 89 4,8% |
| Good | RM18 | | | | | | | | 18 100% | | 18 1% |
| Good | RM19 | | | | | | 37 100% | | | | 37 2% |
| Total | | 541 29,1% | 801 43,1% | 72 3,9% | 270 14,5% | 26 1,4% | 6 0,3% | 37 2% | 89 4,8% | 18 1% | 1860 100% |

*Table 7.2. Distribution of products by raw materials.*

| Raw material source | type | flake | blade | bladelet | waste | CTE | tool | flake | Blade | bladelet | pre- | Total |
|---|---|---|---|---|---|---|---|---|---|---|---|---|
| | | | | Lithic product | | | | | | Core | | |
| RAM | RM1 | 85 18,5% | 56 12,2% | 86 18,7% | 171 37,2% | 13 2,8% | 47 10,2% | 1 0,2% | | 5 1,1% | | 464 100% |
| | RM2 | 1 14,3% | 1 14,3% | 2 28,6% | 2 28,6% | | 1 14,3% | | | | | 7 100% |
| | RM3 | 2 16,7% | 2 16,7% | | 8 66,7% | | | | | | | 12 100% |
| | RM4 | 11 19% | 7 12,1% | 6 10,3% | 29 50% | 2 3,4% | 3 5,2% | | | | | 58 100% |
| DH | RM5 | 94 16,3% | 65 11,3% | 112 19,4% | 234 40,6% | 15 2,6% | 49 8,5% | 1 0,2% | 2 0,3% | 3 0,5% | 1 0,2% | 576 100% |
| | RM6 | 11 30,6% | 5 13,9% | 5 13,9% | 10 27,8% | | 4 11,1% | | 1 2,8% | | | 36 100% |
| | RM7 | 10 20,4% | 4 8,2% | 18 36,7% | 10 20,4% | 1 2% | 6 12,2% | | | | | 49 100% |
| | RM8 | 7 25% | 1 3,6% | 9 32,1% | 2 7,1% | 2 7,1% | 4 14,3% | | 1 3,6% | 1 3,6% | 1 3,6% | 28 100% |
| | RM9 | 1 50% | | | 1 50% | | | | | | | 2 100% |
| | RM11 | 26 23,6% | 13 11,8% | 13 11,8% | 39 35,5% | 4 3,6% | 14 12,7% | | | 1 0,9% | | 110 100% |
| DC | RM12 | 15 33,3% | 3 6,7% | 4 8,9% | 16 35,6% | | 6 13,3% | 1 2,2% | | | | 45 100% |
| | RM13 | 4 14,8% | 4 14,8% | 4 14,8% | 8 29,6% | 1 3,7% | 4 14,8% | 1 3,7% | 1 3,7% | | | 27 100% |
| NM | RM14 | 54 20% | 19 7% | 68 25,2% | 85 31,5% | 5 1,9% | 29 10,7% | 2 0,7% | 2 0,7% | 6 2,2% | | 270 100% |
| SH | RM15 | 6 23,1% | 2 7,7% | 9 34,6% | 1 3,8% | 2 7,7% | 6 23,1% | | | | | 26 100% |
| OII | RM16 | 2 33,3% | | | 1 16,7% | | 3 50% | | | | | 6 100% |
| unknown | RM17 | 11 12,4% | 13 14,6% | 16 18% | 27 30,3% | 2 2,2% | 18 20,2% | | | 2 2,2% | | 89 100% |
| | RM18 | 5 27,8% | 1 5,6% | 5 27,8% | 3 16,7% | | 2 11,1% | | | 2 11,1% | | 18 100% |
| | RM19 | 4 10,8% | 3 8,1% | 18 48,6% | 6 16,2% | | 5 13,5% | | | 1 2,7% | | 37 100% |
| | total | 349 18,8% | 199 10,7% | 375 20,2% | 653 35,1% | 47 2,5% | 201 10,8% | 5 0,3% | 8 0,4% | 21 1,1% | 2 0,1% | 1860 100% |

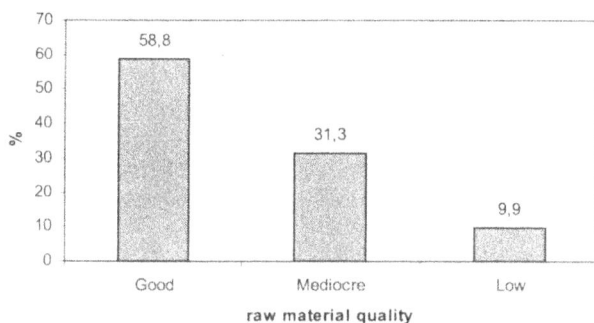

*Figure 7.1. Frequency of raw materials by quality.*

## Blade production

### Blade core configuration

The blade production is based on good quality flints. Within good quality flint group RM5 is dominant (Table 7.2.). Two flint types, RM9 of mediocre quality and RM16 of good quality were not used in blade production.

A few cores show that their lateral sides were shaped from the back and from the striking platform (Figure 7.4: 1, 3.). A total of 29.1% of the blades are cortical. This low percentage highlights an effective decortication prior to blade debitage. Although, the cores themselves exhibit that their back frequently remained cortical. The core fronts were set up on the narrow part of the nodules.

According to the following evidences, two modalities existed to prepare the blade core front to beginning the blade debitage. The first was the cresting, as illustrated by crest blades (n=3) (Figure 7.5: 4.), sub-crest blades (n=2) (Figure 7.5: 5.), and cresting remains on cores (2 specimens). The second modality has rare evidences in the assemblage. It is when natural cortical ridges of flint nodules are removed without preparation in order to create the debitage surface (Figure 7.5: 3.).

The striking platforms of the cores were prepared by the removal of a single flake. It was rarely cortical, as indicated by the high number of plain blade butts (Figure 7.2).

## Blade debitage

The striking platform of the blade cores remained plain during the debitage as indicated by the high frequency of plain butts (Figure 7.2.).

Abraded overhangs characterize 62.4% of the blades. The butts are dominantly thin (56.3% are thinner than 2 mm). The impact point is visible on 31.5% of the blades. In a total of 82.4% of these cases the impact point is minor. A total of 28.8% of the blades have no bulb. The bulb appears as diffused on 47.6% of the blades. The rest of the blades, 23.6%, have convex bulbs. Lipping is characteristic to 25.6% of the blades. These vestiges evidence the use of soft hammer technique.

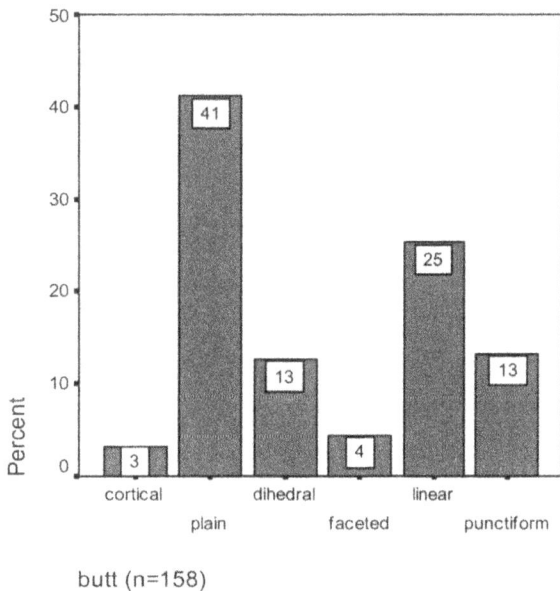

butt (n=158)

***Figure 7.2.*** *Butt types of blades.*

The size of the blades is varied. Most fall between 45 and 60 mm.

The core front, according to the shape of the core tablets, was mostly semi-circular during blade debitage (Figure 7.6: 1.).

The preponderance of blades with parallel and expanding edges indicates that the cores had debitage surfaces with parallel sides during most part of the blade

debitage. In profile, the blades are dominantly curved (Table 7.3.).

A total of 85.7% of the cores have a single striking platform and 56% of the blades bear unidirectional dorsal scars (Figure 7.3.). These vestiges indicate that the orientation of the blade debitage was primarily unidirectional. The opposite removals on blades are definitely in connection with opposite debitage and there is only a single core with opposite striking platforms. However, this core exploitation is uncommon, and the presence of non-unidirectional scars on blades may mostly be remnants of cores' side and debitage surface shaping.

***Table 7.3.*** *Blade edges-profile crosstabulation.*

| Edges | Profile | | | Total |
|---|---|---|---|---|
| | straight | curved | twisted | |
| parallel | 11 | 16 | 2 | *29* |
| converging | 3 | 6 | 2 | *11* |
| expanding | 10 | 14 | | *24* |
| irregular | 6 | 2 | | *8* |
| *Total* | *30* | *38* | *4* | *72* |

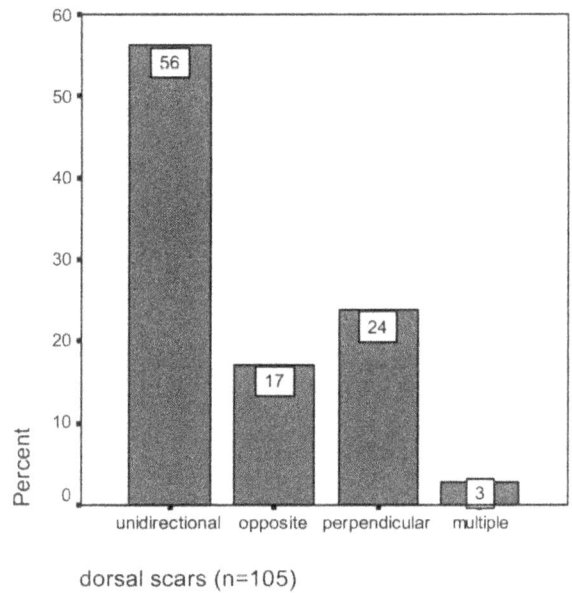

dorsal scars (n=105)

***Figure 7.3.*** *Direction of dorsal scars on blades.*

## Accidents during blade debitage

A total of 64.8% of the blades are broken. Most fragments are distal (52.4%), while mesials make up 21.7% and proximals 27.9%. It is not possible to distinguish between knapping and post knapping breaks, since all are *clear* breakages, and no *languette* pieces were found.

Hinge accidents make up 7.5% of the blade assemblage while plunging items make up 6.5%. Breaks and hinges are characteristic to the exploitation of RAM blade cores (51% of RAM blades are broken against 41.9% of DH blades; 30.76% of RAM blades are hinged against 12.77 % of DH blades).

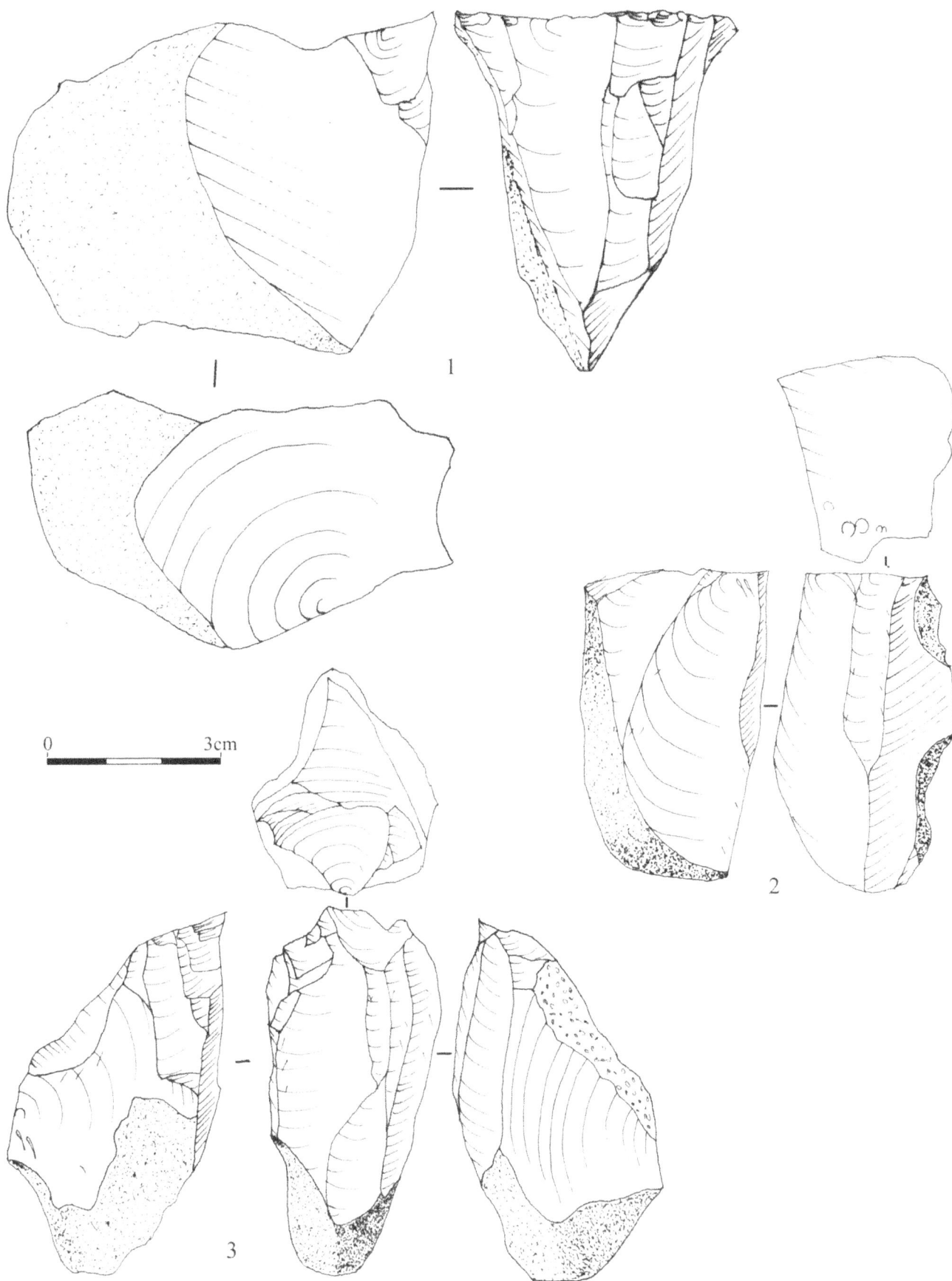

**Figure 7.4**. *Blade cores.*

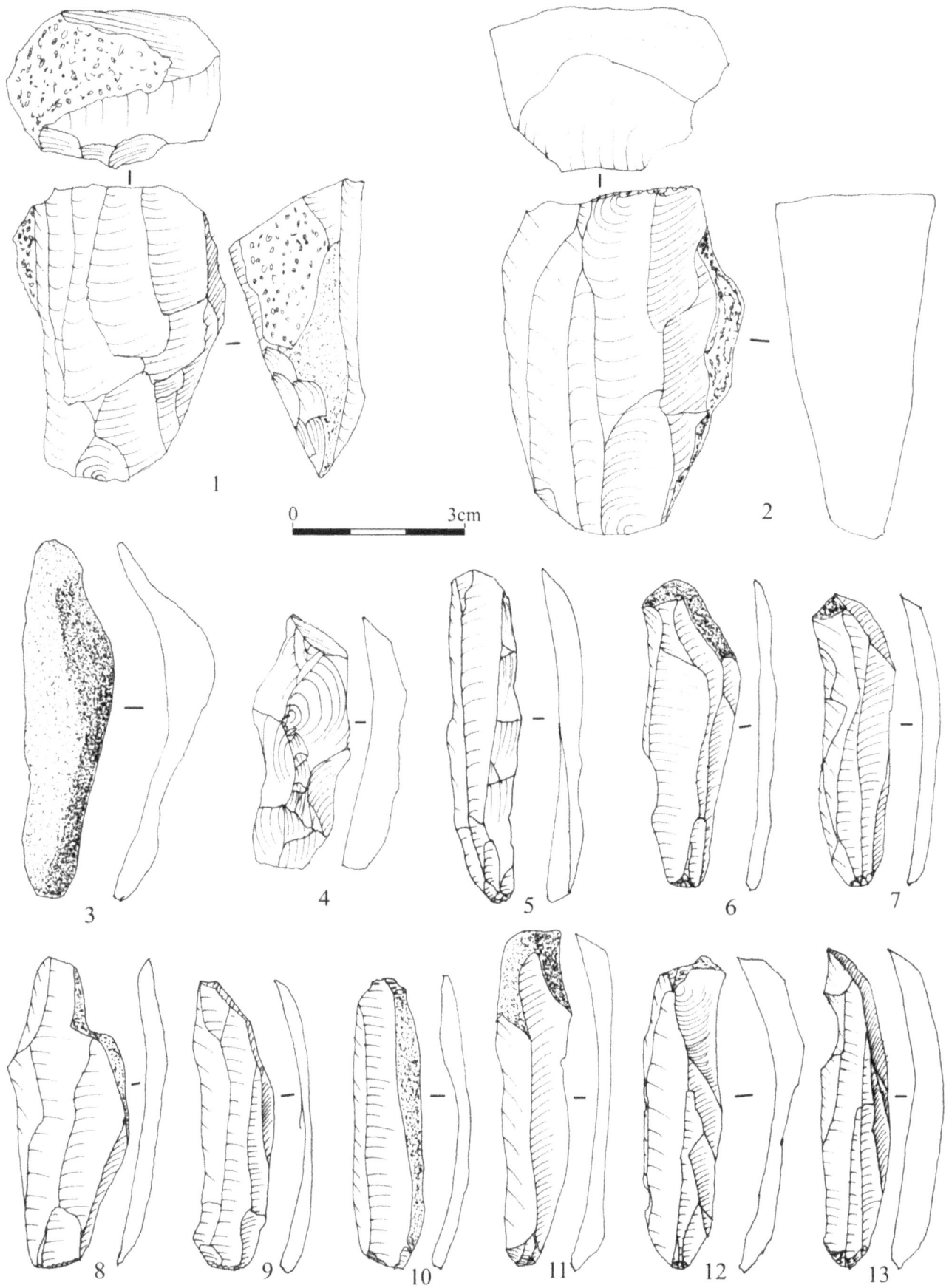

*Figure 7.5.* Blade core (1, 2); fully cortical blade (3); crest blade (4); sub-crest blade (5), blade (6-13).

## Blade core maintenance

During blade production, the cores' striking platforms were rejuvenated by rejuvenating flake removals (n=8) (Figure 7.6: 2.), and core tablet removals (n=2) (Figure 7.6: 1.). These removals were frequently made from the sides of the cores and not from the front (Figure 7.4: 1., 7.5: 1, 2.).

The debitage surface convexity was maintained by neo-cresting (13 neo-crest blades). The neo-cresting was made at the distal part of the cores (Figure 7.6: 3, 4.).

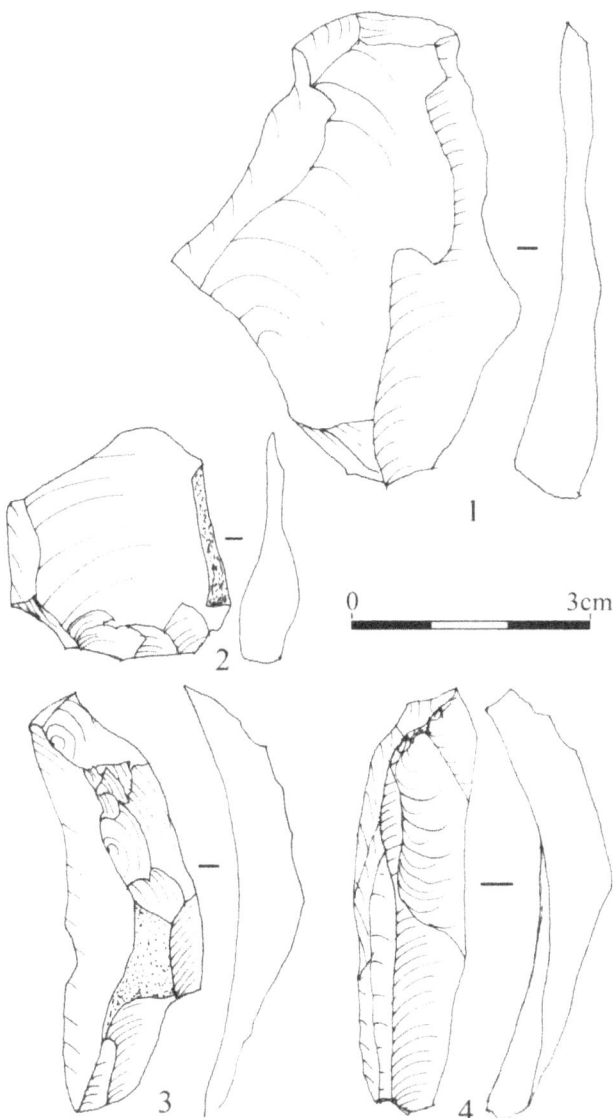

**Figure 7.6.** *core tablets (1); core striking platform rejuvenating flake (2); neo-crest blade (3, 4).*

## Blade core discard

The discarded blade cores have semi-circular and wide front with parallel lateral sides (Table 7.4.). Each core is cortical. Of the 8 blade cores 6 have single striking platforms, one has opposite platforms and one item did not preserve striking platform.

**Table 7.4.** *Crosstabulation of front shape and sides of the blade cores.*

| Front | Sides | | Total |
|---|---|---|---|
| | converging | parallel | |
| narrow | 1 | 1 | 2 |
| semi-circular | | 3 | 3 |
| wide | 1 | 2 | 3 |
| Total | 2 | 6 | 8 |

There are 3 cores which do not bear any crucial accidents on their debitage surfaces (Table 7.5.). Two cores bearing hinge scars were rejuvenated on their striking platforms, but further removals from the debitage surface were not made. On two other hinge scars bearer cores, neo-cresting was the last action performed.

One of the reasons of core discard is the crucial hinge accident. In some cases the hinges did not force the knapper to discard the core as is illustrated by the presence of hinge scars on 21 blades. The other reason of core discard is that cores reached a small size which was not appropriate for continuing removing blades.

**Table 7.5.** *Crosstabulation of maintenance type and last removal type on blade cores.*

| Maintenance | Removal | | | Total |
|---|---|---|---|---|
| | ordinary | hinge | irregular | |
| rejuvenating flake | | 2 | | 2 |
| neo-cresting | | 2 | | 2 |
| no data | 3 | | 1 | 4 |
| Total | 3 | 4 | 1 | 8 |

## Bladelet production

### Bladelet core configuration

The bladelet production is based on good quality flints. Within good quality flint group RM5 is dominant (Table 7.2.). Three flint types, RM3 of low quality, RM9 of mediocre quality, and RM16 of good quality are not present among bladelets.

The bladelet debitage took place in a joint sequence with the blade debitage in the cases of the exploitation of RM1, RM5 and RM14. From RM1, no blade cores are left behind, while considerable amount of blades are present (Table 7.2.). The other two raw materials yielded a large number of blades and the presence of blade cores is scarce.

In addition to the joint debitage sequence of blades and bladelets, according to the preserved original surfaces of the flint nodules, there was a tendency to collect small nodules for bladelet cores. These were, small, *ca* 5 cm sized flint nodules.

Vestiges of bladelet core configuration methods are scarce. A few cores show that the lateral sides were shaped striking the proximal core part (Figure 7.9: 1.). The back of the bladelet cores were not shaped. The configuration removals were restricted to clean the core front and its environment, and the cortex was not entirely removed from the bladelet cores. A total of 8.6% of the entire bladelet assemblage are cortical. The cortex on the bladelets usually appears at the distal part and on one of the dorsal halves along the total length.

The striking platform was created by the removal of a single flake. In the preparation of the debitage surface of the bladelet cores, contrary to the blade cores, neither cresting nor cortical ridge removals were made. The debitage surface was probably created by a few flake removals. The bladelet debitage took place habitually on cores with wide or semi-circular fronts.

## Bladelet debitage

Most bladelets have linear butts (Figure 7.7.). The butt thickness is less than 1mm in 55.8% of the cases. The overhangs are abraded on 56.2% of the bladelet removals. Impact points are present on 20.2% of the bladelets. These indicate that soft hammer technique was used for the most part in the debitage.

**Table 7.6.** *Crosstabulation of bladelet profile, and the shape of the edges.*

| Profile | Edges | | | | Total |
|---------|----------|------------|-----------|-----------|-------|
|         | parallel | converging | expanding | irregular |       |
| straight | 35 | 22 | 22 | 7 | 86 |
| curved | 45 | 22 | 24 | 2 | 93 |
| twisted | 11 | 12 | 8 | 2 | 33 |
| Total | 91 | 56 | 54 | 11 | 212 |

The profile of the bladelets is dominantly curved with parallel edges (Table 7.6.). Parallel-edged bladelets are also frequently straight. The preponderance of bladelets with parallel edges, and also the number of expanding-edged bladelets indicate that the cores had debitage surfaces with parallel sides during most part of the debitage.

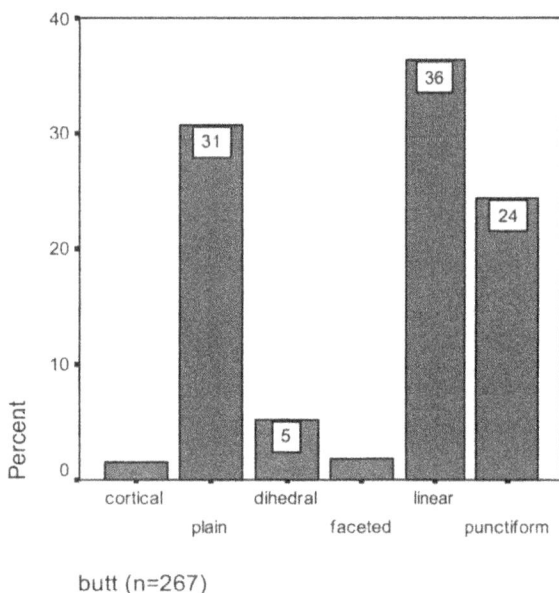

butt (n=267)

**Figure 7.7.** *Butt types of bladelets.*

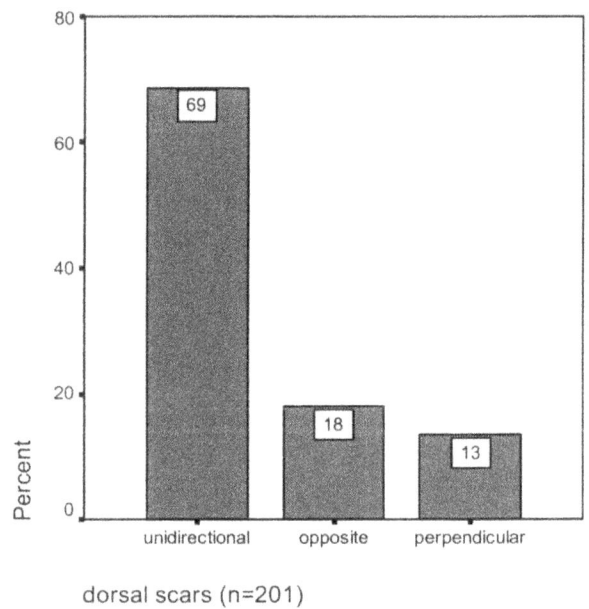

dorsal scars (n=201)

**Figure 7.8.** *Direction of dorsal scars on bladelets.*

A total of 62.5% of the cores have a single striking platform and 69% of the bladelets bear unidirectional dorsal scars (Figure 7.8.). These vestiges indicate that the orientation of the bladelet debitage was primarily unidirectional. Some of the opposite removals are definitely in connection with opposite debitage. However, this core exploitation is uncommon. One core shows that secondarily its lateral side was exploited. Sometimes the core back became the new debitage surface (Figure 7.9: 4.).

## Accidents during bladelet debitage

A total of 49.6% of the bladelets are broken. Distal fragments make up 54.3%, mesials 25.3%, and proximals 20.4%. All breaks are "clear", thus it is impossible to distinguish between knapping and post-knapping breaks. Hinges make up 6.1% and plunging items only 1.9% of the bladelets.

## Bladelet core maintenance

During bladelet production, the cores' striking platforms were rejuvenated by rejuvenating flake removals (n=3) (Figure 7.9: 21, 22.).

The debitage surface convexity maintaining remains are 14 neo-crest bladelets (Figure 7.9: 17-19.).

Sometimes, plunging blades were removed from the direction of the distal end, probably in order renew the entire debitage surface (Figure 7.9: 15, 20.).

Hinge accidents were rarely remedied by virtue of a single core bearing signs of hinge reparation endeavor. This core after the hinge accident received strikes at distal end in order to remove the entire debitage surface.

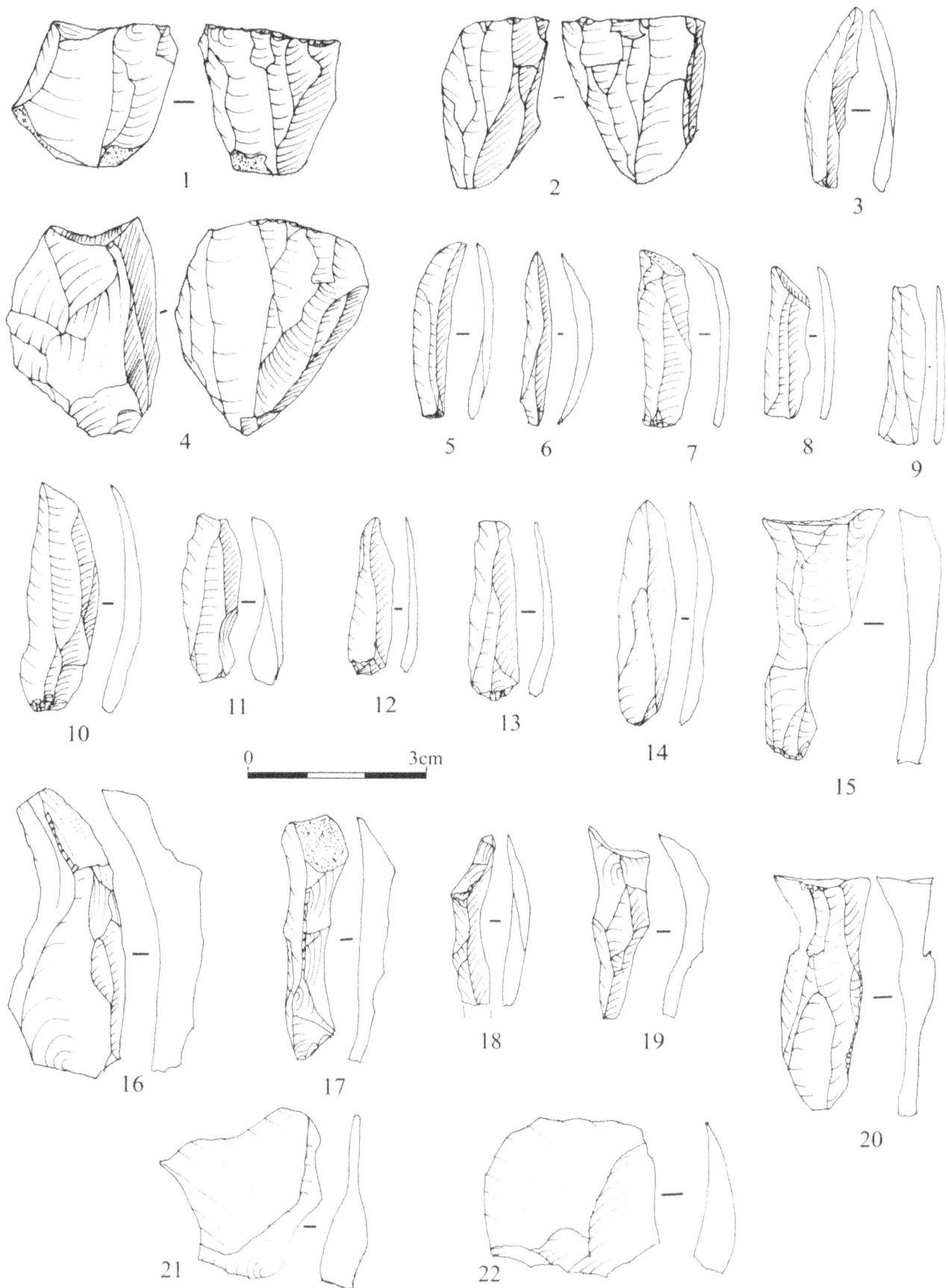

**Figure 7.9.** *Bladelet core (1, 2, 4); bladelet (3, 5-14); core debitage surface rejuvenating removal (15, 20); core tablet (16); core striking platform rejuvenating flake (21, 22); neo-crest bladelet (17-19).*

## Bladelet core discard

Fifty percent of the core assemblage are smaller than 28.6 mm. The front of the cores is usually semi-circular and the lateral sides of the debitage surface are converging (Table 7.7.). Of the 21 bladelet cores 13 items are cortical.

The cores were discarded in different stages of debitage. The striking platforms were rarely rejuvenated after hinge accidents (n=1). Another core, which is devoid of accidents, had been neo-crested before abandoned. The remaining cores were discarded immediately after hinge removals (n=5) and after ordinary removals (n=13).

Most bladelet cores represent the very end of the debitage. The smallest cores (17.2 to 24.3 mm) typically are devoid of accidents, while all hinge bearer cores are greater than 24.3 mm.

*Table 7.7. Crosstabulation of front shape and sides of bladelet cores.*

| Front | Sides | | | Total |
|---|---|---|---|---|
| | converging | parallel | No data | |
| narrow | 2 | | 1 | *3* |
| semi-circular | 7 | 4 | 1 | *12* |
| wide | 2 | 4 | | *6* |
| *Total* | *11* | *8* | *2* | *21* |

## Flake production

Flakes are present from every raw material (Table 7.2.). They are abundant among RM1, RM5, and RM14. The number of flakes is extremely high in comparison to that of the flake cores.

Two cores of RM14 show scars of flake debitage. The RM1, RM5, and the RM13 cores originally belonged to blade production and only a few flakes were removed from them by debitage. The flake cores have single striking platforms and the orientation of their debitage is unidirectional.

Flakes derive straight from laminar cores' debitage surfaces, as is evidenced by the presence of unidirectional scar bearer flakes with parallel ridges (2.86% of the flakes).

Abraded overhangs characterize 23.2% of the flakes. The flake butts are dominantly, 65.1%, thicker than 2 mm. The impact point is visible on 52.2% of the flakes. In 24.7% of these cases the impact point is large. A total of 18% of the flakes have no bulb. The bulb appears as diffused on 41.3% of the flakes. The rest of the flakes, 40.7%, have convex bulbs. Lipping is characteristic to 25.5% of the flakes. These evidence the use of both soft and hard hammer technique. The butt of the flakes is predominantly plain.

A total of 7.4% of the flakes are broken. Distal fragments make up 59.2%, mesials 4.1%, and proximals 63.3%. Hinge flakes (9.8%), and plungings (1.7%) are present, too.

## Tool blank selection and tools

### Blade tool blanks

A total of 19.9% of the blades are tools. Most blade tool blanks are of RM1, RM14 and RM5 (Table 7.8.). A total of 25.5% of the blade tool blanks are cortical. In profile the blades are curved or straight with parallel and expanding edges likewise the unretouched blanks. Included among tool blanks is one neo-crest blade.

### Blade tools

Blades make up 25.3% of the tool kit. Most blade tool blanks are retouched items, end-scrapers, burins and backed items. The retouched blades habitually have partial retouch with scaled and marginal removals. Rarely both edges of the blades are retouched. Blade endscrapers are simple with converging and semi-converging retouch in most cases, rarely they have scaled retouched lateral edge (Figure 7.10: 38, 39.). The backed blades are arched and curved in most cases (Figure 7.10: 42.). The backing is dominantly unipolar, only one arch-backed blade has bipolar retouch. Burins on blades are on break and rarely on truncation. Blades also appear as blanks of geometric microliths, such as trapeze-rectangle and straight backed-straight and oblique truncated items (Figure 7.10: 9, 10.). There is one blade that was truncated on both ends obliquely. It resembles to a geometric trapeze.

### Bladelet tool blanks

A total of 22.8% of the bladelets are tools. Bladelet tool blanks are mostly of RM5 and RM1 (Table 7.8.). It is of interest that from OII flint only bladelets were selected for making tools. Bladelet tool blanks are devoid of cortex except a single specimen. Most bladelet tool blanks are straight in profile (edges shape are not taken into account on the reason of high percentage of blunting retouch), which is in striking contrast with the high presence of curved bladelets among unretouched blanks.

*Table 7.8. Tool blanks by raw material.*

| Raw material | | Tool blank | | | |
|---|---|---|---|---|---|
| source | type | flake | blade | bladelet | *Total* |
| RAM | RM1 | 14 | 12 | 21 | *47* |
| | RM2 | | 1 | | *1* |
| | RM4 | | 1 | 2 | *3* |
| DH | RM5 | 2 | 8 | 39 | *49* |
| | RM6 | 1 | 2 | 1 | *4* |
| | RM7 | | | 6 | *6* |
| | RM8 | 1 | 3 | | *4* |
| DC | RM11 | 2 | 4 | 8 | *14* |
| | RM12 | 2 | 2 | 2 | *6* |
| | RM13 | 1 | 1 | 2 | *4* |
| NM | RM14 | 9 | 11 | 9 | *29* |
| SH | RM15 | | 3 | 3 | *6* |
| OII | RM16 | | | 3 | *3* |
| unknown | RM17 | 3 | 1 | 14 | *18* |
| | RM18 | 1 | | 1 | *2* |
| | RM19 | | 2 | 3 | *5* |
| | burnt | 4 | 4 | 8 | *16* |
| | *Total* | *40* | *55* | *122* | *217* |

## Bladelet tools

Most tools were made of bladelets, making up 56.2% of tool kit. Bladelets are usual tool blanks of geometric microliths (Table 7.9.). For shaping geometrics direct retouching was primarily applied. Bipolar backing is rare (4 specimens) and was made consistently discontinuously on the edge (Figure 7.10: 1, 7, 13, 15.). The backing retouch largely modified the width of the blanks, extending up to the thickest part. Most geometrics are the so called "proto-trapezes", which have straight back and oblique truncation (Figure 7.10: 12, 13, 15-17, 22-25.). Usually, their distal end is truncated and the proximal is snapped off. The next most abundant type of geometrics is the straight backed and straight truncated tool (Figure 7.10: 14, 18, 20, 21.). These were made similarly to the "proto-trapezes". Among the fully retouched geometric forms, trapeze-rectangles are the preponderant (Figure 7.10: 1-11.). These are the longest and narrowest items among geometrics. Trapeze, rectangles and triangles occur in smaller number (Figure 7.10: 26-31.). Four proximal microburins may indicate that fully retouched geometrics forms were obtained by that technique, since typical microburin scars are not found on "proto-trapezes". There are 4 blunt-backed lunates in the assemblage, which are most probably intrusive from Natufian levels, as they always occur in Geometric Kebaran assemblages at sites occupied by Natufian as well (e.g. Hayonim terrace; Valla 1989). However, they also are found in clear Geometric Kebaran context (L. Maher personal communication 2004).

The backed bladelets have straight backs, shaped by direct retouch (Figure 7.10: 32, 33.). Only two specimens have bipolar backing. Three backed bladelets were broken during retouching the back, exhibiting typical fracture of Krukowski microburin (Figure 7.10: 17.).

The edge retouch on bladelets is partial for the most part. Fine alternate retouch prevalently appear on bladelets, forming Dufour bladelets (Figure 9.23: 11.).

Truncations also are characteristic to the bladelet tools. These are oblique and straight.

Points, such as microgravettes, solely were made of bladelets (Figure 7.10: 34, 35.). Their retouch was delicately made direct and abrupt.

Notches are most frequent among bladelet tools. These are habitually single. The only borer was also made of bladelet (Figure 7.10: 36.).

## Flake tool blanks

A total of 6% of the flakes are tools. They are of RM1 and RM14 (Table 7.8.). Flakes, contrary to the laminar tool blanks, are more often cortical (25% of them).

## Flake tools

Flakes make up 18.5%, the smallest percentage of the tool kit. Flakes are primary blanks of retouched items. Retouched flakes have mostly partial marginal retouch. Among burins, they are mostly on break and transversal. Three types of side scrapers, straight, convex and *déjeté* were made of flakes. As endscrapers, mainly simple was made of them with converging front retouch for most part. Flakes are also characteristic blanks of the denticulates (Figure 7.10: 43.).

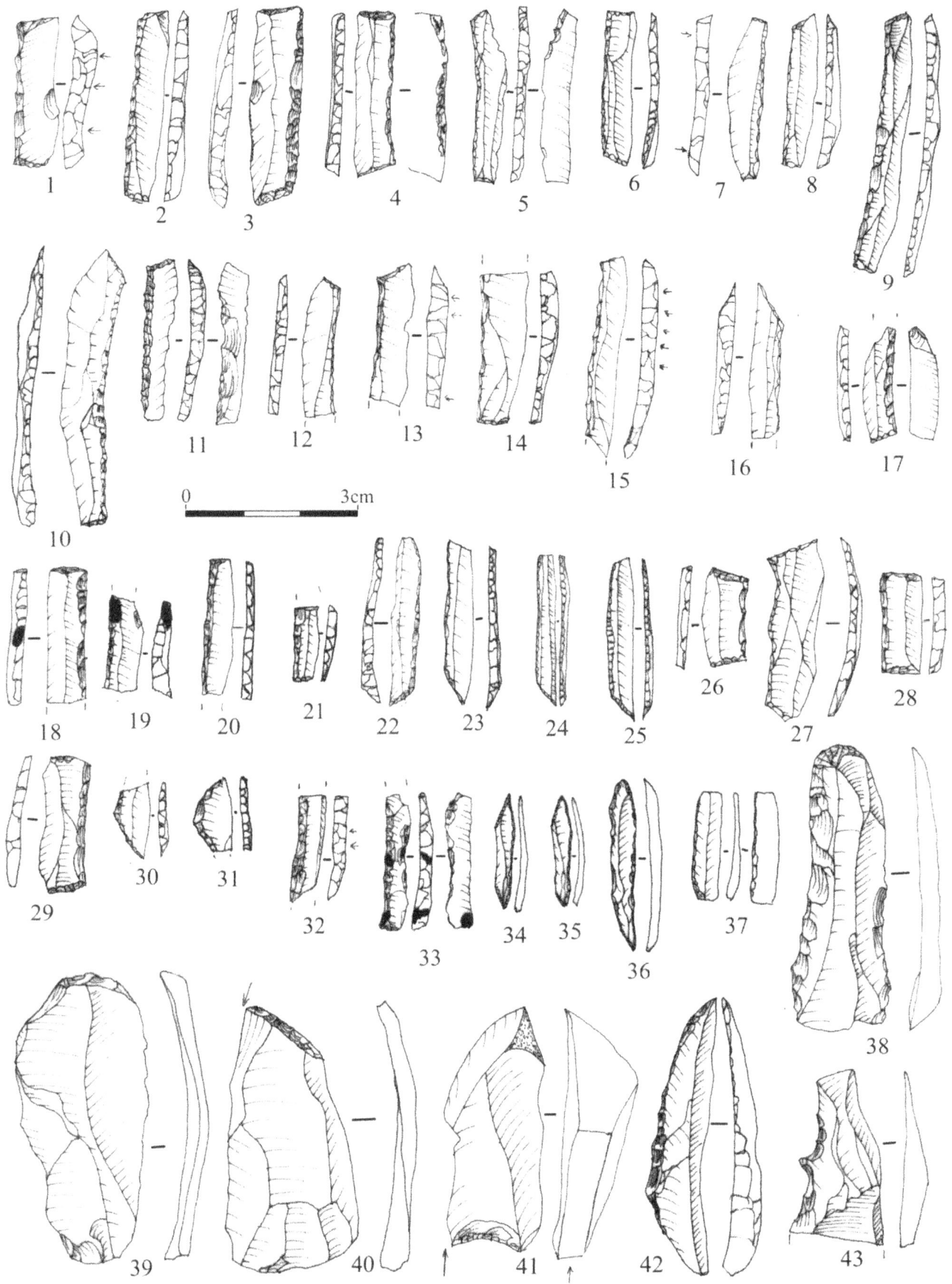

*Figure 7.10.* Trapeze-rectangle (1-11); backed, obliquely truncated bladelet (12, 13, 15-17, 22-25); backed truncated bladelet (14, 18, 20, 21); trapeze (26, 27); rectangle (28, 29); triangle (30, 31); backed bladelet (32, 33); microgravette (34, 35); borer (36); dufour bladelet (37); endscraper (38, 39); burin on truncation (40, 41); curve backed blade (42); denticulate (43).

*Table 7.9. Tool type list of the Geometric Kebaran assemblage.*

| Tool types | | Blank | | | Total | |
|---|---|---|---|---|---|---|
| | | flake | blade | bladelet | # | % |
| Endscrapers | simple | 3 | 5 | | 8 | 3,7 |
| | on retouched blank | 1 | 2 | | 3 | 1,4 |
| | ogival | 1 | | | 1 | 0,5 |
| | double | 1 | | | 1 | 0,5 |
| | atypical | | 1 | | 1 | 0,5 |
| | *Sub-total* | *6* | *8* | | *14* | *6,5* |
| Burins | carinated | 1 | | | 1 | 0,5 |
| | dihedral | 1 | | | 1 | 0,5 |
| | angled dihedral | 1 | | | 1 | 0,5 |
| | on break | 5 | 4 | 1 | 10 | 4,6 |
| | on oblique truncation | | 2 | | 2 | 0,9 |
| | on concave truncation | | 1 | | 1 | 0,5 |
| | transversal | 3 | | | 3 | 1,4 |
| | *Sub-total* | *11* | *7* | *1* | *19* | *8,8* |
| Retouched items | continuous scaled | 2 | | 1 | 3 | 1,4 |
| | discontinuous scaled | 1 | | | 1 | 0,5 |
| | discontinuous marginal | | 2 | 1 | 3 | 1,4 |
| | partially scaled | 3 | 8 | 2 | 13 | 6,0 |
| | partially marginal | 7 | 8 | 5 | 20 | 9,2 |
| | discontinuously alternating scaled | | 1 | | 1 | 0,5 |
| | both edges continuous scaled | | 1 | | 1 | 0,5 |
| | both edges continuous marginal | | 1 | | 1 | 0,5 |
| | alternate | | 1 | 3 | 4 | 1,8 |
| | *Sub-total* | *13* | *22* | *12* | *47* | *21,7* |
| Backed items | straight | | 1 | 29 | 30 | 13,8 |
| | straight partially | | 1 | 2 | 3 | 1,4 |
| | curved | | 2 | 3 | 5 | 2,3 |
| | curved partially | | | 3 | 3 | 1,4 |
| | arch | | 3 | 3 | 6 | 2,8 |
| | *Sub-total* | | *7* | *40* | *47* | *21,7* |
| Truncations | double | | 1 | | 1 | 0,5 |
| | straight | | 2 | 2 | 4 | 1,8 |
| | oblique | | | 3 | 3 | 1,4 |
| | concave | | 1 | 1 | 2 | 0,9 |
| | *Sub-total* | | *4* | *6* | *10* | *4,6* |
| Points | microgravette | | | 3 | 3 | 1,4 |
| | *Sub-total* | | | *3* | *3* | *1,4* |
| Geometrics | straight backed – straight truncated | | 1 | 15 | 16 | 7,4 |
| | straight backed – obliquely truncated | | 1 | 20 | 21 | 9,7 |
| | rectangle | | | 3 | 3 | 1,4 |
| | trapeze – rectangle | | 2 | 7 | 9 | 4,1 |
| | symmetrical trapeze | | | 1 | 1 | 0,5 |
| | triangle | | | 3 | 3 | 1,4 |
| | lunate | | | 4 | 4 | 1,8 |
| | *Sub-total* | | *3* | *54* | *57* | *26,3* |
| Borers | | | | 1 | 1 | 0,5 |
| | *Sub-total* | | | *1* | *1* | *0,5* |
| Notches | single | 1 | 1 | 4 | 6 | 2,8 |
| | two or more | | | 1 | 1 | 0,5 |
| | *Sub-total* | *1* | *1* | *5* | *7* | *3,2* |
| Denticulates | | 5 | 3 | | 8 | 3,7 |
| | *Sub-total* | *5* | *3* | | *8* | *3,7* |
| Side scrapers | straight | 1 | | | 1 | 0,5 |
| | convex | 1 | | | 1 | 0,5 |
| | dejete | 1 | | | 1 | 0,5 |
| | *Sub-total* | *3* | | | *3* | *1,4* |
| Divers | splintered tool | 1 | | | 1 | 0,5 |
| | *Sub-total* | *1* | | | *1* | *0,5* |
| *Total* | | *40* | *55* | *122* | *217* | *100* |

# THE LATE NATUFIAN ASSEMBLAGE
# LAYER V, AREA G-H/12-13

## Raw material

The raw materials of the assemblage derive from five flint sources (Table 8.1). Deir Hannah formation (DH) yielded the majority of the raw materials, among which the good quality RM5 is dominant. This raw material is the most abundant in the whole assemblage.

Nahal Mearot good quality flints (NM) make up the second largest group of raw material.

Ramat Menashe (RAM) flints, the closest source to Raqefet, make up the third largest group of raw material. Among them the mediocre quality RM1 is dominant. RM1 constitutes the second most abundant raw material type in the assemblage.

Shamir formation good quality raw materials (SH) derived from the farthest part of the Carmel to Raqefet. They constitute a small portion of the assemblage, as well as Daliyat ha Carmel low quality raw materials (DC).

Good quality raw materials of unknown origin make up a quite large portion of the assemblage, larger than that of SH raw materials.

Based on the presence of first flakes in the assemblage, RM5, RM7, RM8, and RM15 were brought to the site as fully cortical nodules. The remaining raw materials were roughed-out with various extents off-site. RM9 and RM18 are present only with the bladelets themselves, therefore they were brought in ready-made.

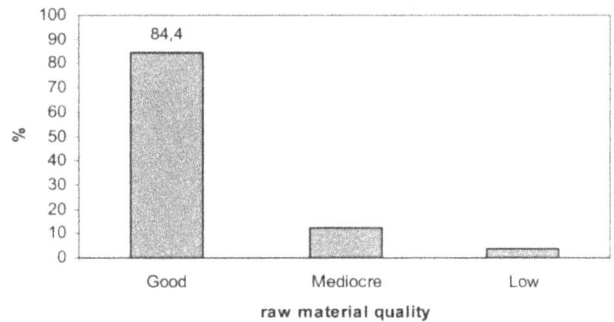

*Figure 8.1. Frequency of raw materials by quality.*

In sum, the raw material acquisition focused on good quality raw materials, while mediocre and especially low quality flints make up the smallest part of the assemblage (Figure 8.1).

*Table 8.1. Frequency of raw material types by sources.*

| Raw material | | Raw material source | | | | | | | | Total |
|---|---|---|---|---|---|---|---|---|---|---|
| quality | type | RAM | DH | DC | NM | SH | unknown | | | |
| Mediocre | RM1 | 118 86,1% | | | | | | | | 118 11,5% |
| Low | RM 2 | 6 4,4% | | | | | | | | 6 0,6% |
| Low | RM 3 | 3 2,2% | | | | | | | | 3 0,3% |
| Low | RM 4 | 10 7,3% | | | | | | | | 10 1% |
| Good | RM 5 | | 436 72,3% | | | | | | | 436 42,4% |
| Low | RM 6 | | 2 0,3% | | | | | | | 2 0,2% |
| Good | RM 7 | | 82 13,6% | | | | | | | 82 8% |
| Good | RM 8 | | 76 12,6% | | | | | | | 76 7,4% |
| Mediocre | RM 9 | | 1 0,2% | | | | | | | 1 0,1% |
| Mediocre | RM 11 | | 6 1% | | | | | | | 6 0,6% |
| Low | RM 12 | | | 7 46,7% | | | | | | 7 0,7% |
| Low | RM 13 | | | 8 53,3% | | | | | | 8 0,8% |
| Good | RM 14 | | | | 196 100% | | | | | 196 19% |
| Good | RM 15 | | | | | 33 100% | | | | 33 3,2% |
| Good | RM 17 | | | | | | | 22 100% | | 22 2,1% |
| Good | RM 18 | | | | | | | | 5 100% | 5 0,5% |
| Good | RM 19 | | | | | 18 100% | | | | 18 1,7% |
| Total | | 137 13,3% | 603 58,6% | 15 1,5% | 196 19% | 33 3,2% | 18 1,7% | 22 2,1% | 5 0,5% | 1029 100% |

**Table 8.2.** *Frequency of lithic products by raw material.*

| Raw material | | Lithic product | | | | | | Core | | | Total |
|---|---|---|---|---|---|---|---|---|---|---|---|
| Source | Type | blade | bladelet | flake | waste | CTE | tool | Flake | blade | bladelet | |
| RAM | RM1 | 16<br>13,6% | 16<br>13,6% | 33<br>28% | 25<br>21,2% | 6<br>5,1% | 9<br>7,6% | 2<br>1,7% | 2<br>1,7% | 9<br>7,6% | 118<br>100% |
| | RM2 | | 1<br>16,7% | 1<br>16,7% | 4<br>66,7% | | | | | | 6<br>100% |
| | RM3 | | 2<br>66,7% | 1<br>33,3% | | | | | | | 3<br>100% |
| | RM 4 | | | 5<br>50% | 4<br>40% | | 1<br>10% | | | | 10<br>100% |
| DH | RM 5 | 14<br>3,2% | 27<br>6,2% | 64<br>14,7% | 294<br>67,4% | 8<br>1,8% | 13<br>3% | 3<br>,7% | 2<br>,5% | 11<br>2,5% | 436<br>100% |
| | RM 6 | | | 1<br>50% | | | 1<br>50% | | | | 2<br>100% |
| | RM 7 | 4<br>4,9% | 20<br>24,4% | 26<br>31,7% | 16<br>19,5% | 4<br>4,9% | 6<br>7,3% | | | 6<br>7,3% | 82<br>100% |
| | RM 8 | 4<br>5,3% | 19<br>25% | 23<br>30,3% | 9<br>11,8% | 4<br>5,3% | 4<br>5,3% | 3<br>3,9% | | 10<br>13,2% | 76<br>100% |
| | RM 9 | | 1<br>100% | | | | | | | | 1<br>100% |
| | RM 11 | 2<br>33,3% | | 3<br>50% | 1<br>16,7% | | | | | | 6<br>100% |
| DC | RM 12 | | 1<br>14,3% | 4<br>57,1% | | 2<br>28,6% | | | | | 7<br>100% |
| | RM 13 | 1<br>12,5% | 1<br>12,5% | 3<br>37,5% | | | 3<br>37,5% | | | | 8<br>100% |
| NM | RM 14 | 4<br>2% | 26<br>13,3% | 35<br>17,9% | 97<br>49,5% | 3<br>1,5% | 14<br>7,1% | 3<br>1,5% | 1<br>,5% | 13<br>6,6% | 196<br>100% |
| SH | RM 15 | | 12<br>36,4% | 7<br>21,2% | 9<br>27,3% | 4<br>12,1% | | | | 1<br>3% | 33<br>100% |
| unknown | RM 17 | 3<br>13,6% | 6<br>27,3% | 6<br>27,3% | 4<br>18,2% | 1<br>4,5% | | | | 2<br>9,1% | 22<br>100% |
| | RM 18 | | 4<br>80% | | 1<br>20% | | | | | | 5<br>100% |
| | RM 19 | 1<br>5,6% | 3<br>16,7% | 6<br>33,3% | 8<br>44,4% | | | | | | 18<br>100% |
| Total | | 49<br>4,8% | 139<br>13,5% | 218<br>21,2% | 472<br>45,9% | 33<br>3,2% | 50<br>4,9% | 11<br>1,1% | 5<br>,5% | 52<br>5,1% | 1029<br>100% |

## Blade production

### *Blade core configuration*

The blade production is connected to good quality flints. Within good quality flint group RM5 is dominant (Table 8.2.). RM2, RM3, RM4, RM6, and RM12 of low quality, RM9 of mediocre quality, RM15 and RM18 of good quality are not present in blade production.

No blade cores preserved the original shape of the raw material nodule and sets of configuration, as well. The majority of the cortex is found on flakes from the flint nodule (70% of the cortical items are flakes and only 22.8% of the blades are cortical).

There are no crest blades in the assemblage. The debitage surface was created in most of the cases by flake removals, and the longitudinal ridges created by flake scars guided the first blade removals. The striking platforms of the cores were prepared by the removal of a single flake. It was rarely cortical, as indicated by the plain blade butts (Figure 8.2.).

### *Blade debitage*

The striking platform of the blade cores remained plain during the debitage as indicated by the high frequency of plain butts.

Abraded overhangs characterize 64.8% of the blades. The butts are dominantly, 73.5% of the blades, are thinner than 2 mm. The impact point is visible on 19.6% of the blades. In a total of 85% of these cases the impact point is minor. A total of 27.5% of the blades have no bulb. The bulb appears as diffused on 50% of the blades. The rest of the blades, 22.5%, have convex bulbs. Lipping is characteristic to 13.7% of the blades. These vestiges evidence the use of soft hammer technique.

**Table 8.3.** *Blade edges-profile crosstabulation.*

| Profile | Edges | | | | Total |
|---|---|---|---|---|---|
| | parallel | converging | expanding | irregular | |
| straight | 1 | 2 | | | 3 |
| curved | 4 | | 6 | 1 | 11 |
| twisted | 1 | | 1 | | 2 |
| Total | 6 | 2 | 7 | 1 | 16 |

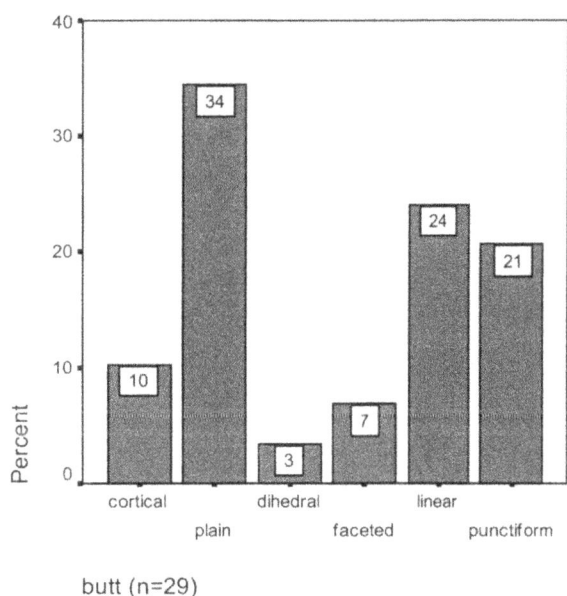

butt (n=29)

**Figure 8.2.** *Butt types of blades.*

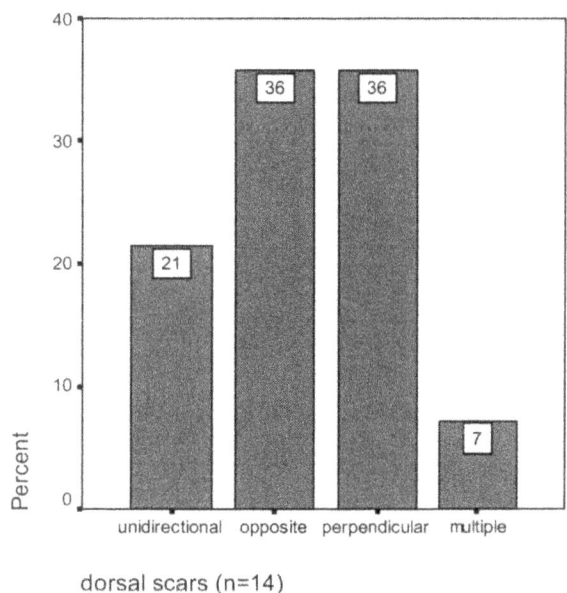

dorsal scars (n=14)

**Figure 8.3.** *Direction of dorsal scars on blades.*

The core front, according to the shape of the core tablets, was mostly semi-circular in the debitage (Figure 8.4: 11.).

The preponderance of blades with parallel and expanding edges indicates that the cores had debitage surfaces with parallel sides during most part of the blade debitage. In profile, the blades are dominantly curved. (Table 8.3.).

All cores have a single striking platform, but 21% of the blades bear unidirectional dorsal scars and 36% opposite (Figure 8.3.). These vestiges would indicate that the orientation of the blade debitage frequently

changed, but in the light of the dominancy of blade cores with single striking platforms this conclusion is ambiguous. The presence of non-unidirectional scars on blades is also remnants of cores' side and debitage surface shaping.

## Accidents during blade debitage

The breakage rate is very high among blades (73.3% of the items are broken). Distal fragments make up 59%, mesials 11.4% and proximals 29.6% of the broken blades. All breaks are "clear", thus it is impossible to distinguish between knapping and post-knapping breaks.

Other accidents are very rare. There is a single proximal fragment of plunging blade, while hinged blades are missing. However, hinge accident occurred in the debitage, evidenced by six flakes bearing hinged blade scars.

## Blade core maintenance

During blade production, the cores' striking platforms were rejuvenated by rejuvenating flake removals (n=1) and core tablet removals (n=6) (Figure 8.4: 11.).

The debitage surface convexity was maintained by neo-cresting (2 neo-crest blades) (Figure 8.4: 7.). The neo-cresting was habitually made at the distal part of the cores.

Hinge scars were remedied by flake removals detached from the direction of the striking platform and the distal end of the cores.

## Blade core discard

Four of the discarded blade cores have semi-circular and one has a wide front. Among the semi-circular fronted cores 3 have parallel sides and one has converging (Table 8.4.). The wide debitage surface core also has parallel sides. Of the 5 blade cores 4 items are cortical.

**Table 8.4.** *Crosstabulation of front shape and the sides of the blade cores.*

| Sides | Front | | Total |
|---|---|---|---|
| | semi-circular | wide | |
| converging | 1 | | *1* |
| parallel | 3 | 1 | *4* |
| *Total* | *4* | *1* | *5* |

The blade cores were discarded in different stages of debitage. There is a core with hinge scar on the debitage surface. This was prepared for knapping by overhang removal and striking platform rejuvenation. The intended removal was not performed; the core was discarded probably on the reason of the hinge scar. Other cores also bear hinge accidents, although their hinges are not last removals, except two items. The majority of the abandoned cores do not bear crucial accidents.

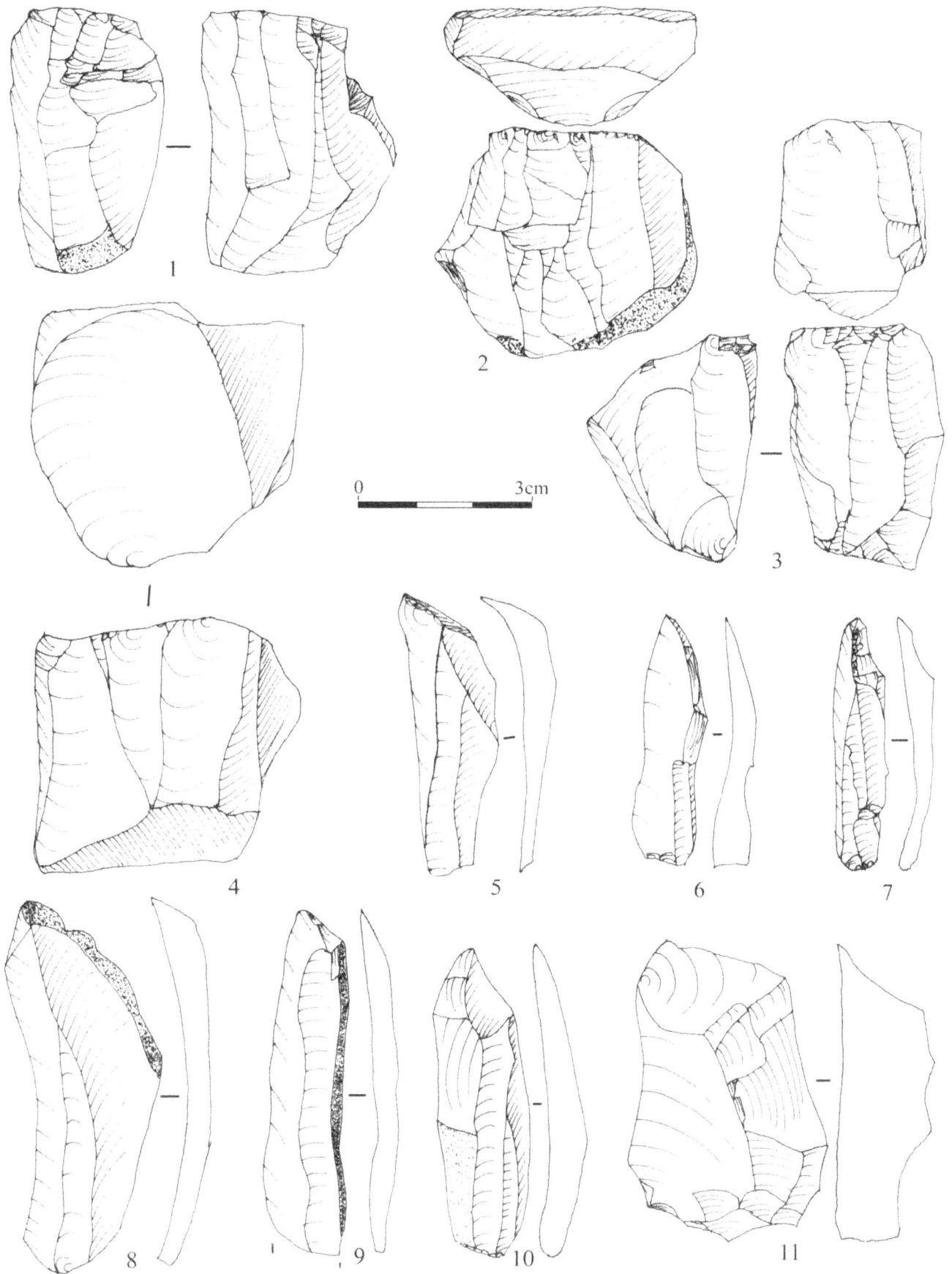

**Figure 8.4.** *Blade core (1-4); blade (5, 8, 9); subcrest blade (6, 10); neo-crest blade (7); core tablet (11).*

## Bladelet production

### Bladelet core configuration

The bladelet production is based on good quality flints. Within good quality flint group RM5 and RM14 are dominant (Table 8.2.). Several raw materials, RM2, RM3, RM9, RM12, and RM18, were used solely for the bladelet production. Three flint types, RM4 and RM6 of low quality and RM11 of mediocre quality were not used in bladelet production.

The bladelet debitage took place in a joint sequence with the blade debitage in the cases of the exploitation of RM5, RM7, RM8, RM14, RM17, and RM19. From RM7, RM8, RM17, and RM19 no blade cores are left behind, while blades are present (Table 8.2.). The other two raw materials yielded blades and a number of bladelets but the presence of blade cores is scarce.

According to the preserved original surfaces of the flint nodules, also there was a tendency to collect small nodules for making cores to the bladelet production. In four cases thick flakes are the core blanks.

Vestiges of bladelet core configuration methods are scarce. A few cores show that their lateral sides were shaped from the back and the proximal core part. The configuration removals were restricted to clean the core front and its environment, thus the cortex was not entirely removed from the bladelet cores. A total of 14.9% of the entire bladelet assemblage are cortical. The cortex on the bladelets usually appears at the distal part and on one of the dorsal halves along the total length.

The striking platforms were created by the removal of a single flake. In a few instances the debitage surfaces were created by cresting, since only a single sub-crest bladelet can be found in the assemblage, which is an indirect evidence of this modality. Contrary, the majority of the debitage surfaces of the cores were created by simple flake removals from the striking platform.

Six bladelet cores show indicative signs of heat treatment (Inizan *et al* 1976; Inizan *et al* 1995). These are most recognized from RM5, since the color of the raw material is changed from yellowish-brow/brown to red. Some of these cores are totally shiny, others have matt surfaces cut by shiny negative scars. In addition to the cores, products also bear these signs. Experiments must verify this observation, yet.

### Bladelet debitage

Most bladelets have punctiform butts (Figure 8.5.). The butt thickness is less than 1 mm in 60.8% of the cases. The overhangs were abraded on 64.8% of the bladelet removals. Impact points are present on 19.6% of the bladelets. These indicate that soft hammer technique was used for the most part in the debitage. Bladelets of RM17 were removed solely by hard stone hammer technique.

The profile of the bladelets is dominantly straight, in lesser cases curved (Table 8.5.). Items with twisted profile account for almost the one-third part of the bladelets. The straight bladelets have mostly parallel edges and the curved bladelets have dominantly expanding edges. The preponderance of bladelets with parallel and expanding edges indicates that the cores had debitage surfaces with parallel sides during most part of the debitage.

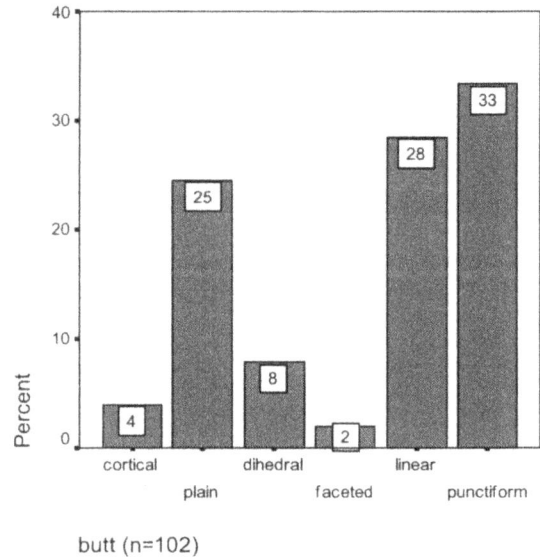

butt (n=102)

**Figure 8.5.** *Butt types of bladelets.*

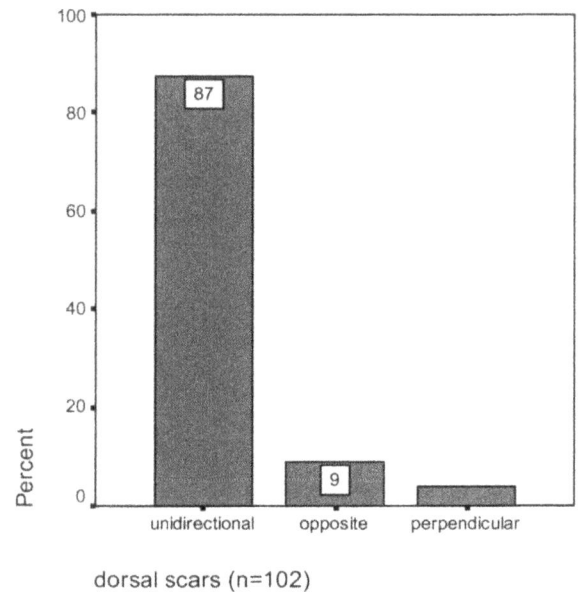

dorsal scars (n=102)

**Figure 8.6.** *Direction of dorsal scars on bladelets.*

**Table 8.5.** *Crosstabulation of bladelet profile and the shape of the edges.*

| Profile | Edges | | | | Total |
|---|---|---|---|---|---|
| | parallel | converging | expanding | irregular | |
| straight | 16 | 10 | 11 | 4 | *41* |
| curved | 12 | 7 | 16 | | *35* |
| twisted | 4 | 8 | 10 | 1 | *23* |
| *total* | *32* | *25* | *37* | *5* | *99* |

88

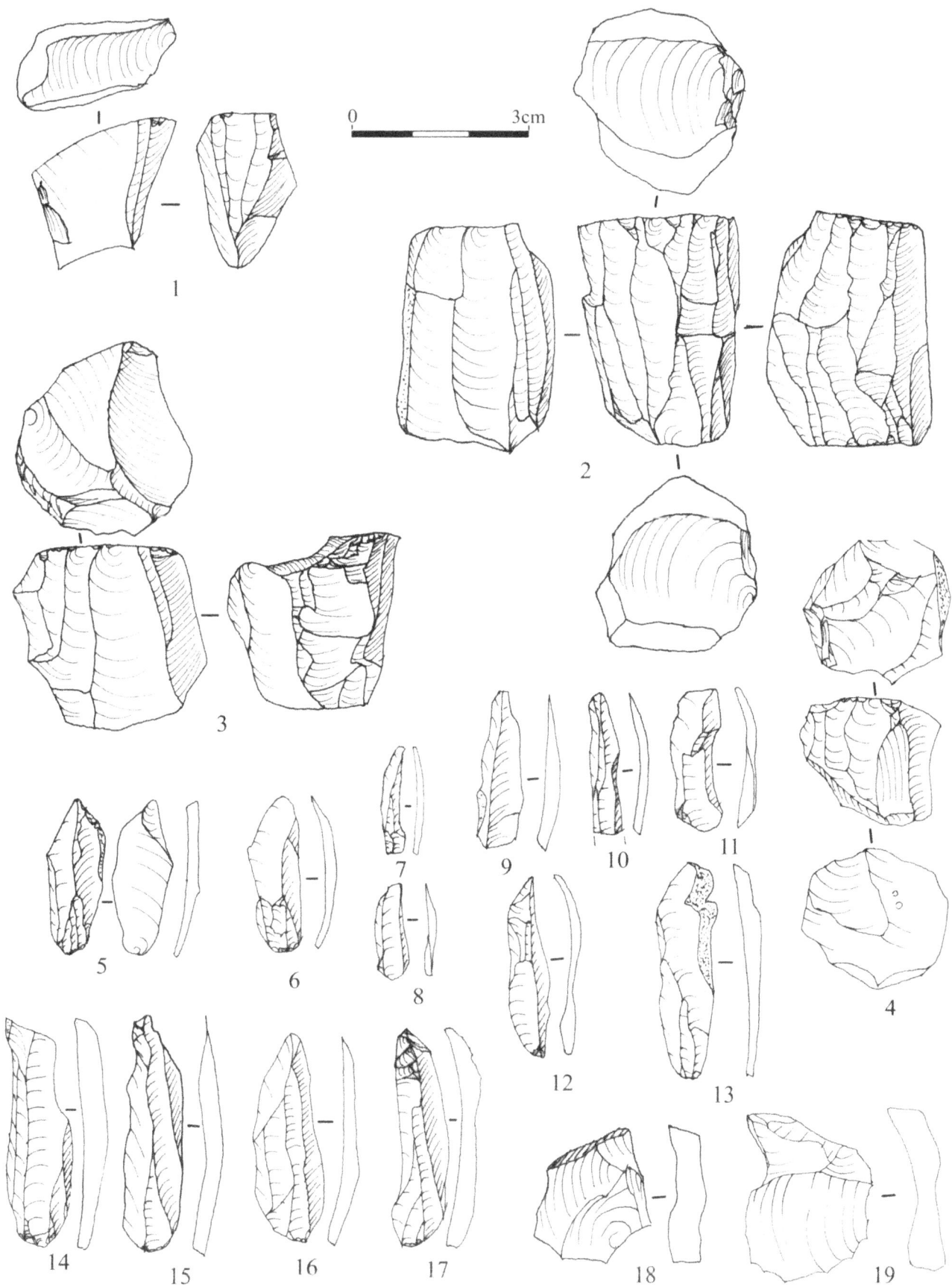

**Figure 8.7.** *bladelet core (1-4); bladelet (5-16); neo-crest bladelet (17); bladelet core tablet (18, 19).*

A total of 75.1% of the cores have a single striking platform and 87% of the bladelets bear unidirectional dorsal scars (Figure 8.6.). These vestiges indicate that the orientation of the bladelet debitage was primarily unidirectional. Some of the opposite removals are definitely in connection with opposite debitage (17.3% of cores). However, this core exploitation is uncommon. Other cores (3.8%) were turned by 90 degrees, in order to use the lateral side as a new debitage surface. The remaining cores (3.8%) show vestiges of exploitation from more than two directions.

### Accidents during bladelet debitage

A total of 42.5% of the bladelets are broken. Distal fragments make up 50.7%, mesials 21.9% and proximals 27.4%. All breaks are "clear", thus it is impossible to distinguish between knapping and post-knapping breaks. Hinge and plunging bladelets items are scarce and total 1.8% (n=3) and 1.2% (n=2) of the unbroken bladelets.

### Bladelet core maintenance

During bladelet production, the cores' striking platforms were rejuvenated by rejuvenating flake removals (n=11), and core tablet removals (n=14) (Figure 8.7: 18, 19.). Ten core tablets and six rejuvenating flakes have been removed by hard stone hammer technique. The remaining pieces do not bear clear markers of their knapping technique.

There are six flakes with dorsal bladelet hinge scars. These were probably detached to repair hinge scar damage on bladelet core debitage surfaces. The debitage surface convexity was maintained by neo-cresting (3 neo-crest bladelets).

### Bladelet core discard

The fronts of the discarded bladelet cores is usually wide, in a fewer cases semi-circular and narrow (Table 8.6.). The sides of the semi circular-fronted cores are dominantly parallel while that of the narrow-fronted cores are converging. The wide-fronted cores have parallel or converging sides. Of the 52 bladelet cores 31 are cortical.

Five cores were rejuvenated by flake removals on their striking platforms prior to discard. Among these, in two cases, the rejuvenations were accomplished after hinge accidental removals on the debitage surfaces. Of the 52 cores, 16 specimens were used for obtaining flakes after the last bladelet removal. This flaking abolished most of the features of the bladelet cores. A total of 18 items were discarded after hinge accidents, 15 items after ordinary removals and 8 items after irregular removals.

**Table 8.6.** *Crosstabulation of front shape and sides shape of the bladelet cores.*

| Front | Sides | | Total |
|---|---|---|---|
| | converging | parallel | |
| narrow | 7 | 3 | 10 |
| semi-circular | 2 | 9 | 11 |
| wide | 8 | 7 | 15 |
| Total | 17 | 19 | 36 |

## Flake production

RM9 and RM18 are not present with flakes (Table 8.2.). Flakes are abundant among RM1, RM5, and RM14. The number of flakes is extremely high in comparison to that of the flake cores.

All cores, except one from RM5 that originally belonged to blade production and only a few flakes were removed by debitage, show scars of flake debitage (Figure 8.8.). In addition, 16 bladelet cores were used furthermore to remove minute sized flakes. (Taking into account these cores, the number of flake cores may be raised from 11 to 27.) Eight of the flake cores signify unidirectional, two opposite and one multiple orientation of debitage.

Flakes derive straight from laminar cores' debitage surfaces, as is evidenced by the presence of unidirectional scar bearer flakes with parallel ridges (16% of the flakes). Abraded overhangs characterize 22.3% of the flakes. The butts are dominantly thick (63.2% are thicker than 2 mm). The impact point is visible on 51.6% of the flakes. In 39.7% of these cases the impact point is large. A total of 24% of the flakes have no bulb. The bulb appears as diffused on 37.3% of the flakes. The rest of the flakes, 38.7%, have convex bulbs. Lipping is characteristic to 21.3% of the flakes. These evidence the use of both soft and hard hammer technique. The butt of the flakes is predominantly plain.

A total of 21.6% of the flakes are broken. Distal fragments make up 67.2%, mesials 8.6%, and proximals 24.2%. Hinge flakes (9.6%), and plungings (0.7%) are present, too.

## Tool blank selection and tools

### Blade tool blanks

A total of 15.9% of the blades are tools. Most of these are of RM14 (Table 8.7.). Blades of RM4 and RM13 were not used as tool blanks. A total of 20% of the blade tools are cortical. Their shape is variable.

### Blade tools

Blades make up only 2% of the tool kit. Most blade tools are retouched items (Table 8.8.). The retouch is typically scaled with various extents on the edge. Blades appear among burins, backed items, truncations, sickle blades and denticulates with a single specimen, respectively. The backed item bears sickle shine (Figure 8.8: 3.).

### Bladelet tool blanks

A total of 13.1% of the bladelets are tools. Bladelet tool blanks are of RM5 and RM14 good and high quality flints in most cases (Table 8.7.). RM4 and RM13 were not used for making bladelet tools. Of the 22 bladelet tools 20 specimens are devoid of cortex. Their edges are typically parallel or expanding with straight or curved profile likewise those of the unretouched blanks.

## Bladelet tools

Bladelets make up the majority of the tool kit (43.1%). Most bladelet tools are geometric microliths (Table 8.8.).

The overwhelming majority of the geometrics are blunt backed lunates (Figure 8.8: 9-16.). Two items bear signs of heat treatment. The backing of the lunates is direct on five items (Figure 8.8: 10, 11, 13-15.) and bipolar on three (Figure 8.8: 9, 12, 16.). Their size ranges between 12.3 and 18.2 mm.

Other geometrics were made in smaller number, and their retouch is consistently direct. A typical waste product of the geometric microlith production is the microburin. This is present only by a single item in the assemblage.

The remaining bladelet tool types are present in small number. Among them, truncations were typically made of bladelets on the distal end of the blank. A few backed items are also present (n=2). There are 3 wastes of backed bladelet or geometric microlith production (Figure 8.8: 4-6.). Their form resembles shouldered tools. One of their ends is broken. On the basis of these it can be concluded that the process of backed bladelet production started with a concave abrupt retouch on a blade or bladelet close to the distal or proximal end on one of the edges. The retouch as blunting was extended longitudinally along the edge and crosswise almost up to blank's thickest part. After backing, the blank intentionally was broken. This breakage surface does not resemble microburin. The method is similar to that of recovered from Negev Geometric Kebaran assemblages (Marder 2002).

## Flake tool blanks

A small portion, 7.1% of the flakes is tools. Flake tool blanks are mostly of RM1, RM5 and RM14 (Table 8.7.). The mediocre quality RM13 was solely used fro flake tool blanks. A total of 52.6% of the flake tools are cortical.

## Flake tools

Flakes make up 37.3% of the tool kit. Most flake tool blanks are denticulates and flakes are sole blanks of endscrapers. Denticulates are the thickest tools (Figure 8.8: 20.). One of the endscrapers, an ogival with scaled front retouch has retouch on its edges proximal part resembling a sort of hafting preparation (Figure 8.8: 18.). The carinated endscraper has large scaled and laminar removals on front (Figure 8.8: 19.). The truncation burins are cortical (Figure 8.8: 17.). A dihedral burin was made on a heat treatment signs bearer flake.

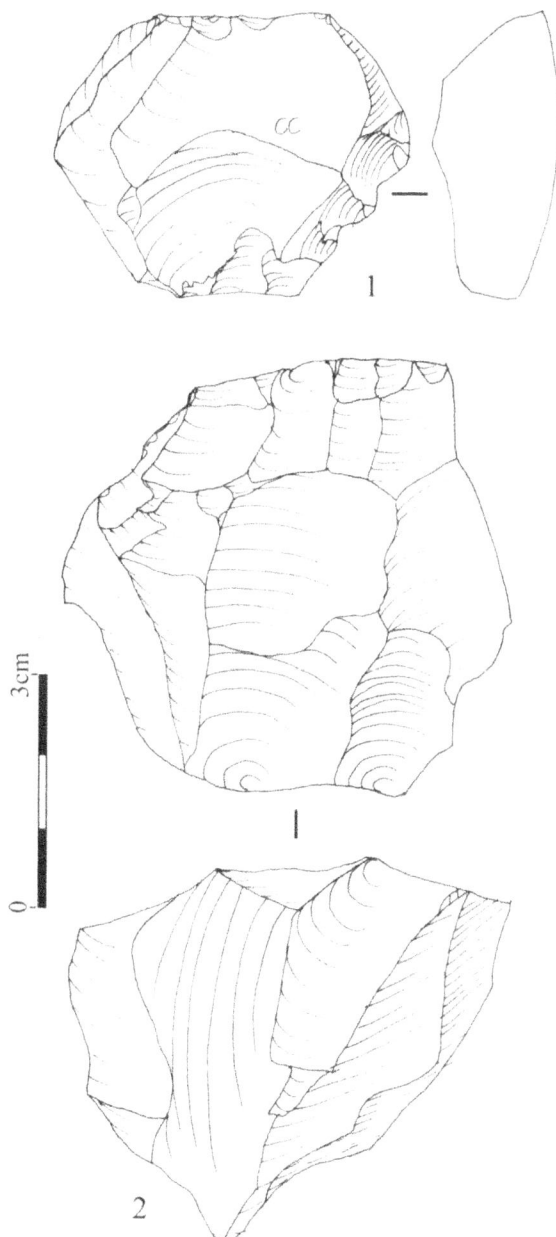

**Figure 8.8.** Flake cores.

**Table 8.7.** Distribution of blanks by raw material.

| Raw material | | Tool blank | | | Total |
|---|---|---|---|---|---|
| Source | Type | blade | bladelet | flake | |
| RAM | RM1 | 1 | 3 | 5 | 9 |
| | RM4 | | | 1 | 1 |
| DH | RM5 | 2 | 7 | 4 | 13 |
| | RM7 | 1 | 4 | 1 | 6 |
| | RM8 | 2 | 1 | 1 | 4 |
| DC | RM13 | | | 3 | 3 |
| NM | RM14 | 4 | 6 | 4 | 14 |
| | burnt | | 1 | | 1 |
| Total | | 10 | 22 | 19 | 51 |

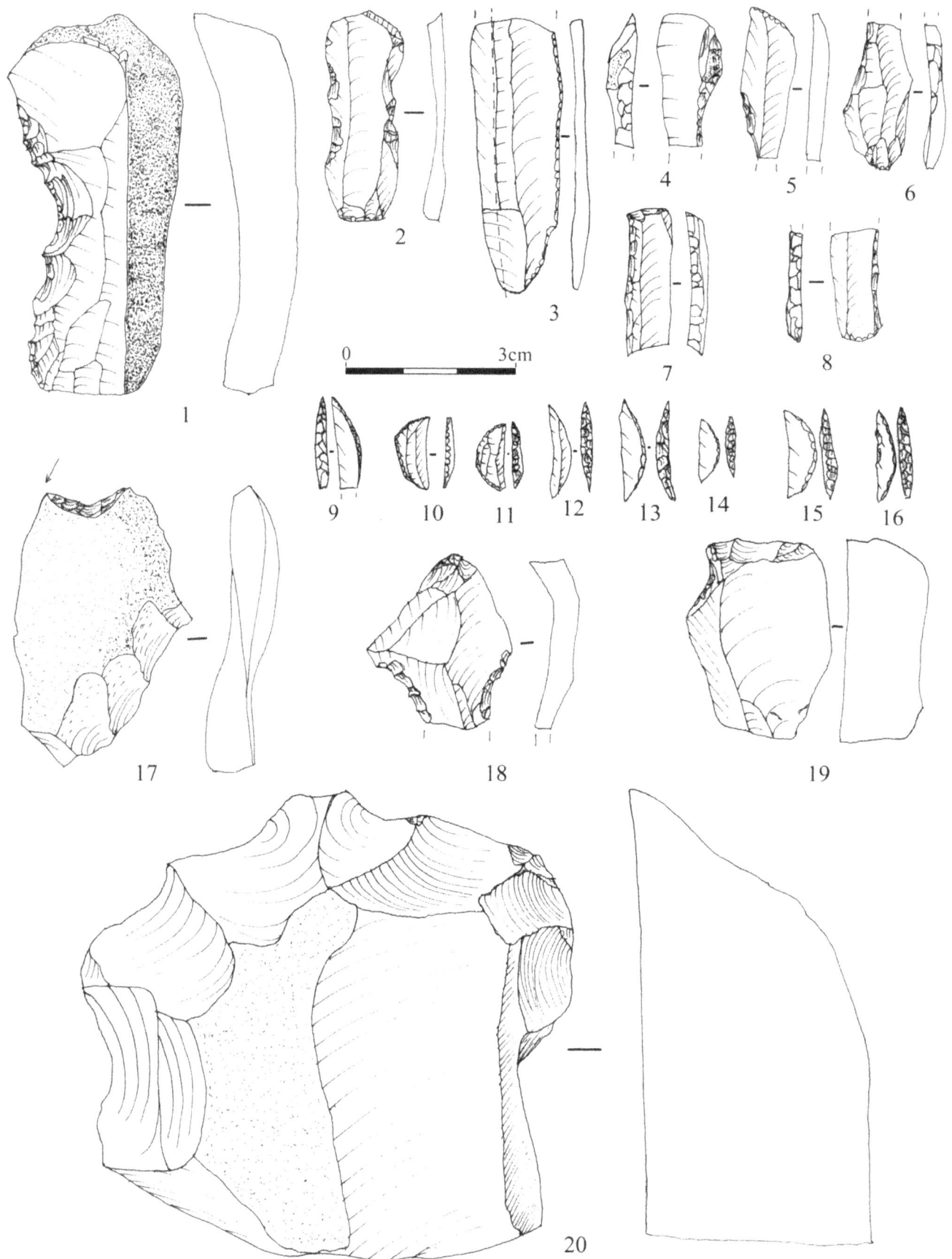

***Figure 8.9.*** *denticulate blade (1, 2); sickle blade (3); back bladelet production residue (4-6); backed-truncated bladelet (7); backed bladelet (8); blunt backed lunate (9-16); burin on concave truncation (17); endscraper (18, 19); denticulate flake (20).*

*Table 8.8.* Tool type list of the Late Natufian assemblage.

| Tool types | | Blank | | | Total | |
|---|---|---|---|---|---|---|
| | | blade | bladelet | flake | # | % |
| Endscrapers | simple | | | 1 | 1 | 2 |
| | ogival | | | 1 | 1 | 2 |
| | carinated | | | 1 | 1 | 2 |
| | *Sub-total* | | | *3* | *3* | *5,9* |
| Burins | on break | 1 | | | 1 | 2 |
| | on concave truncation | | | 2 | 2 | 3,9 |
| | transversal | | | 1 | 1 | 2 |
| | dihedral | | | 1 | 1 | 2 |
| | *Sub-total* | | | *4* | *5* | *9,8* |
| Retouched | continuous scaled | 1 | | | 1 | 2 |
| items | partial scaled | 2 | | 1 | 3 | 5,9 |
| | Alternating partial scaled | | | 1 | 1 | 2 |
| | continuous marginal | 1 | 1 | 1 | 3 | 5,9 |
| | partial marginal | | | 1 | 1 | 2 |
| | discontinuous scaled | 1 | | | 1 | 2 |
| | alternate | 1 | | | 1 | 2 |
| | *Sub-total* | *6* | *1* | *4* | *11* | *21,6* |
| Backed | straight | | 1 | | 1 | 2 |
| items | curved partial | | 1 | | 1 | 2 |
| | backed sickle blade | 1 | | | 1 | 2 |
| | *Sub-total* | *1* | *2* | | *3* | *5,9* |
| Truncations | straight | 1 | | | 1 | 2 |
| | oblique | | 2 | | 2 | 3,9 |
| | concave | | 1 | | 1 | 2 |
| | *Sub-total* | *1* | *3* | | *4* | *7,8* |
| Geometrics | straight backed and straight truncated | | 2 | | 2 | 3,9 |
| | symmetrical trapeze | | 1 | | 1 | 2 |
| | blunt backed lunate | | 8 | | 8 | 15,7 |
| | triangle | | 1 | | 1 | 2 |
| | *Sub-total* | | *12* | | *12* | *23,5* |
| Notches | double | | 1 | 1 | 2 | 3,9 |
| | multiple | | 1 | | 1 | 2 |
| | single | | 1 | 1 | 2 | 3,9 |
| | *Sub-total* | | *3* | *2* | *5* | *9,8* |
| Denticulates | | 1 | 1 | 5 | 7 | 13,7 |
| | *Sub-total* | *1* | *1* | *5* | *7* | *13,7* |
| Bec | | | | 1 | 1 | 2 |
| | *Sub-total* | | | *1* | *1* | *2* |
| *Total* | | *10* | *22* | *19* | *51* | *100* |

# CHAPTER 9: VARIABILITY IN LITHIC TECHNOLOGIES OF RAQEFET UPPER PALAEOLITHIC AND EPIPALAEOLITHIC

## Raw material acquisition

Figures 9.1. and 9.2. present the cumulative curves of the raw material composition of the industries studied. The earliest assemblage of the sequence, of layer IV in area B-G/18-23, is characterized by mediocre quality flint use of local sources, especially of Ramat Menashe. The Levantine Aurignacian often exploited the same area, however mostly low quality flints were collected. The Late Kebaran shows a similar raw material procurement strategy to the indeterminate Early Upper Palaeolithic. A common feature of these industries is that RM1 is the prevalent raw material.

After the Late Kebaran, there is radical change in the raw material procurement strategy. This has two components: 1) The Geometric Kebaran and the Late Natufian based their lithic production on good quality flints, thus they habitually exploited the Deir Hannah formation for RM5 (Figure 9.3.). The shift from mediocre to good quality raw materials (Figure 9.4.) may be explained by the fact that good quality flints are better controlled during knapping due to lack of inclusions and cracks. This may be illustrated by the Geometric Kebaran assemblage, in which the fragmentation ratio of mediocre quality RAM blades is higher than that of the good quality DH blades. 2) The appearance of distant flints (Shamir formation flints from 15 km) in the Geometric Kebaran and in the Late Natufian in larger quantity than earlier. The Geometric Kebaran has artifacts from the farthest flint source (OII raw material) from near the Galilee Sea area. The presence of distant flints undoubtedly document human group mobility between territories, which is increased in the Late Epipalaeolithic times. Moreover, this indicates a higher level of insistence to raw materials in flint knapping in comparison to the sole local flint user technologies such as the indeterminate Early Upper Palaeolithic, the Levantine Aurignacian, and the Late Kebaran.

It is also noticeable, that in the Upper Palaeolithic in the case of selecting raw material nodules for blade production, there was an attention paid to find nodules in proper shape to get the blade production started with minimal or no investment in core shaping. This approach is missing from the Epipalaeolithic. Contrary to the Upper Palaeolithic, in bladelet production of the Epipalaeolithic, when raw nodules were directly used for cores, the original shape of flint is taken into account during selection.

## Blank productions

### Blade production

Uniformly, the most common raw materials tend to appear with the highest frequency in the production of all

products. One assemblage, the Levantine Aurignacian, displays a targeted procurement for RM3 in the production of large blades. This raw material is found in the largest size on the field.

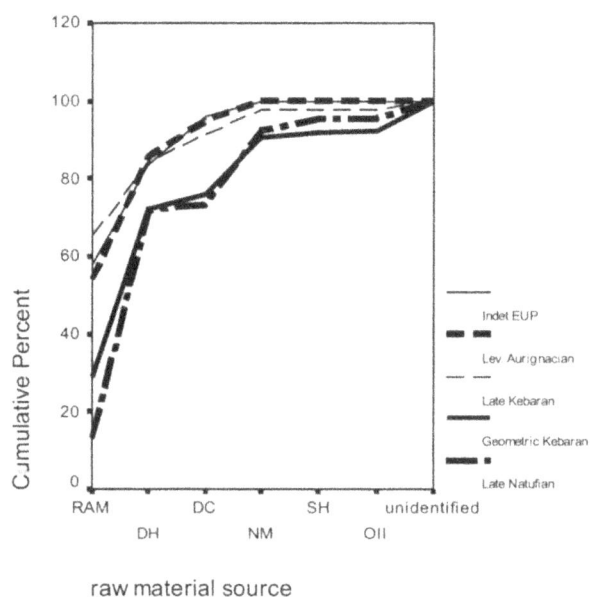

*Figure 9.1.* Cumulative curve of raw material composition by flint source(RAM, Ramat Menashe; DH, Deir Hannah formation; DC, Daliyat ha Carmel; NM, Nahal Mearot; SH, Shamir formation; OII, Ohalo II).

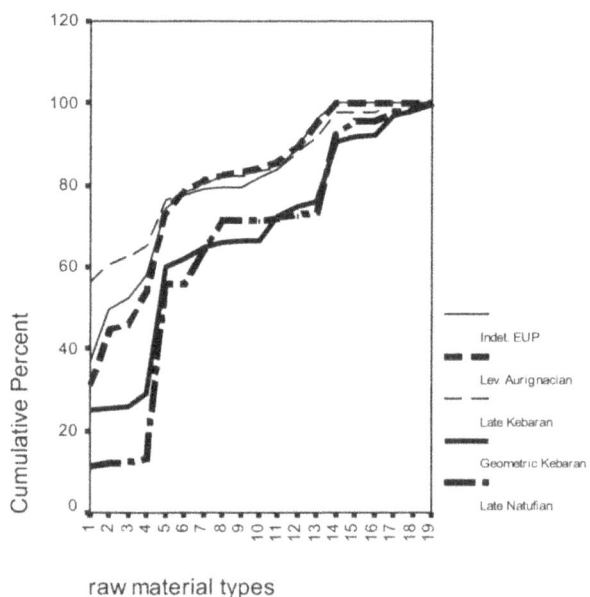

*Figure 9.2.* Cumulative curve of the raw material composition by type.

94

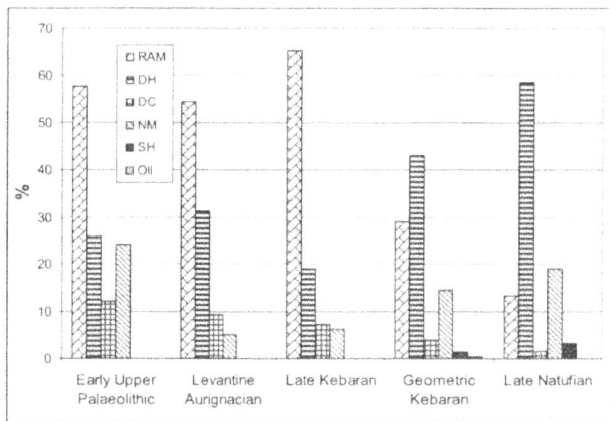

**Figure 9.3.** *Frequency of raw materials by source in the studied assemblages (RAM, Ramat Menashe; DH, Deir Hannah formation; DC, Daliyat ha Carmel; NM, Nahal Mearot; SH, Shamir formation; OII, Ohalo II).*

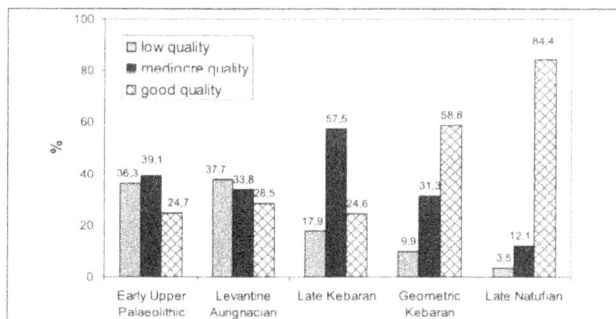

**Figure 9.4.** *Frequency of raw materials by quality in the studied assemblages.*

Both Upper Palaeolithic industries paid attention to raw material selection, in order to find flint nodule forms having longitudinal ridges that could have been exploited without core performing using the natural givens of the stone. With this concept the investment of energy in core performing was well lowed. In addition to the selection of apt shape of nodule for blade production, the Levantine Aurignacian utilized a wider spectrum of blade core blanks that consists of used up flake cores and large flakes. The Epipalaeolithic industries technically behaved the opposite, those rather performed core performing.

Basically, the concept of laminar debitage made up a single sequence to obtain blanks from the size of blade to that of bladelet. It is present in every industry, and characteristic to all but the Levantine Aurignacian. The Levantine Aurignacian has a well distinguishable blade debitage, separate from bladelet debitage, and moreover displays a greater variability of blade products with three distinct operational schemes. This makes it unique in terms of the organization of laminar lithic production.

Comparing the number of cortical blades to non-cortical ones, the degree of core decortication prior to blade debitage can be described. These data compared between assemblages show which lithic industry

performed decortication the most and the least. According to these data, the Levantine Aurignacian performed blade core decortications with the lowest degree in core configuration (Figure 9.5.). Except the Late Kebaran, the blade core decortication strongly characterizes the Epipalaeolithic industries, and it was the most frequent in the Late Natufian.

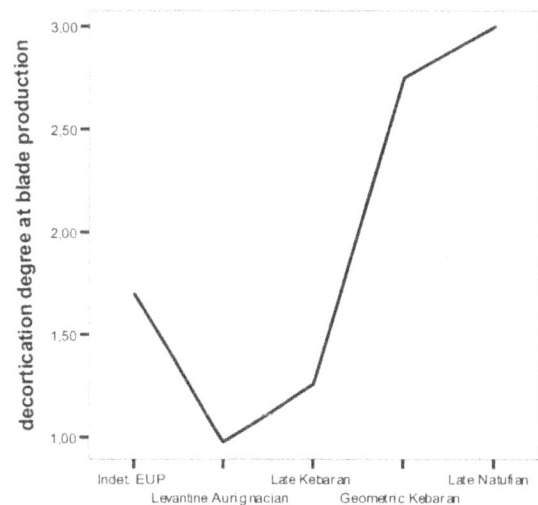

**Figure 9.5.** *Degree of decortication in blade productions of the assemblages studied. Values are counted by non-cortical/cortical blades.*

The Epipalaeolithic blade cores were frequently shaped on their lateral sides with flake removals detached from the direction of the core back. This led to a core configuration that was apt for producing laminar blanks from large to small size in a single sequence.

In all industries, the narrow part of the raw material nodules were chosen to be the front of the blade cores for the most part. Core front cresting is rare in the Upper Palaeolithic, more frequent in the Late Kebaran and Geometric Kebaran and apparently absent in the Natufian. As a uniform feature in core configuration, the striking platforms of the cores were prepared by the removal of a single flake.

Soft hammer knapping technique dominates all industries' blade debitage, but that of the Levantine Aurignacian. Here, the soft hammer technique was used to remove fine blades from wide-fronted cores and with the hard stone hammer technique a large portion of the blades, especially thick and heavy ones, were obtained.

The blade debitage was dominantly unidirectional in every industry. As a negligible practice, opposite or bi-directional debitage occurred almost everywhere.

The shape of blade through the Upper Palaeolithic-Epipalaeolithic sequence is almost perfectly constant (Table 9.1.). Blades with parallel edges were most often produced, but only the Late Natufian blades have typically expanding edges. The profile of the blades is less continuous. It is straight in the Levantine

Aurignacian and in the Late Kebaran, and curved in the rest of the industries.

The blade cores were habitually kept in their initial shape during the debitage. The Geometric Kebaran is the only assemblage where the debitage surfaces of the blade cores became flat and wide in the course of the debitage.

*Table 9.1.* The most frequent blade shape in the assemblages studied.

|  | Profile | Edges |
|---|---|---|
| **Late Natufian** | Curved | Expanding |
| **Geometric Kebaran** | Curved | Parallel |
| **Late Kebaran** | Straight | Parallel |
| **Levantine Aurignacian** | Straight | Parallel |
| **Indet. Early Upper Palaeolithic** | Curved | Parallel |

The blade core maintenance was commonly used in every industry. Its main modalities (neo-cresting, core tablet and rejuvenating flake removals) did not change throughout the Upper Palaeolithic and Epipalaeolithic. However, the core maintenance modalities were practiced in different degrees. The most frequent use of neo-cresting can be observed in the indeterminate Early Upper Palaeolithic and Late Kebaran (Figure 9.6.). Platform rejuvenation was frequent in every industry with the exception of the Late Kebaran (Figure 9.7.).

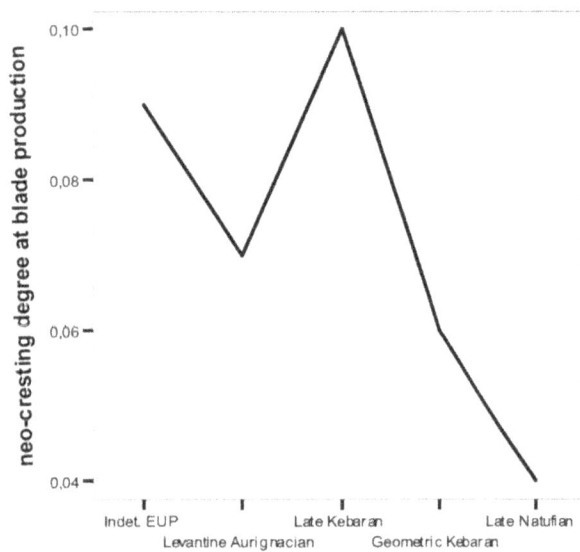

*Figure 9.7. Degree of platform rejuvenation in blade productions of the assemblages studied. Values are counted by blade core tablets + rejuvenating flakes/blade cores.*

## Bladelet production

In the Indeterminate Early Upper Palaeolithic and the Late Kebaran mediocre quality flints were used for bladelet production, while in the Levantine Aurignacian, Geometric Kebaran and Late Natufian good quality raw materials dominate. The raw material exploited for bladelet production dominate other debitages of the assemblages, except the Levantine Aurignacian, in which the flake and blade productions are based on mediocre and low quality flints. This means that the bladelet debitage in the Levantine Aurignacian required a different selection among raw materials.

Three types of bladelet core blanks were used in the studied assemblages. The first is small sized raw material nodules. This was often of RM5 flint in every assemblage since it can be found on the field as small nodules with appropriate shape for bladelet cores. In this case, the bladelet core shaping was restricted to the striking platform, to the core front and its environment. Accordingly, the decortication degree is higher in bladelet productions than in blade productions. The most intensive decortication was made in the indeterminate Early Upper Palaeolithic, Geometric Kebaran and Late Natufian industries (Figure 9.8.).

The second type of bladelet core blank is the thick flake. This characterizes best the Levantine Aurignacian. The configuration of these cores was restricted to the striking platform.

The third type of bladelet core blank is the used up blade core. This is characteristic to the Indeterminate early Upper Palaeolithic and Epipalaeolithic industries and not illustrative of the Levantine Aurignacian.

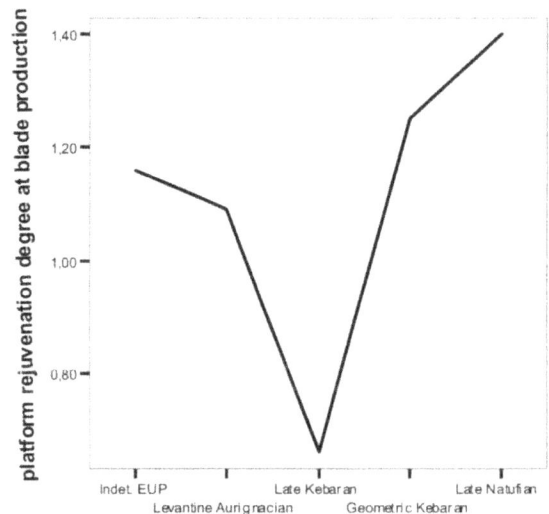

*Figure 9.6. Degree of neo-cresting in blade productions of the assemblages studied. Values are counted by neo-crest/ordinary blades.*

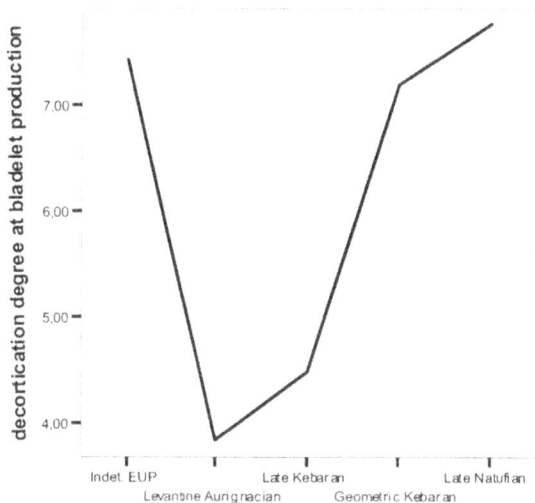

**Figure 9.8.** *Degree of decortication in bladelet productions of the assemblages studied. Values are counted by non-cortical/cortical bladelets.*

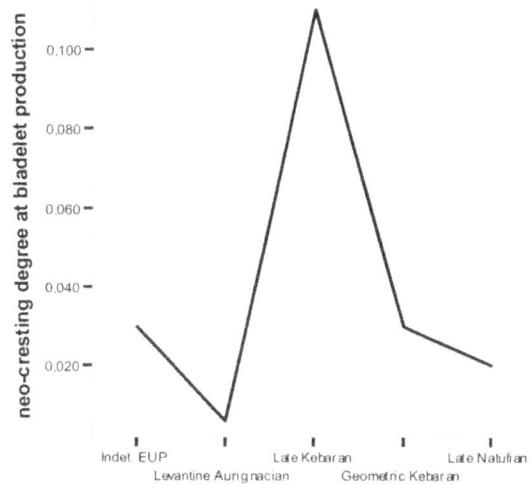

**Figure 9.9.** *Degree of neo-cresting in bladelet productions of the assemblages studied. Values are counted by neo-crest/ordinary bladelets.*

Cresting of bladelet cores was performed in the Late Kebaran and Geometric Kebaran. In the other industries the debitage commenced with using ridges created by flake removals. Sings of flint heat treatment for pre-formed cores in the Late Natufian is a major technical innovation in flint knapping. Its use may be for gaining better quality flint for better control over the raw material being knapped.

In the bladelet production of every studied industry the soft hammer technique and unidirectional debitage is dominant. Bladelets with straight profile appear in significant amount in the Indeterminate Early Upper Palaeolithic, Levantine Aurignacian and the Late Natufian. In the whole sequence of Raqefet, bladelets with parallel edges and curved profile were most often produced. Bladelets with converging edges are characteristic only to the indeterminate Early Upper Palaeolithic (Table 9.2.). Twisted bladelets, which are thought to be entailed Aurignacian technology (Bergman 2003; Copeland 2003; Chazan 2001), do not dominate any of the industries studied. Their highest frequency is recorded in the Late Kebaran industry (32.6% of the bladelet assemblage as against 25.9% in the Levantine Aurignacian) at Raqefet.

The Levantine Aurignacian and the Late Natufian did not involve neo-cresting within the chain of operation of the debitage for debitage surface correction, while it is strongly present in the Late Kebaran and, with moderate frequency, in the indeterminate Early Upper Palaeolithic and Geometric Kebaran (Figure 9.9.). The rejuvenation of core striking platform is frequent in the indeterminate Early Upper Palaeolithic, Late Kebaran and Late Natufian, and infrequent in the Geometric Kebaran and the Levantine Aurignacian (Figure 9.10.).

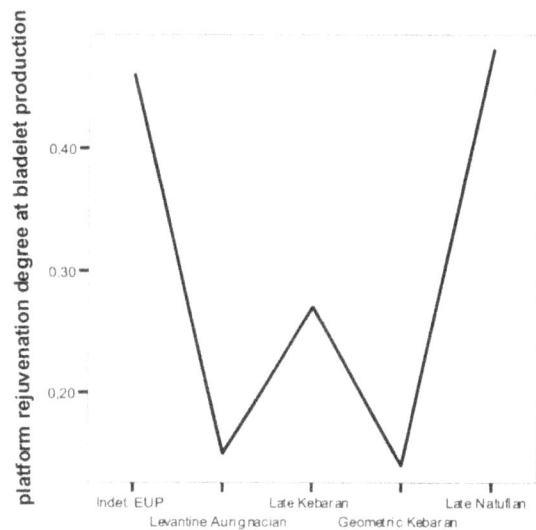

**Figure 9.10.** *Degree of platform rejuvenation in bladelet productions of the assemblages studied. Values are counted by bladelet core tablets + rejuvenating flakes/bladelet cores.*

Rejuvenation of striking platforms, neo-cresting of debitage surface, and abrasion of overhang occurred even before core discard. This action is characteristic to the Epipalaeolithic industries but to those of the Upper Palaeolithic. Since the Epipalaeolithic industries are highly dominated by bladelets and the main knapping activity is the bladelet production, it may be obvious that the knapper was about to try all possibilities to produce bladelets. A common reason for core discard is the hinge accident. These cores are usually bigger than those without. The smallest cores bearing no accidents most likely were discarded on the reason of critical diminishing of the size of the exploitable debitage surface.

**Table 9.2.** *The most frequent bladelet shape in the assemblages studied.*

|  | Profile | Edges |
|---|---|---|
| **Late Natufian** | Straight | Parallel |
| **Geometric Kebaran** | Curved | Parallel |
| **Late Kebaran** | Curved | Parallel |
| **Levantine Aurignacian** | Curved | Parallel |
| **Early Upper Palaeolithic** | Curved | Converging |

## Knapping accidents in laminar production

Solely the Levantine Aurignacian exhibits indispensable traits of knapping breaks, such as *languette* fragments, *nacelle* and *siret* accident. In addition, this industry represents the participation of unskilled stone tool makers in the lithic production by the intensive repetition of hinges on cores. The percentage of hinge and plunging accidents in the blade production is highest in the Late Kebaran. This is a biased data, since the blades are few in the Late Kebaran and the focus in lithic production was put on bladelets, which are perfectly made. The Late Natufian exhibits the least number of accidents.

## Flake production

Every industry of Raqefet contains a relative high amount of flakes. However, frequent use of flake debitage is recognized only in the Levantine Aurignacian and in the Late Natufian. The Levantine Aurignacian flake debitage was performed according to two methods. The first method is when several surfaces of the cores were flaked. This flaking kept the core in cube or globular shapes. The debitage resulted in thick removals with steep distal termination. The second method of flake debitage took place with simple removals on single platform cores. The Late Natufian flake debitage is similar to the second modality of the Levantine Aurignacian. The Indeterminate Early Upper Palaeolithic, Late Kebaran and Geometric Kebaran industries hardly have intended flake debitage. The majority of their flakes are by-products (core rejuvenating and shaping flakes) of the blade and bladelet production.

## Tool blank selection and tools

Generally, the most frequently produced blanks are present in the tool kit with the highest frequency. The Levantine Aurignacian tool blanks are mostly flakes, in the Late Kebaran and Geometric Kebaran those are bladelets, and in the Late Natufian bladelets and flakes (Table 9.3.). The Indeterminate Early Upper Palaeolithic industry is distinct from this feature. Although fine blades and bladelets are frequent, they were rarely used as blanks of tools as against the flakes of the blade debitage by-products, such as core tablets and decortical flakes. The blades and bladelets, whose production requires more skills than that of the flakes, were most likely taken away.

It is of interest that the shape of the blanks does not always correspond with that of the tools. For example, in the Indeterminate Early Upper Palaeolithic the blank blades have often parallel edges while the blade tools are made of blades having converging edges. In the Late Kebaran and Geometric Kebaran, the blank bladelets often have curved profile, while straight bladelets dominate the tools. This may refer to that the blank items are left over after tool blank selection. In the other industries such differences between the shape of retouched and unretouched blanks are not observed.

Some relations between tool types and blanks can be observed. Denticulates and sidescrapers were made of flakes. The prevalent blanks of the end-scrapers are flakes, while in the Geometric Kebaran those are mostly blades. Burins were predominantly made on flakes, except in the Indeterminate Early Upper Palaeolithic, where blades dominate. In the Geometric Kebaran and in the Late Natufian, bladelets of good quality flints were used for making microliths and geometric tools, while flakes and blades from lower quality raw materials were selected for making non-microlithic tools.

## Retouching

Endscrapers, burins, retouched items, truncations and notches were made in every industry (Table 9.3.) by different types of retouch. In the lithic industries studied here, the simple endscrapers were made by typical fan shaped converging retouch, with the exception of the Late Kebaran, which often used scalar form removals. Nosed, shouldered and carinated endscrapers are solely characteristic to the Levantine Aurignacian. Their retouch is unique, which is characterized by tiny small bladelet-like removals.

In the production of burins, the dihedral type characterizes the Upper Palaeolithic, while in the Epipalaeolithic the truncation burin is more frequent.

In regard to retouched items, also there is a contrast between the Upper Palaeolithic and the Epipalaeolithic. The former made frequently heavy retouch while the latter fine retouch.

Notches habitually were made by the series of small removals. Clactonian notching is characteristic only to the Levantine Aurignacian.

The microlithic tools of the Epipalaeolithic industries were produced with different approaches. In the Late Kebaran, the blank forms closely parallel the finished microlithic tools in shape and size. Thus, the blunting removed only a small portion of the blank. This minimal blank shape modification in retouching is believed to stem from the „Upper Palaeolithic mindset" of the Early Ahmarian that produced el-Wad points of pointed blank blade/lets the shape of which was predetermined by the organization of the debitage (Belfer-Cohen and Goring-Morris 2002). Contrary to this, in the Late Natufian and the Geometric Kebaran, the blunting modified largely the original blank shape, and the back of their microliths was created near the longitudinal axis of the blank, at the thickest part of the blank. This intensive blank shape modification, including also microburin technique, is viewed as the true Epipaleolithic tool making concept (Belfer-Cohen and Goring-Morris 2002).

## Conclusion

In the lithic technology of the Upper Palaeolithic-Epipalaeolithic sequence of Raqefet 1) tendencies can be observed such as: shift from mediocre to good quality flints use towards the end of the Epipalaeolithic (Geometric Kebaran and the Late Natufian), including the appearance of flint heat treatment as means for gaining better quality raw material (Late Natufian); increased bladelet production by the Epipalaeolithic; the retouching of the microlithic tools with extent blank shape modification appears with the Geometric Kebaran and linger on the Late Natufian; making blades and bladelets in a single operational sequence; 2) changes can be observed such as: increased flake debitage in the Levantine Aurignacian and then in the Late Natufian; hard hammer technique in Levantine Aurignacian blade debitage; varied frequency of core platform and debitage surface rejuvenation, and other small parts of the operational sequence; 3) consistency can be observed only on very general levels such as the performance of blade and bladelet debitage in each culture.

On the basic level of the lithic technology (the organization of blanks debitages and blank use for tools) three fundamental operational schemes can be revealed (Figure 9.11.):

**Scheme 1** shows that raw material nodules (bold lines) are used for blade and bladelet debitages. Flake debitage is not performed. The cores of the blade debitage are also used for bladelet debitage (dashed line). Flakes (thin line) and blades (dotted line) of the blade production, and bladelets (dotted-dashed line) of the bladelet production are used as tool blanks. This pattern characterizes the Early Upper Palaeolithic, Late Kebaran and Geometric Kebaran.

In **Scheme 2**, raw material nodules are used for flake, blade and bladelet debitages. In addition, flakes from the flake debitage are selected for making blade and bladelet cores. Blanks of each debitage are used for tool making. This scheme solely characterizes the Levantine Aurignacian.

**Scheme 3** shows that raw material nodules are introduced into flake, blade and bladelet debitages. Cores of the blade debitage also are used in the bladelet debitage. Blanks of each debitage are used for tool making. In addition, flakes from the blade debitage are used as blanks of tools. This scheme solely characterizes the Late Natufian.

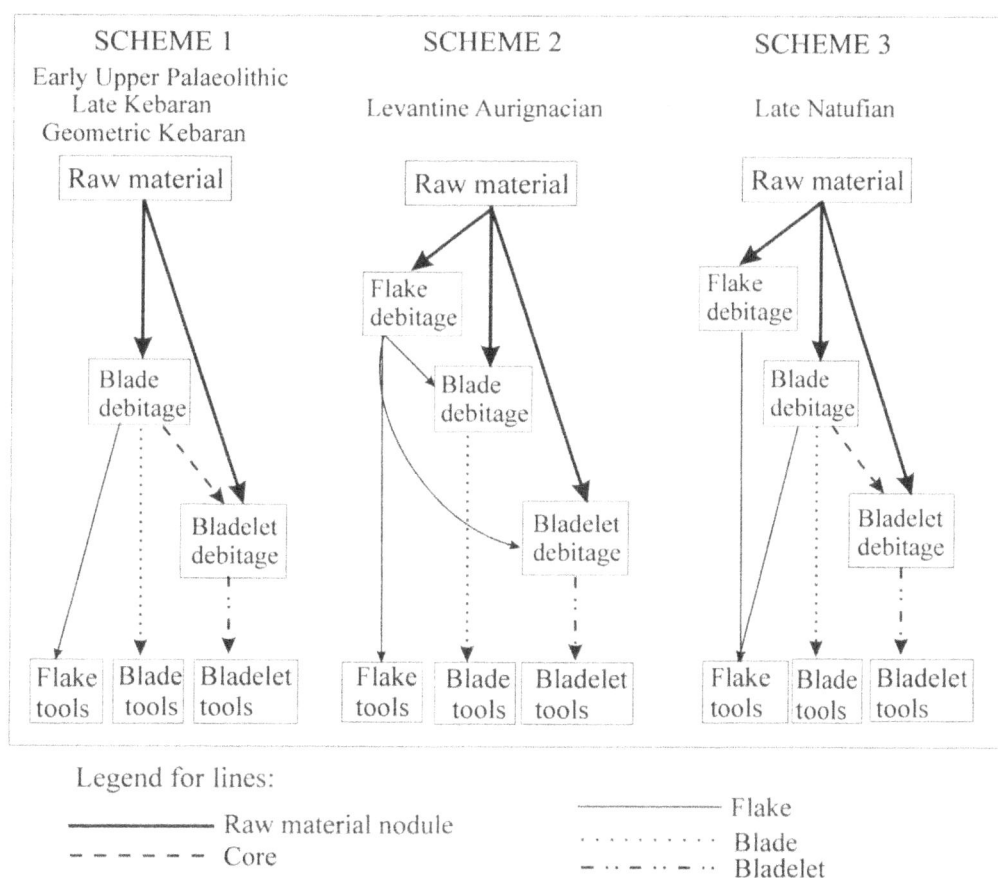

*Figure 9.11. Operational scheme patterns of Raqefet assemblages studied.*

*Table 9.3*: Most frequent blanks of major tool types in the assemblages studied.

| Major tool types | Indet. Early Upper Palaeolithic | Levantine Aurignacian | Late Kebaran | Geometric Kebaran | Late Natufian |
|---|---|---|---|---|---|
| End-scrapers | Flake | Flake | Flake | Blade | Flake |
| Burins | Blade | Flake | Flake | Flake | Flake |
| Retouched items | Flake | Flake | Bladelet | Blade | Blade |
| Backed items | - | Flake | Bladelet | Bladelet | Bladelet |
| Truncations | Blade | Flake | Bladelet | Bladelet | Bladelet |
| Points | - | Blade | Bladelet | Bladelet | - |
| Geometric microliths | - | - | Bladelet | Bladelet | Bladelet |
| Borers | - | Flake | - | Bladelet | - |
| Notches | Flake | Flake | Flake | Bladelet | Bladelet |
| Denticulates | Flake | Flake | - | Flake | Flake |
| Side scrapers | Flake | Flake | Flake | Flake | - |
| Diverse | Flake | Flake | Flake | Flake | Flake |
| Composite tools | Blade | Flake | Bladelet | - | - |

# CHAPTER 10: A BRIEF SURVEY OF THE LEVANTINE UPPER PALAEOLITHIC AND EPIPALAEOLITHIC LITHIC TECHNOLOGY AND RAQEFET CAVE

## Early Upper Palaeolithic

### Early Ahmarian

The first fully fledged Upper Palaeolithic culture of the Levant is the Early Ahmarian. This culture is named after the site of Erq el-Ahmar in the Judean desert. Chronologically, it follows the "Transitional period" that is characterized by Levallois point-shaped elongated laminar production with Upper Palaeolithic volumetric debitage concept and tool kit (Volkman 1983; Azoury 1986, Ohnuma 1988; Škrdla 2003). The Early Ahmarian precedes and also is contemporaneous with the Levantine Aurignacian. Its time span ranges from 43/42 kyear BP to 26 kyear BP (Belfer-Cohen and Goring-Morris 2003).

In the 1980s the Ahmarian was defined according to techno-typological features. Assemblages characterized by blades and the frequent presence of blade blanks in tool kits were classified as members of the "Ahmarian" culture (Gilead 1981) or "Ahmarian tradition" (Marks 1981). Lately, the naming of "Ahmarian tradition" was proposed to be changed to "Levantine Leptolithic Lineage", which includes the Transitional/Emiran/Initial Upper Palaeolithic and the Epipalaeolithic (Marks 2003).

Early Ahmarian lithic technologies can be illustrated from Nahal Nizzana XIII (Davidzon and Goring-Morris 2003), Ksar 'Aqil levels 17-16 (Azoury 1986; Williams 2003a), Boker A (Monigal 2003), Ücagizli Cave B, B1-B4, C (Kuhn 2004), and Qafzeh Cave E (Bar-Yosef and Belfer-Cohen 2004):

1) Laminar core configuration

According to refitted assemblages in the Negev, Boker A and Nahal Nizzana XIII, ovoid raw material nodules were collected for laminar production. At Boker A, the investment of energy into core configuration was low. The decortication was limited to cleaning only the face from which blades would be detached and, perpendicular to this, what would become the striking platform (Monigal 2003). In contrary, at Nahal Nizzana XIII, the blade cores underwent an expansive core shaping (Davidzon and Goring-Morris 2003). What is common in these technologies is that the core front cresting was not part of the knapping concept. In contrast to above assemblages, Qafzeh E is characterized by rare core shaping and frequent front cresting (the cortical blades outnumber two times the cortical flakes and there is a relative large number of crest blades) (Bar-Yosef and Belfer-Cohen 2004). From Ücagizli Cave Ahmarian front cresting and strong decortication is mentioned (Kuhn et al 2003; Kuhn 2004).

2) Laminar debitage

At Nahal Nizzana XIII, the reconstructed knapping sequences evidence a laminar debitage commenced with blade removals and finished with bladelet sized products (Davidzon and Goring-Morris 2003). Distinct, but somewhat "secondary" bladelet debitage using thick flakes removed during core configuration as blanks for bladelet cores also was observed at Nahal Nizzana XIII (ibid.). Boker A also contains conjoins yielding first blades than bladelets and, in addition, there are core conjoins that comprises only bladelets, and conjoins that comprises only blades (Monigal 2003). Nahal Nizzana XIII and Boker A are dominated by unidirectional blade debitage (Davidzon and Goring-Morris 2003, Monigal 2003;), while Ücagizli, B, B1-B4, C, Qafzeh E and Ksar 'Aqil 17-16 are characterized by bidirectional blade debitage (Kuhn et al 2003; Kuhn 2004; Bar-Yosef and Belfer-Cohen 2004; Williams 2003a; Azoury 1986).

Universal features among the Early Upper Palaeolithic assemblages discussed here are: 1) the production of elongated and pointed blades and bladelets by soft hammer knapping technique (Davidzon and Goring-Morris 2003; Marks 2003); 2) the intensive laminar production and no flake debitage. The flakes are the by-products of the laminar debitage almost in every case.

Typologically, the Early Ahmarian is abundant of finely retouched bladelets. In the tool kit, end-scrapers frequently made on core tablets, cortical flakes and blades are also frequent, burins are rarer (Marks 2003). The Early Ahmarian *"fossile directure"* is the el-Wad point (Belfer-Cohen and Goring-Morris 2003), which was made on curved blade or bladelet with fine retouch at the tip or along one or both edges of the blank (Bar-Yosef and Belfer 1977).

### Other Early Upper Palaeolithic industries?

Lately, the classification of all Early Upper Palaeolithic blade production dominated industries as Early Ahmarian has been questioned. Based on lithic studies on sites of Jordan, Kerry and Henry (2003) noticed that most likely a wider variety of archaeological cultures characterizes this period Kebara Cave units III-IV assemblages also were challenged, and suggested that more than two Early Upper Palaeolithic cultures were present in the Levant (Williams 2003a; Belfer-Cohen and Goring-Morris 2003). Further north, the identification of lithics of Ücagizli Cave layers C/D, D, E is also ambiguous (Kuhn 2004). Although the Early Upper Palaeolithic layers of Umm el-Tlel in Syria are designated to Ahmarian and Levantine Aurignacian (Ploux and Soriano 2003), the assemblages do not resemble any of the two cultures of this period. Both assemblages are dominated by unidirectional bladelet production and retouched bladelets in tool kit. The differences between them are present by the debitage modes of bladelet production. While the "Ahmarian" is characterized by straight and pointed bladelet production from cores prepared by front cresting, the "Aurignacian" is abundant of twisted bladelets produced from cores resembling carinated burin.

*Table 10.1.* The first Levantine Upper Palaeolithic chronology and the division of Ksar 'Aqil's Upper Palaeolithic sequence (modified after Belfer-Cohen and Bar Yosef 1999).

| Phase (Neuville & Garrod) | Flint tools | Ksar 'Aqil | London 1969 |
|---|---|---|---|
| VI<br>Kebaran | Numerous truncated and pointed bladelets | 1<br>5 | Kebaran |
| V<br>Atlitian | Polyhedral and truncated burins | 6<br>7 | Levantine Aurignacian C |
| IV<br>Upper Aurignacian<br>Upper Antelian | Aurignacian endscrapers (carinated<nosed), few el-Wad points | 8<br>9<br>10 | Levantine Aurignacian B |
| III<br>Middle Aurignacian<br>Lower Antelian | Aurignacian endscrapers (carinated>nosed), many el-Wad points | 11<br>12<br>13 | Levantine Aurignacian A |
| II<br>Unnamed | Pointed blades, endscrapers, burins | 15 | Ksar 'Aqil Phase B |
| I<br>Emiran | Emireh points, Levallois, blades | 21<br>25 | Ksar 'Aqil Phase A |

Besides the Early Ahmarian, lithic assemblages under the term Levantine Aurignacian also turned out to be variegated. For example, Ksar 'Aqil levels 13-11, habitually believed to belong to the Levantine Aurignacian (Levantine Aurignacian A), indeed are different from the classical Levantine Aurignacian to the extent that their cultural affinity is uncertain (Bergman 1987; Bergman and Goring-Morris 1987; Belfer-Cohen and Goring-Morris 2003).

Technologically, the above assemblages are dissimilar. Although in laminar production at Ksar 'Aqil 13-11 and at Kebara III-IV decortication, core shaping and front cresting were performed, the former used unidirectional debitage whilst the latter used bidirectional debitage (Bergman 1987; Tostevin 2000; Williams 2003a). In tool kits, endscrapers, burins, el-Wad points and retouched bladelets can be found (Bergman 1987; Bar-Yosef and Belfer Cohen 1996; Kuhn *et al* 2003; Williams 2003a).

Umm el-Tlel, contrary to the other assemblages, is strictly bladelet dominated in debitage and toolkit (Ploux and Soriano 2003). This feature fits better the Epipalaeolithic than the Upper Palaeolithic

*Synthesis*

The Early Upper Palaeolithic, non-Levantine Aurignacian, lithic technologies exhibit five modalities in terms of laminar production. The first involves an intensive core decortication without front cresting and with unidirectional debitage. This characterizes Nahal Nizzana XIII (Davidson and Goring-Morris 2003). The second modality is characterized by the lack of core shaping and front cresting, and unidirectional debitage. This is observed at

Boker A (Monigal 2003). In the third modality front cresting, decortication and bi-directional opposite debitage were used. This characterizes Ksar 'Aqil 17-16, Kebara III-IV and Üçağizli B, B1-B4, C (Ohnuma 1988; Tostevin 2000; Williams 2003; Kuhn 2004; Kuhn *et al* 2003). The fourth modality is characterized by cresting, decortication and unidirectional debitage (Ksar 'Aqil 13-11). What is overall to all above sites is that blade/lets with converging edges were frequently used as tool blanks. The fifth modality is present in the bladelet debitage dominated Umm el-Tlel "Ahmarian" and "Aurignacian" layers (Ploux and Soriano 2003).

In respect of the organization of lithic technology, Raqefet Indeterminate Early Upper Palaeolithic corresponds best to Boker A (Monigal 2003) and Ksar 'Aqil levels 13-11 (Bergman 1987). The main similarities between them are given by the predominant use of unidirectional laminar debitage, the lack of pronounced flake debitage, the presence of *chaînes opératoires* for both blade and bladelet productions. Dissimilarities between them are given by the frequent decortication and front cresting at Ksar 'Aqil 13-11, and the predominant use of laminar blanks for tools in Ksar 'Aqil 13-11 and Boker A. Similarly to all above sites, the blade tool blanks are frequently converging-sided items.

Above comparisons show that the Raqefet Indeterminate Early Upper Palaeolithic does not fit neatly to any of the other Early Upper Palaeolithic laminar technologies and there is no an overall laminar production method in the Early Ahmarian and non-Levantine Aurignacian Early Upper Palaeolithic cultural entities of the Levant. Raqefet Indeterminate Early Upper Palaeolithic industry also refers to that the period under consideration in the Levant may have been more variegated than formerly thought.

## Levantine Aurignacian

The Aurignacian was named after the European Upper Palaeolithic Aurignacian (Neuville 1934; Garrod and Bate 1937; Garrod 1953). The chronological range of the Aurignacian is restricted to a well defined period between 36 and 27 kyear BP. Radiocarbon dates were obtained from Kebara Cave, Ksar 'Aqil, Hayonim Cave and Raqefet Cave (Bar-Yosef 1991; Bar-Yosef *et al* 1996; Higgs *et al* 1975; Lengyel *et al* 2006; Mellars and Tixier 1989).

In the first Upper Palaeolithic chronology of the Levant, the Aurignacian was divided into two stages (Garrod 1953) (Table 10.1):

1) Middle Aurignacian, which was characterized by scrapers on thick flakes or blocks with nose-shape made by fine lamellar retouch, carinated scrapers, *burin busqué*, and "Font-Yves" points;

2) Lower Aurignacian, which was not significantly different from the preceding horizon: carinated end-scrapers remained constant while the nosed end-scrapers became more abundant, and Font Yves points were less frequent.

Later, Garrod (1957a) argued that the Aurignacian in the Levant is different from the European Aurignacian and changed the Aurignacian naming to Antelian after Antelias Cave in Lebanon.

Garrod's classification was used till the end of the 1960s. A conference organized by Wenner-Gren Foundation in London in 1969 aimed to make clear the Upper Palaeolithic division of the Levant on the basis of Ksar 'Aqil Upper Palaeolithic layers (Bergman 1987). Researchers in agreement rejected Garrod's naming of Antelian. They decided to divide the Aurignacian feature bearer industries of Ksar 'Aqil into three groups, Levantine Aurignacian A (layers 13-11), Levantine Aurignacian B (layers 10-8), and Levantine Aurignacian C (layers 7-6) (Bergman 1987). This division was under

refinement for long time and never became strictly adopted by the researchers as was established in 1969 (Table 10.2.).

After investigations in the Negev a new classification scheme was proposed for the Aurignacian in the 1980s. Every lithic industry technologically dominated by flakes over blades and typologically by end-scrapers and burins or both ($\geq ca$ 50%), as well as by the low quantity of bladelet tools ($\geq ca$ 20%) became ranged among the assemblages of the "Levantine Aurignacian" culture (Gilead 1981) or "Levantine Aurignacian tradition" (Marks 1981). According to several scholars, the assemblages of this classification (open-air sites of the Negev and Sinai) did not exhibit most characteristics of the Aurignacian (Belfer-Cohen 1995; Bar-Yosef and Belfer-Cohen 1996). Several of them are undated surface collections, and the high proportion of Aurignacian-like tools may have been part of an Epipalaeolithic tool-kit, as was recognized from the excavations at Nahal Neqarot rock shelter in Central Negev (Belfer-Cohen *et al* 1991). Thus, Gilead's method to classify the Levantine Aurignacian never became fully accepted by the researchers investigating Levantine prehistory (Belfer-Cohen and Bar-Yosef 1981; Belfer-Cohen and Goring Morris 1986; Belfer Cohen 1995).

After Bergman's (1987) paper on Ksar 'Aqil "Levantine Aurignacian" sequence, it turned out that the master pieces of Levantine Aurignacian industries are not developmentally related. Only two layers (8-7) share features with other Levantine Aurignacian assemblages, the rest do not (Bergman and Goring-Morris 1987).

According to a recent technological analysis (Williams 2003a, 2003b), the lithic assemblages of the "Levantine Aurignacian tradition" consist of three separate lithic industrial units. Thus, there is a "carinated industry" (Ksar 'Aqil phase 6-7, Arkov, D27A, Ein Aqev, G11, K9A, Har Horesha I), a "non-carinated flake-blade-scraper industry" (Ksar 'Aqil Phase 5, Kebara I-II, Hayonim D, Sefunim 8), and a "non-carinated flake burin industry" (Nahal Ein Gev I, Fazael IX).

*Table 10.2. The cultural division of Ksar 'Aqil layers 13-6 from the 1969 conference to the late 80s. Headline: 1 – Ksar 'Aqil Layers; 2 - Division of 1969 (after Bergman 1987); 3 – Copeland and Hours 1971; 4 - Hours et al 1973; 5 - Copeland 1975; 6 - Besancon et al 1977; 7 - Ziffer 1981; 8 – Bergman 1987; 9 - London 1987 (after Bergman and Goring-Morris 1987); 10 - Marks and Ferring 1988. Captures of abbreviations: LA A – Levantine Aurignacian A; LA B - Levantine Aurignacian B; LA C - Levantine Aurignacian C.*

| 1 | 2 | 3 | 4 | 5 | 6 | 7 | 8 | 9 | 10 |
|---|---|---|---|---|---|---|---|---|---|
| 6 | LA C | LA Cii | Atlitian | LA C | LA C | LA C | Stage 6 | | |
| 7 | LA C | LA Ci | Atlitian | LA C | LA C | LA C | Stage 5 | Levantine | Evolved Levantine |
| 8 | LA C | LA Ci | LA B | LA B | LA B | LA Bii | Stage 5 | Aurignacian | Aurignacian |
| 9 | LA B | LA Bii | LA B | LA B | LA B | LA Bii | Stage 4 | Ahmarian | Early |
| 10 | LA B | LA Bi | LA B | LA B | LA B | LA Bi | Stage 4 | | Levantine |
| 11 | LA A | | LA A | LA A | LA A | LA Bi | Stage 3 | | Aurignacian |
| 12 | LA A | | LA A | LA A | LA A | LA A | Stage 3 | | |
| 13 | LA A | | Eboulis complex | LA A | LA A | LA A | Stage 3 | | |

Umm el-Tlel in Syria also is introduced as Aurignacian site (Ploux and Soriano 2003). Since its assemblages primarily contain remains of bladelet production, most tools are retouched bladelets and no Aurignacian type of endscrapers and blades, these cannot be classified Levantine Aurignacian (Belfer-Cohen and Goring-Morris 2003).

Recently, only a few sites of the Levant are regarded as "real" Levantine Aurignacian (Belfer-Cohen and Bar-Yosef 1999; Bar-Yosef 2000; Belfer-Cohen and Gorring-Morris 2003). These are caves (Antelias, Yabrud II, Kebara, El-Wad, Sefunim, Raqefet, Hayonim) and a rock shelter (Ksar 'Aqil) (Belfer-Cohen and Gorring-Morris 2003).

Complex lithic technology studies on Levantine Aurignacian sites are rare. Some data can be gathered from Hayonim D (Belfer-Cohen and Bar-Yosef 1981; Wiseman 1993; Williams 2003), Kebara I-II (Tostevin 2000; Williams 2003a), Sefunim 8 and 10 (Ronen 1984; Williams 2003a) and Ksar 'Aqil 8 (Bergman 1987).

The Aurignacian blade debitage is characterized by the use of poor core preparation. The front of the cores in most cases lacks crest preparation at Hayonim D (Wiseman 1993), at Kebara I-II (Williams 2003a) and at Ksar 'Aqil 8 (Bergman 1987). It is in striking contrast to the above sites that Sefunim 8 assemblage exhibits blade core decortication since blades are typically devoid of cortex. In addition crest blades are also frequent (Ronen 1984; Williams 2003).

The Levantine Aurignacian blade technology seems to be characterized by the frequent use of hard hammer technique, as reported from Hayonim D (Wiseman 1993, Chazan 2001), and from Ksar 'Aqil 8 (minor use of overhang abrasion and robust blade production) (Bergman 1987). Besides robust blades, fine ones were also produced by soft hammer technique (Bergman 1987; Wiseman 1993; Marks 2003). The Levantine Aurignacian prevalently used unidirectional blade debitage. The only deviance assemblage is Sefunim 8, the blades of which have a notable presence of bi-directional dorsal scars. In addition, single platform blade cores are present in descending frequency (Williams 2003a).

In bladelet production, the Levantine Aurignacian habitually made use of thick flakes as blanks of cores. This is evidenced in Ksar 'Aqil 8 and Hayonim D (personal observations), but not reported from Kebara I-II and Sefunim 8 and 10. The Aurignacian end-scraper retouching is commonly associated with the production of twisted bladelets. These bladelets are the blanks of Dufour and other retouched bladelets (Bergman 2003; Chazan 2001; Copeland 2003).

The widespread feature of all Levantine Aurignacian industries is the strong flake production. The Aurignacian flake debitage, according to Bergman (1987), is opportunistic since most of the flake cores have several debitage surfaces (multi platform flake cores) and their shape is cube or globular.

The blank selection mirrors a strong preference for flakes and for heavy blades (Belfer-Cohen and Bar-Yosef 1981; Bergman 1987; Bergman and Goring-Morris 1987). The blanks of the typical Aurignacian tools such as carinated, thick nosed and shouldered end-scrapers are thick flakes at every industry. The use of core trimming elements such as core tablets also is present in Levantine Aurignacian toolkits. The retouching of blanks was most frequently made by large scalar removals on blades and flakes, and the Aurignacian type end-scrapers are frequently retouched by tiny laminar removals. Bladelets and fine blades were delicately retouched into Dufour bladelets and el-Wad points.

Raqefet Aurignacian assemblage is characterized by the features of the Levantine Aurignacian. In contrast with Bergman's opinion (1987), the Levantine Aurignacian flake debitage cannot be regarded opportunistic on the basis of Raqefet lithic technology study. One of the flake debitages primarily took place according to a multidirectional debitage scheme aiming to produce thick flakes. The other is a simple, unidirectional debitage. The Sefunim Cave assemblages show strong difference from all others. This deviance probably reflects a different Aurignacian technical behavior, or simply the Aurignacian designation to these assemblages cannot be maintained.

Above discussion shows, with the exception of Sefunim, that the Levantine Aurignacian in comparison with other Early Upper Palaeolithic cultures in the Levant is technologically uniform. This signifies a stern adherence to tradition of technical behavior.

## Late Kebaran

At the onset of the Upper Palaeolithic periodization of the Levant, the term Kebaran was originally coined to incorporate non-Natufian microlithic dominated assemblages of the late Upper Palaeolithic (Garrod 1953) (phase VI of Neuville 1951). Garrod proposed to call this period Epipalaeolithic (Garrod 1957b). Then, the term Epipalaeolithic became to incorporate microlithic dominated industries: Kebaran, Geometric Kebaran and Natufian (Bar-Yosef 1970).

On the basis of microlithic tool types, the Kebaran was divided into four clusters (Bar-Yosef 1981): A) with narrow micropoints and a large number of items with basal truncation; B) with curved and pointed backed retouched bladelets sometimes with basal truncation; C) with narrow micropoints and obliquely truncated backed bladelets; D) with dominance of obliquely truncated backed bladelets, sometime along with narrow curved bladelets shaped by semi-abrupt retouch.

The Kebaran complex today consists of two chronologically and typologically distinct entities (Bar-Yosef 1981). The early phase of the Kebaran (*ca* 19,5-16,5 kyear BP.) is characterized in each sub-region by the dominance of various types of microliths: in the Galilee and Carmel area narrow curved micropoints and obliquely truncated bladelets; in the southern coastal plain narrow and broad curved micropints; in the western Negev arch backed bladelets and broad micropoints; and in the lower Jordan Valley curved backed bladelets are abundant (Bar-Yosef and Vogel 1987). In the late phase of the Kebaran (*ca* 16,5-14,5 kyear BP.), the frequency of obliquely truncated and backed bladelets (Kebara points) is consistently higher than that of other microliths (*ibid.*; Fellner 1995). This latter seems to be the only overall feature of the Kebaran.

The Kebaran chronologically covers the early Epipalaeolithic period (*ca* 19,5-14,5 kyears BP). Besides the Kebaran, other cultures also appear in this period. The Masraqan characterized by finely retouched Outchata bladelets postdates the Kebaran. East to the Rift valley, the Nebekian coeval with at least part of the Masraqan. The Nebekian (Azraq region) is characterized by curved pointed arch-backed bladelets (Goring-Morris 1995, Belfer-Cohen and Goring-Morris 2003). Nebekian is followed by the Qalkhan (Azraq and Nahal Lavan) characterized by wide tools and large blade blanks and the Qalkhan point. Nizzanan ("Triangle industry" of Fellner 1995) with scalene and isoceles triangles is coeval with the Late Kebaran. It is found east to the Jordan and in Ksar Akil (phase III) and at Nahal Oren VII (Goring-Morris 1995; Goring-Morris and Belfer-Cohen 1998).

Up to date, little is known about Kebaran lithic technology. Data is available only from the Late Kebaran in the Negev (Marder 2002). The lithic technology presented herein is from Shunera XVII after Marder 2002.

The Late Kebaran of Shunera XVII collected habitually high and excellent quality raw materials for producing microlithic tools. Nodule sizes were slightly larger than fist-sized. No cresting or partial was made in core configuration. The natural flat narrow lateral side of the nodule was chosen as striking platform. Blank manufacture was achieved by systematic sequential removals of mainly elongate (>50 mm) incurvate blade blanks from the narrow part of the cores (N-fronted concept). The abrasion of overhang was widely applied during blank production. Therefore, soft hammer technique was used. The debitage was predominantly unidirectional. The blanks are most frequently bladelets. The retouching of obliquely truncated backed bladelets (or else Kebara point) reduced a large portion of the width in order to narrow the blank (Marder 2002). Massive denticulated blades were made off-site on coarse grained cherty flint.

The assemblage of Raqefet exhibits several features observed at Shunera XVII. Significant dissimilarities between Raqefet and Shunera XVII are the use of mediocre quality flints and the habitual use of front cresting at Raqefet and the more invasive retouch in shaping backed-obliquely truncated bladelets at Shunera XVII. Latter difference shows there was a tendency to produce more predetermined blanks closely paralleling the finished microlithic tools in shape and size at Raqefet. A significant similarity between the two assemblages is the close resemblance of the organization of the lithic technology with the Early Upper Palaeolithic. Above observations may allow deducing the presence of a technologically variegated Late Kebaran in the Levant, the debitage organization of which apparently stem from the local Early Upper Palaeolithic.

## Geometric Kebaran

In the course of the Epipalaeolithic research in the Levant, the Geometric Kebaran first was part of the Kebaran (phase VI) and later it became a separate entity, based on its typological characteristics (Bar-Yosef 1970). It was divided into A and B phases. Phase A's most characteristic tool group was the geometric microliths, consisting of trapezes, rectangles, trapeze-rectangles and triangles. Phase B was characterized by obliquely truncated microliths, trapeze-rectangles, triangles, and, in addition, lunates (*ibid.*). Later, the term Geometric Kebaran B was eliminated from the Epipalaeolithic and the phase A became the only Geometric Kebaran taxonomic unit (Bar-Yosef 1981; Bar-Yosef and Vogel 1987). But still, there is a typological dissimilarity between Geometric Kebaran sites of Southern and Northern Israel. A few Negev sites are characterized by large geometric tools while northern sites are solely characterized by narrow geometric tools (Goring-Morris 1995). Geometric Kebaran remains from caves were apparently missing. It was only lately recognized that Geometric Kebaran groups occupied caves and their remains usually are found mixed into Natufian and Kebaran deposits, as the high frequency of typical Geometric Kebaran forms shows (e.g. Kebara and el-Wad caves) (Belfer-Cohen and Goring- Morris *in press*).

Today, the Geometric Kebaran is a middle Epipalaeolithic culture, dated to 14,5-12,5 kyear BP, and contemporaneous with the Mushabian (*ca* 14-13 kyears BP) characterized by arch backed points and the Ramonian (earlier called Negev Kebaran, 13-12,5 kyears BP) characterized by obliquely truncated and backed bladelet with a straight to concave back (Ramon point), in the Negev (Goring-Morris 1987, 1995).

Geometric Kebaran lithic technology study is also scars, and can be presented only from Negev sites after Marder 2002.

At Shunera XIIB chalcedony raw material was collected for microlithic tools. In addition, regular, mediocre quality flint collected from the immediate vicinity of the site was used for the manufacture of microliths and end-scrapers. At Azariq XVI, fine-grained good and high quality flints were collected to the production of geometric microliths, end-scrapers, burins, retouched blades, notches and denticulates with one *chaîne opératoire*. Wide variety of nodules in terms of shape was collected. At Azariq XVIII a large variety of flints, from poor to high quality were collected. High quality fine-grained flints were used for microlithic production

At Shunera XIIB large portion of the original raw material was removed during core shaping. Two steps of shaping-out were carried out. First the front crest preparation and then the flanks shaping were performed. At Azariq XVI and XVIII front cresting is extremely rare. Instead, a natural ridge was removed from the front. At the former site the laminar core was minimally shaped and at the latter intensive core decortication was practiced. At Shunera XIIB, relatively a few blanks were produced from each core. Before core discard, a new striking platform was prepared opposed to the original one. In other cases, the utilization of a large part of the core's circumference by separately employing the front and the left side was observed.

At Azariq XVI and XVIII the laminar debitage was unidirectional on wide debitage surfaces. Primarily parallel-sided blades were produced. At the former site abrasion was systematically applied throughout the whole knapping operation, while at the latter that was uncommon. At Azariq XVIII, at the end of the laminar production the core debitage surface was narrowed in order to obtain narrow bladelets. Elongated blades were produced from poor to medium quality raw materials with bidirectional debitage for end-scrapers.

The tool production of the Geometric Kebaran is very standardized (Belfer-Cohen and Goring-Morris 2002).Among the sites, at Azariq XVI, large blanks were used for making end-scrapers and smaller blanks for making microlithic tools. During microlithic production, on one hand, the blanks were snapped without use of microburin technique, as well as at Shunera XIIB, and on the other hand the microliths' ends were notched and broken. Often more than one microliths were produced from each blank. The burins were shaped by flaking between one to five successive spalls. End-scrapers were produced off-site, from coarse-grained raw materials, as well as massive denticulates and multiple tools.At Azariq XVIII, elongated blades were selected in order to make more than one microliths from each blank. The blades were modified into elongated microliths. Massive tools were made of blanks from coarse-grained cherty flints.

Negev Geometric Kebaran sites share most characteristics with Raqefet. The tenor to collect good quality flints, decortication, front cresting, unidirectional organization of the blade debitage often on wide-fronted cores, the use of more than one surfaces of bladelet cores at the end of the bladelet debitage, the insignificant use of microburin technique for obtaining geometric microliths as against snapping, the use of invasive retouching in shaping geometric microliths, and the end-scraper production from blades characterize the Raqefet Geometric Kebaran technology, as well. Among Negev sites, Shunera XIIB is the most similar to Raqefet Geometric Kebaran. A significant difference between Negev Geometric Kebaran and Raqefet is that large microliths were not produced at Raqefet. This confirms earlier stated dissimilarity between northern and southern Geometric Kebaran sites in Israel (Goring-Morris 1995). The Geometric Kebaran operational scheme is the same as that of the Late Kebaran in Raqefet. This may allow deducing the Geometric Kebaran emerges from the Late Kebaran.

## Late Natufian

The Natufian was the first local prehistoric culture in the Levant. It was named by Garrod (1932) after wadi Natuf where its first excavated site Shukba cave was located. Since the industry contained microlithic tools likewise the European Mesolithic period, Garrod dated it to the Mesolithic (*ibid.*).

In Garrod's work (1957b) the Natufian was divided into three stages (herein only lithic evidences are listed). The Lower Natufian was characterized by lunates, sickle blades, geometrics, and ridge-back retouch (Helwan). The Middle Natufian typologically did not differ greatly from the Lower one. Lunates were still abundant but the Helwan retouch was very rare. A new element in the Middle Natufian was the microburin. In the Upper Natufian the lunates became rare and the Helwan retouch was almost entirely absent. The most important Upper Natufian stone tool type was the flint arrowhead (Khiam point).

The division of the Natufian and its characterization was changed after Garrod. The assemblages characterized by Khiam points became an individual industry called Khiamian (Echegaray 1978) of the PPNA period. Examining the Natufian in the level of specific technology, a new twofold chronological-cultural arrangement was suggested (Bar-Yosef and Valla 1979). Observations on radiocarbon dates, stratigraphic situation, microburin, Helwan lunates and other lunates were taken into account for this classification. The Early Natufian stage was characterized by the high frequency of Helwan lunates and the Late Natufian by the diminished size of lunates and the decreased frequency of Helwan retouch. Later, the Natufian became divided into three stages (Valla 1984, 1987, 1995). The Early stage (12,500 BP-11,500 BP) is characterized by the strong presence of Helwan lunates (more than 50% among the lunates) in the size of 19-28 mm. In the late Natufian (11,500 BP-10,750 BP) lunates are smaller, the Helwan retouch use in lunate shaping appears at less than 50% of the lunates. The size of the lunates falls between 20 and 15 mm. In the Final stage (10,750-10,250 BP) the Helwan retouch is nearly absent and the size of the lunates is the smallest (15-13 mm) in comparison to the earlier Natufian periods.

The Natufian complex chronologically covers the late Epipalaeolithic period (*ca* 12,5-10,2 kyears BP). There are geographic varieties of Natufian in the Southern Levant. In the desert area the Early Natufian is joined with the Terminal Ramonian (characterized by Helwan lunates and Ramon points). The Final Natufian "counterpart" in the Negev is called Harifian characterized by small blunt backed lunates and Harif points (10,750-10,100 BP) (Goring-Morris 1987, 1995).

Detailed technology studies on Natufian assemblages are available from Negev Early Natufian/Terminal Ramonian sites (Marder 2002), from Eynan (Valla *et al* 1998, 2001) and Mureybet (Calley 1986) final Natufian sites.

Negev Early Natufian/Terminal Ramonian sites display good and high quality flint procurement for producing blade/lets. The cores were shaped with raw material splitting and underwent systematic decortication. In the core configuration sings of heat treatment occurs at Nahal Sheker 23 and Azariq XV (Marder 2002). Mureybet Final Natufian is characterized by fine grained flint exploitation. Neither intensive core shaping nor cresting was made in core configuration (Calley 1986).Eynan Final Natufian assemblage also shows that small fine grained nodules with homogeneous texture were collected. The decortication took place before bladelet removals. The cores most likely underwent heat treatment as weak sings refer to it (Valla *et al* 1998, 2001).

At Negev Early Natufian/Terminal Ramonian sites, unidirectional debitage, intensive abrasion of the overhang, and core rejuvenation was performed during the debitage (Marder 2002). At Mureybet, the form of the raw material affected the debitage which exhibits no standardization and no precise scheme of bladelet production (Calley 1986). At Eynan, short, wide and flat bladelets were produced with converging lateral edges, using abrasion and soft stone hammer technique. The debitage was unidirectional without involving precisely planned laminar blank production. Sometimes, the striking platforms were moved on the cores, but the debitage remained unidirectional. The laminar debitage maintained the cores themselves without neo-cresting. The hinge accident rarely occurred. Bladelet cores were used furthermore for producing flakes (Valla *et al* 1998, 2001).

Flake debitage use was observed at Eynan. Habitually coarse grained flints were exploited using unidirectional debitage with hard hammer technique (Valla *et al* 1998, 2001).

Information concerning blank selection and tool making is available from the Negev sites and Eynan. At Negev Early Natufian/Terminal Ramonian sites, the microburin technique was highly used in geometric microlith production (Marder 2002). At Eynan, blanks for microlithic and geometric tools were selected among bladelets while flakes were used for retouched, notched and denticulated tools (Valla *et al* 1998, 2001).

Eynan Final Natufian (Valla *et al* 1998, 2001) exhibits most similarities to Raqefet Late Natufian, with fine-grained raw material exploitation, core decortication before bladelet removals, lack of front cresting, signs of flint heat treatment, unidirectional laminar debitage, lack of neo-cresting, rare hinge accidents, use of bladelet cores for producing flakes, and a pronounced flake debitage. However, Raqefet Late Natufian shows more organized laminar debitage, also in comparison to Mureybet Final Natufian.

The indicative signs of flint heat treatment, first appeared in the Early Natufian/Terminal Ramonian (Nahal Sheker 23 and Azariq XV in Marder 2002), represent a drastic technological change in Levantine Palaeolithic. It continues in the Late Natufian of Raqefet and in the Final Natufian of Eynan (Valla *et al* 1998, 2001). This technological innovation in Levantine prehistory was initiated by Natufian groups, as well as the sedentary life way, variegated burial customs, habitual artistic activity, and the domestication of animals (Belfer-Cohen 1991).

# SUMMARY

Raqefet Cave is situated close to the southeast corner of Mount Carmel in wadi Raqefet. Excavations were conducted by Eric Higgs from the University of Cambridge and Tamar Noy of the Israel Museum between 1970 and 1972. The excavation procedure, using wet sieving, was designed for the collection of a quantitatively comprehensive sample of artefact remains without bias for size or other factors. Therefore the lithic assemblages of Raqefet cave are fully suitable for technology study.

The thesis views lithic assemblages as product of technical behavioural phenomenon. The method used in thesis derives from French lithic studies. The study reconstructs operational sequences *(chaîne opératoire)* of past stone knapping activities. The reconstruction of operational sequences leads to the recognition of operational schemes that guided the stone knapper in making tools. Thus the theoretical and practical components of stone knapping compose up the lithic technology.

In the indeterminate Early Upper Palaeolithic, primarily, local raw material sources with mediocre quality flints were exploited. Flints in the size of *ca* 10-15 cm nodules were brought to the site in unknapped or tested state. Raw materials from sources yielding larger nodules were pre-processed off-site. Some raw materials were brought to the site in the form of ready made blanks. Decortication of flint nodules is rare.

The stone knapping focuses on fine blade (50-60 mm long) production for end-scrapers and retouched items, and bladelet (20-40 mm long) production with converging lateral edges for retouched items. Flake tools, such as end-scrapers and burins, are frequent and usually made on products of laminar core shaping and rejuvenation.

For blade production, the raw material procurement paid attention to the selection of nodules in appropriate shape, since evidences for extensive core pre-forming and cresting are rare. The narrow parts of the raw material nodules are used as debitage surfaces. The debitage is unidirectional, using consistently a single front and a single striking platform of the core. Soft hammer technique is habitually used to remove the blades, especially in the case of good quality raw material exploitation.

The bladelet production on one hand stems from further use of exploited blade cores. On the other hand, it is performed separately from the blade production. In latter case small raw material nodules are selected for making bladelet cores. The cores in bladelet production undergo minimal shaping-out. Bladelets are detached from both wide and narrow-fronted cores. The debitage is unidirectional, using consistently a single front and a single striking platform of the core. Soft hammer technique is used to remove bladelets.

Flake debitage is occasional. The frequent necessity for flakes as tool blanks is habitually satisfied by using the products of laminar core shaping and rejuvenation.

In the Levantine Aurignacian, local flint sources with low and mediocre quality flints are habitually exploited. These raw materials are available in the largest size in the environment of Raqefet. The nodules are brought to the site in a natural shape and most of the knapping, including pre-forming, is performed on-site. Decortication of flint nodules is rare.

The stone knapping focuses on producing thick (15-20 mm) flakes with steep distal termination for end-scrapers and notches-dencticulates, while thinner flakes (5-15 mm) are used for notches, burins and retouched tools. Large blades (60-120 mm long) are used for denticulates, retouched tools and end-scrapers, while fine blades with slightly curved profile (40-50 mm long) and converging lateral edges for el-Wad points. The bladelet tools are made of 20-40 mm long fine curved blanks with converging lateral edges.

Large flint nodules are used for flake production. This uses two methods. The first method is to produce thick tool blanks from cube or globular-shaped cores with changing orientation of debitage. The second, unidirectional debitage method produces the thinner tool blanks.

For blade production raw stone nodules are selected according to an appropriate shape for long and large blades which needed no or minimal investment in core preparation. The blade production is unidirectional, using consistently a single front and a single striking platform of the core. Rejected flake cores also are used for blade production, and vice versa. In addition, thick flakes from initial flaking also are used as blade cores. Large straight blade tool blanks are produced from narrow-fronted cores mainly by hard hammer knapping technique. Fine blade blanks are produced from wide-fronted cores by soft hammer knapping technique.

The bladelet production is not the continuation of the blade debitage. Small raw nodules and thick flakes are the blanks of bladelet cores. The bladelet core front habitually is narrow or semi-circular, in order to make narrow and long bladelet tool blanks. This concept does not plan to remove several series of bladelets from a single core. In the case of knapping accidents, instead of rejuvenation, the bladelet cores were often replaced by new ones and the debitage restarted.

In the Late Kebaran, primarily, local raw material sources with mediocre quality flints are exploited. The raw materials are brought to the site in pre-worked state and the essential part of the knapping takes place at the site. Decortication of flint nodules is rare.

The lithic production focuses on obtaining thin, elongated and straight 20-40 mm long bladelets for backed, backed-truncated and retouched tools. Blades are rarely tools, while flakes are abundant among burins and end-scrapers.

The bladelet production basically is performed in a joint sequence with the blade debitage. The cores are systematically prepared with cresting on their fronts, and frequently on their back. The narrow parts of the cores are used as debitage surfaces. The debitage is unidirectional, using consistently a single front and a single striking platform of the core. The debitage of both the blades and bladelets is performed by soft organic hammer technique. The debitage surface and the flank of the cores are reshaped and the striking platform is renewed during the debitage, in order to keep the cores in appropriate shape for future bladelet production. The bladelet blanks are predetermined in shape in order to minimize the energy investment into retouching that forms the final tool.

Flakes rarely are produced by their own debitage. The necessity for flakes as tool blanks is satisfied by using the products of laminar core shaping and rejuvenation.

In the Geometric Kebaran, the raw materials procurement focuses on locally available good quality flints. The raw material nodules of local sources sometimes are brought to the site in roughed-out state. Flints from distant sources appear in relatively high number and are brought in more pre-processed state and as ready made blanks. Decortication of flint nodules is intensive.

The lithic production primarily makes geometric microliths from straight 30-45 mm long bladelets. Blades and flakes are frequent blanks for end-scrapers, burins and retouched tools.

Blades and bladelets are made in a joint sequence with the bladelet debitage. The laminar cores are decorticated by flake removals. Crest preparation is occasionally used. In blade blank production, the narrow parts of the cores are used initially, and then the debitage takes place on wide fronts. The debitage is unidirectional, using consistently a single front and a single striking platform of the core. During bladelet production wide core fronts are exploited. In bladelet debitage, instead of rejuvenation, the cores are rather used on further surfaces. The laminar products are removed by soft hammer technique. In order to achieve the shape and size of the desired tools (geometrics and backed bladelets), a relative large part of the blanks is removed by retouching.

Flakes are occasionally produced by their own debitage. The necessity for flakes as tool blanks habitually is satisfied by using the products of laminar core shaping and rejuvenation.

In the Late Natufian, especially good quality raw materials are collected from local sources. Decortication of flint nodules is rare, and it took place off-site.

The lithic production focuses on bladelets for making geometric microliths. Flakes are blanks of denticulates, end-scrapers and burins. Blades are used for retouched items.

Blades are produced in a joint sequence with bladelets. The shaped-out flint nodules for bladelet production (most likely) undergo heat treatment. The

laminar debitage is unidirectional, which uses consistently a single front and a single striking platform of the core. All laminar products are obtained by soft hammer technique. The bladelet cores also are used for obtaining flakes.

Flakes for tool blanks are detached by hard hammer technique mainly from unidirectional cores.

On the basic level of the lithic technology (the organization of blanks debitages and blank use for tools) three fundamental operational schemes are revealed from the Upper Palaeolithic-Epipalaeolithic sequence of Raqefet:

Scheme 1 shows that raw material nodules are used for blade and bladelet debitages. Flake debitage is not performed. The cores of the blade debitage also were used for bladelet debitage. Flakes and blades of the blade production, and bladelets of the bladelet production were used as tool blanks. This pattern characterizes the indeterminate Early Upper Palaeolithic, Late Kebaran and Geometric Kebaran. These cultures may have been related to each other in terms of tradition in lithic production.

In Scheme 2, raw material nodules are used for flake, blade and bladelet debitages. In addition, flakes from the flake debitage are selected for making blade and bladelet cores. Blanks of each debitage are used for tool making. This pattern solely characterizes the Levantine Aurignacian.

Scheme 3 shows that raw material nodules are introduced into flake, blade and bladelet debitages. Cores of the blade debitage also are used in the bladelet debitage. Blanks of each debitage are used for tool making. In addition, flakes from the blade debitage are used as blanks of tools. This pattern shows resemblance to Pattern 2, but solely characterizes the Late Natufian.

In the lithic technology of the Upper Palaeolithic-Epipalaeolithic sequence of Raqefet 1) tendencies can be observed such as: shift from mediocre to good quality flints use towards the end of the Epipalaeolithic (Geometric Kebaran and the Late Natufian), including the appearance of flint heat treatment as means for gaining better quality raw material (Late Natufian); increased bladelet production by the Epipalaeolithic; the retouching of the microlithic tools with extent blank shape modification appears with the Geometric Kebaran and linger on the Late Natufian; making blades and bladelets in a single operational sequence; 2) changes can be observed such as: increased flake debitage in the Levantine Aurignacian and then in the Late Natufian; dominance of hard hammer technique in Levantine Aurignacian blade debitage; 3) consistency can be observed only on very general levels such as the performance of blade and bladelet debitage in each culture.

The lithic technologies from Raqefet in comparison to other Levantine sites shows that the Early Upper Palaeolithic non-Aurignacian industries represent a wide inter-site variety of knapping strategies, while the Levantine Aurignacian is technologically uniform; the Levantine Aurignacian lithic technology in terms of strict tradition kept over wide geographical range does not characterize any other Upper Palaeolithic assemblage, thus this behaviour rather fit the Middle Palaeolithic Mousterian or the transitional Emiran-Bohunician which also appeared with a consistent lithic technology over continents; the Late Kebaran and Geometric Kebaran technologically appear to be varied; the Late Natufian has a quite consistent lithic technology and exhibits a great technological innovation with the pyrotechnic modification of the raw materials.

# REFERENCES

Alon, D., Mintz G., Cohen I., Weiner S., Boaretto E. 2002. The use of Raman spectroscopy to monitor the removal of humic substances from charcoal: quality control for $^{14}$C dating of charcoal. *Radiocarbon* 44: 1-11.

Azoury, I. 1986. *Ksar Akil, Lebanon. A Technological and Typological Analysis of the Transitional and Early UpperPalaeolithic Levels of Ksar Akil and Abu Halka*. BAR International Series 289, Oxford.

Bar-Yosef, O. 1970. *The Epi-Palaeolithic Cultures in Palestine*. Ph. D. dissertation, Hebrew University.

Bar-Yosef, O. 1981. The Epi-Palaeolithic Complexes in the Southern Levant. In *Préhistoire du Levant*, C.N.R.S., Paris. pp. 389-408.

Bar-Yosef, O. 1991. The Archaeology of the Natufian layer at Hayonim Cave. In Bar-Yosef, O., Valla, F.R. (eds.) *The Natufian Culture in the Levant*, International Monographs in Prehistory, Ann Arbor. pp. 81-92.

Bar-Yosef, O. 2000. The Middle and Early Upper Paleolithic in Southwest Asia and Neighboring Regions. In Bar-Yosef, O., Pilbeam, D. (eds.) *The Geography of Neandertals and Modern Humans in Europe and the Greater Mediterranean*, Peabody Museum Bulletin 8, Cambridge. pp. 107-156.

Bar-Yosef, O., Belfer, A. 1977. The Lagaman industry. In Bar-Yosef, O., Phillips, J.L. (eds.) *Prehistoric Investigations in Gebel Maghara, Northern Sinai*, Qedem 7, Monographs of the Institute of Archaeology, Hebrew University Jerusalem. pp. 42-84.

Bar-Yosef, O., Belfer-Cohen, A. 1996. Another look at theLevantine Aurignacian. In diCesnola, A., Montet-White, A. (eds.) *The Late Aurignacian*, 13th Congress, UISPP, ABACO Edizioni, Forli. pp. 139-150.

Bar-Yosef, O., Belfer-Cohen, A. 2004. The Qafzeh Upper Paleolithic Assemblages: 70 Year Later. *Eurasian Prehistory* 2 /1: 145-180.

Bar-Yosef, O., Valla, F.R. 1979 L'evolution du Natoufien Nouvelles Suggestions. *Paléorient* 5: 145-152.

Bar-Yosef, O., Vandermeersch, B. 1972. The stratigraphical and cultural problems of the passage from Middle to Upper Paleolithic in Palestinian caves. In Bordes, F. (ed.) *The Origins of Homo Sapiens*, UNESCO, Paris. pp. 221-225.

Bar-Yosef, O., Vogel, J.C. 1987. Relative and absolute chronology of the Epi-Palaeolithic in the Southern Levant. In Aurenche, O., Evin, J., Hours, F. (eds.) *Chronologies in the Near East*, BAR International Series 379, Oxford. pp. 219-245.

Bar-Yosef, O., Arnold, M., Mercier, N., Belfer-Cohen, A., Goldberg, P., Housley, R., Laville, H., Meignen, L., Vogel, J. C., and B. Vandermeersch 1996. The Dating of the Upper Paleolithic Layers in Kebara Cave, Mt Carmel. *Journal of Archaeological Science* 23: 297-306.

Bar-Yosef, O., Vandermeersch, B, Arensburg, B., Belfer-Cohen, A., Goldberg, P., Laville, H., Meignen, L., Rak, Y., Speth, J. D., Tchernov, E., Tillier, A-M., and S. Weiner 1992. The Excavations in the Kebara Cave, Mt. Carmel. Current Anthropology 33/5: 497-550.

Belfer-Cohen, A. 1991. The Natufian in the Levant. *Annual Review of Anthropology* 20: 167-186.

Belfer-Cohen, A. 1995. Problems in Defining a Prehistoric Culture: an Example from the Southern Levant. In Otte, M. (ed.) *Nature et Culture*, E.R.A.U.L. 68. pp. 247-255.

Belfer-Cohen, A., Bar-Yosef, O. 1981. The Aurignacian at Hayonim Cave. *Paléorient* 7/2: 19-42.

Belfer-Cohen, A., Bar-Yosef, O. 1999. The Levantine Aurignacian: 60 years of research. In Davies, W., Charles, R. (eds.) *Dorothy Garrod and the Progress of the Palaeolithic. Studies in the Prehistoric Archaeology of the Near East and Europe*, Oxbow Books. pp. 118-134.

Belfer-Cohen, A., Goring-Morris, A.N. 1986. Har Horesha I: an Upper Palaeolithic site in the central Negev highlands. *Mitekufat Haeven – Journal of the Israel Prehistoric Society* 19: 43-57.

Belfer-Cohen, A., Goring-Morris, A.N. 2002. Why microliths? Microlithisation in the Levant. In Elston, R.G., Kuhn, S.L. (eds.) *Thinking Small: Global Perspectives on Microlithic Technologies*, AP3A, Washington, D.C. pp. 57-68.

Belfer-Cohen, A., Goring-Morris, A.N. 2003. Current Issues in Levantine Upper Palaeolithic Research. In Goring-Morris, A.N., Belfer-Cohen, A. (eds.) *More Than Meets the Eye: Studies on Upper Palaeolithic Diversity in the Near East*, Oxford, Oxbow, pp.1-12.

Belfer-Cohen, A., Goring-Morris, A.N. In press A New Look at Old Assemblages: A Cautionary Tale. NeoLithics conference 2004 April.

Belfer-Cohen, A., Gilead I., Goring-Morris A.N., Rosen, S. 1991. An Epipalaeolithic Rockshelter at Nahal Neqarot in the Central Negev. *Mitekufat Haeven. Journal of the Israel Prehistoric Society* 24: 164-168.

Bergman, C.A 1987. *Ksar Akil, Lebanon. Technological and Typological Analysis of the Later Palaeolithic Levels of Ksar Akil*. Vol II: Levels XIII-VI. BAR International Series 329.

Bergman, C.A. 2003. Twisted Debitage and the Levantine Aurignacian Problem. In Goring-Morris, A.N., Belfer-Cohen, A. (eds.) *More Than Meets the Eye: Studies on Upper Palaeolithic Diversity in the Near East*, Oxford, Oxbow, pp. 185-195.

Bergman, C.A., Goring-Morris, A.N. 1987. Conference: the Levantine Aurignacian with special reference to Ksar Akil, Lebanon, March 27-28, 1987. *Paléorient* 13: 140-145.

Besancon, J., Copeland, P., Hours, F. 1977. Tableux de préhistoire Libanese. *Paléorient* 3 (1975-1977): 5-45.

Calley, S. 1986. *Téchnologie du Débitage a Mureybet, Syrie*. BAR International Series 312, Oxford.

Chazan, M. 2001. Bladelet production in the Aurignacian of Hayonim Cave, Israel. *Palèorient* 27: 81-88.

Copeland, L. 1975. The Middle and Upper Paleolithic of Lebanon and Syria in the light of recent research. In Wendorf, F., Marks, A.E. (eds.) *Problems in Prehistory: North Africa and the Levant*, SMU Press, Dallas. pp. 317-350.

Copeland, L. 2003. The Levantine Upper Palaeolithic: A Commentary on Contributions to the Philadelphia Symposium. In Goring-Morris, A.N., Belfer-Cohen, A. (eds.) *More Than Meets the Eye: Studies on Upper Palaeolithic Diversity in the Near East*, Oxford, Oxbow. pp. 242-248.

Copeland, L., Hours, F. 1971. The later Upper Palaeolithic Material from Antelias Cave, Lebanon: Levels IV-I. Berytus, Archaeological Studies 20: 57-138.

Davidzon, A., Goring-Morris, A.N. 2003. Sealed in Stone: The Upper Palaeolithic Early Ahmarian Knapping Method in the Light of Refitting Studies at Nahal Nizzana XIII, Western Negev, Israel *Journal of The Israel Prehistoric Society* 33: 75-205.

Delage, C. 2001. *Les ressources lithiques dans le nord d'Israël: La question des territoires d'approvisionnement natoufiens confrontée a l'hypothèse de leur sédentarité*. Thèse de doctorat. Université de Paris I-Pantheon-Sorbonne.

Demars, P.-Y. 1992. L'Aurignacien ancien en Périgord: le problème du Protoaurignacien. *Paléo* 4:101-122.

Demars, P.-Y., Laurent, P. 1992. *Types d'outils lithiques du Paléolithique supérieur en Europe*. Cahiers du Quaternaire No7. Presses du CNRS, Paris.

Dortch, C. 1970. *The Late Aurignacian Industries of Levels 8-6 at Ksar 'Akil, Lebanon*. Unpublished MA Thesis, UCL, London.

Echegaray, G.J. 1978. Notes toward a systematization of the Upper Paleolithic in Palestine. In Freeman, L.G. (ed.) *Views of the Past: Essays in Old World Prehistory and Paleoanthropology*, Mouton Publishers, The Hague. pp. 177-191.

Fellner, R. 1995. *Cultural Change and the Epipalaeolithic of Palestine*. BAR International Series 599, Oxford.

Ferring, C.R. 1980. *Technological Variability and Change in the Late Paleolithic of the Negev*. University Microfilms Inter-national, Ann Arbor.

Ferring, C.R. 1988. Technological change in the Upper Paleolithic of the Negev. In Dibble, H.L., Montet-White, A. (eds.) *Upper Pleistocene Prehistory of Western Eurasia*, University Museum, University of Pennsylvania, Philadelphia. pp. 333-348.

Garrard A.N. 1980. *Man-Animal-Plant Relationships During the Upper Pleistocene and Early Holocene*. Unpublished Ph.D. Thesis, University of Cambridge.

Garrod, D. A. E. 1932. A New Mesolithic Industry: The Natufian of Palestine. *Journal of the Royal Anthropological Institute of Great Britain and Ireland* 62: 257-269.

Garrod, D. A. E 1953. The Relations between South-West Asia and Europe in the Later Palaeolithic Age with Special Reference to the Origins of the Upper Palaeolithic Blade Cultures. *Journal of World History* 1: 13-37.

Garrod, D. A. E. 1954. Excavations at the Mugharet Kebara, Mount Carmel, 1931: the Aurignacian industries. *Proceedings of the Prehistoric Society* 20: 155-192.

Garrod, D.A.E. 1957a. Notes sur le Paléolithique supérieur du Moyen Orient. *Bulletin de la Société Préhistorique Française* 55: 239-445.

Garrod, D.A.E. 1957b. The Natufian Culture: The Life and Economy of a Mesolithic People in the Near East. Proceedings of the British Academy 43: 211-227.

Garrod, D.A.E. and D.M.A. Bate 1937. *The Stone Age of Mount Carmel* : Volume 1. Clarendon Press: Oxford.

Geneste, J.-M. 1991. Systèmes techniques de production lithique: variations techno économiques dans les processus de réalisation des outillages paléolithiques. *Techniques et culture* 17–18: 1-35.

Gilead, I. 1981. Upper Palaeolithic tool assemblages from the Negev and Sinai. In Sanlaville, P., Cauvin, J. (eds.) *Préhistoire du Levant*, CNRS, Paris. pp. 331-342.

Goldberg, P., Bar-Yosef, O. 1998. Site formation processes in Kebara and Hayonim caves and their significance in Levantine prehistoric caves. In Akazawa, T., Aoki K., Bar-Yosef, O. (eds) *Neandertals and Modern Humans in Western Asia*, Plenum, New York. pp. 107-125.

Goldberg, P., Laville, P. 1988. Le contexte stratigraphique des occupations Paléolithiques de la grotte de Kebara (Israel). *Paléorient* 14/2: 117-123.

Goldberg, P., Laville, P. 1991. Étude géologiques des dépôts de la grotte de Kébara (Mont-Carmel): campagnes 1982–1984. In Bar-Yosef, O., Vandermeersch, B. (eds.) *Le Squelette Moustérien de Kébara 2*, CNRS, Paris. pp. 29-41.

Goring-Morris, A.N. 1980. *Late Quaternary Sites in Wadi Fazael, Lower Jordan Valley*. Unpublished MA thesis, Hebrew University, Jerusalem.

Goring-Morris, A.N. 1987. *At the Edge: Terminal Pleistocene Hunter-Gatherers in the Negev and Sinai*. BAR International Series 361, Oxford.

Goring-Morris, A.N. 1995. Complex hunter-gatherers at the end of the Paleolithic (20,000–10,000 BP). In Levy, T.E. (ed.) *The Archaeology of Society in the Holy Land*, Leicester University Press, London. pp. 141-168.

Goring-Morris, A.N., Marder, O., Davidzon A., Ibrahim, F. 1998. Putting Humpty Dumpty together again: preliminary observations on refitting studies in the eastern Mediterranean. In Milliken, S. (ed.) *From Raw Material Procurement to Tool Production: The Organisation of Lithic Technology in Late Glacial and Early Postglacial Europe*, BAR International Series 700, Oxford. pp. 149-182.

Haudricourt, A-G. 1987. *La Technologie Science Humanie. Recherches d'Histoire et Ethnologie des Techniques*. Paris.

Higgs, E.S., Garrard, A.N., Noy, T., Ziffer, D. 1975. Report on Excavation at Rakefet, Mount Carmel, Israel. Unpublished Raqefet Archives.

Hours, F. 1974. Remarques sur l'utilisation de listes-types pour l'étude du Paléolithique supérieur et de l'Epipaléolithique du Levant. *Paléorient* 2/1: 3-15.

Hours, F., Copeland, L., Aurenche, O. 1973. Les industries paléolithique du Proche-Orient, essai de correlation. *L'Anthropologie* 77: 229-280, 437-496.

Inizan, M.-L., Roche, H., Tixier, J. 1976. Avantages d'un traitement thermique pour la taille des roches siliceuses. *Quaternaria* XIX (1975-1976): 1-18.

Inizan, M.-L., Reduron, M., Roche, H., Tixier, J. 1995. *Technologie de la Pierre taillé 4*, Meudon: CREP. Nanterre.

Karlin, C., Julien, M. 1994. Prehistoric technology: a cognitive science? In Renfrew, C., Ezra, B., Zubrow, W. (eds.) *The ancient mind: elements of cognitive archaeology*, New directions in archaeology, Cambridge, University Press. pp. 152-165.

Kaufman, D. 1986. A Proposed Method for Distinguishing Between Blades and Bladelets. *Lithic Technology* 15/1: 34-40.

Kaufman, D. 1987. Interassemblage Variability of Metric Attributes from Lithic Assemblages of The Late Upper Paleolithic of Israel. *Mitekufat Haeven. Journal of the Israel Prehistoric Society* 20: 37-49.

Kaufman, D. 1989. Observations on the Geometric Kebaran: A view from Neve David. In Bar-Yosef,, O. Vandermeersch, B. (eds.) *Investigations in South Levantine Prehistory. Prehistoire du Sud-Levant*. BAR international series 497. pp. 275-285.

Kerry, K.W., Henry, D.O. 2003. Tor Fawaz (J403): An Upper Palaeolithic Occupation in the Jebel Qalkha Area, Southwest Jordan. In Goring-Morris, A.N., Belfer-Cohen, A. (eds.) *More Than Meets the Eye: Studies on Upper Palaeolithic Diversity in the Near East*, Oxford, Oxbow. pp. 171-184.

Kuhn, S.L. 2004. Upper Paleolithic raw material economies at Üçağizli cave, Turkey. *Journal of Anthropological Archaeology* 23: 431-448.

Kuhn, S.L., Stiner, M.C., Kerry, K.W., Güleç, E. 2003. The Early Upper Palaeolithic at Üçağizli Cave (Hatay, Turkey): Some Preliminary Results. In Goring-Morris, A.N., Belfer-Cohen, A. (eds.) *More Than Meets the Eye: Studies on Upper Palaeolithic Diversity in the Near East*, Oxford, Oxbow. pp. 106-117.

Lemonnier, P. 1992. *Elements for an Anthropology of Technology*. Anthropological Papers No. 88, Museum of Anthropology, University of Michigan, Ann Arbor.

Lengyel, G. 2005. *Lithic technology of the Upper Palaeolithic and Epipalaeolithic of Raqefet Cave, Mount Carmel, Israel.* Unpublished PhD thesis, University of Haifa.

Lengyel, G., Nadel, D., Tsatskin, A., Bar-Oz, G., Bar-Yosef Mayer, D., Beeri, R., Hershkovitz, I. 2005. Back to Raqefet Cave. *Mitekufat Haeven, Journal of the Israel Prehistoric Society* 35: 245-270.

Lengyel, G., Boaretto, E., Fabre, L., Ronen, A. 2006. New AMS 14C dates from the early Upper Paleolithic sequence of Raqefet Cave, Mount Carmel, Israel. *Radiocarbon* 48/2: 253-258.

Maher, L., Banning, E.B. 2002. Geological survey and the Epipalaeolithic in northern Jordan. *Antiquity* 76: 313-314.

Marder, O. 2002. *The Lithic Technology of Epipaleolithic Hunter-Gatherers in the Negev: The Implication of Refitting Studies.* Unpublished PhD dissertation. Hebrew University of Jerusalem.

Marks, A. E. 1981. The Upper Palaeolithic of the Negev. In Cauvin, J., Sanlaville, P. (eds) *Préhistoire du Levant,* C.N.R.S., Paris. pp. 343-352.

Marks, A. E. 2003. Reflections on the Levantine Upper Palaeolithic Studies: Past and Present. In Goring-Morris, A.N., Belfer-Cohen, A. (eds.) *More Than Meets the Eye: Studies on Upper Palaeolithic Diversity in the Near East,* Oxford, Oxbow. pp. 249-264.

Marks, A.E., Ferring, C.R. 1988. The Early Upper Paleolithic of the Levant. In Hoffecker, J.F., Wolf, C.A. (eds.) *The Early Upper Paleolithic, Evidence from Europe and the Near East,* BAR International Series 437, Oxford. pp. 43-72.

Mc Brearty, S., Bishop, L., Plummer, T., Dewar, R., Conard, N. 1998. Tools Underfoot: Human Trampling as an Agent of Lithic Artifact Edge Modification. *American Antiquity* 63/1: 108-129.

Mellars, P., Tixier, J. 1989. Radiocarbon-accelerator dating of Ksar Akil (Lebanon) and the chronology of the Upper Palaeolithic sequence in the Middle East. *Antiquity* 63:761–768.

Monigal, K. 2003. Technology, Economy, and Mobility at the Beginning of the Levantine Upper Palaeolithic. In Goring-Morris, A.N., Belfer-Cohen, A. (eds.) *More Than Meets the Eye: Studies on Upper Palaeolithic Diversity in the Near East,* Oxford, Oxbow. pp. 118-133.

Neuville, R. 1934. Le préhistorique de Palestine. *Revue Biblique* 43: 237-259.

Neuville, R. 1951. *Le Paléolithique et le Mésolithique du Desert de Judée,* Mémoire no. 24. Archives de l'Institut de Paléontologie Humaine, Paris.

Noy, T., Higgs E.S. 1971. Raqefet Cave. *Israel Exploration Journal* 21: 225-226.

Noy, T., Legge, A. J., Higgs, E.S. 1973. Recent Excavations at Nahal Oren, Israel. *Proceedings of the Prehistoric Society* 39: 75-99.

Ohnuma, K. 1988. *Ksar 'Akil, Lebanon. A Technological Study of the Earlier Upper Palaeolithic Levels of Ksar 'Akil, vol. III. Levels XXV–XIV.* BAR International Series 426, Oxford.

Olami, Y. 1984. *Prehistoric Carmel.* Haifa.

Pelegrin, J. 1985. Réflexions sur le comportement technique. In Otte, M. (ed.) *La signification culturelle des industries lithiques,* Studia Prehistorica Belgica 4. BAR International Series 239. pp. 72-88.

Pelegrin, J. 1986 *Technologie lithique: une méthode appliquée a l'étude de deux séries du Périgordien ancien (Roc de Combe, couche 8 – La Cote, niveau III).* Thèse de doctorat. Université de Paris X.

Pelegrin, J. 1995. *Technologie lithique: le Châtelperronien de Roc-de-Combe (Lot) et de La Côte (Dordogne).* Cahiers du Quaternaire No. 20.

Pelegrin, J. 2000. Les techniques de débitage laminaire au Tardiglaciaire : critères de diagnose et quelques réflexions. In Valentin, B., Bodu, P., Christensen, M. (eds.) *L'Europe centrale et septentrionale au Tardiglaciaire. Confrontation des modèles régionaux de peuplement,* pp. 73-86. Actes de la Table-ronde internationale de Nemours 14-15-16 mai 1997. Mémoires du Musée de Préhistoire d'Ile-de-France n°7, A.P.R.A.I.F., Nemours.

Pelegrin, J., Karlin, C., Bodu, P. 1988. «Chaînes opératoires»: un outil pour le préhistorien. In Tixier, J. (ed.) *Journée d'études technologiques en Préhistoire,* Notes et Monographies Techniques N° 25, Éditions du CNRS, Paris. pp. 55-62.

Perlès, C. 1992. In Search of Lithic Strategies. In Gardin, J-C., Christopher, S.P. (eds.) *Representations in Archaeology.* Indiana University Press. pp: 223-247.

Ploux, S., Soriano, S. 2003. Umm el Tlel, une sequence du Paléolithique supérieur en Syrie centrale. Industries lithiques et chronologie culturelle. *Paléorient* 29/2: 5-34.

Roche, H., Tixier, J. 1982. Les accidents de taille. In: *Tailler! Pour quoi faire: préhistoire et technologie lithique II. Recent progress in microwear studies,*

Tervuren, Musée Royal d'Afrique Centrale (Studia Praehistorica Belgica; 2). pp. 65-76.

Ronen, A. 1984. *Sefunim Prehistoric Sites, Mount Carmel, Israel*. BAR Iternational Series 230 (i-ii).

Sarel, J. 2002. *The Middle-Upper Palaeolithic Transition in Israel*: Technological analysis. Unpublished PhD thesis, University of Haifa.

Sarel J. 2004. *The Middle-Upper Paleolithic Transition in Israel*. BAR International Series 1229.

Shahack-Gross, R., Berna, F., Karkanas, P., Weiner, S. 2004. Bat guano and preservation of archaeological remains in cave sites. *Journal of Archaeological Science* 31/ 9: 1259-1272.

Solecki R. L., Solecki, R.S. 1970. A new secondary flaking technique at the Nahr Ibrahim cave site. *Bulletin du Musée de Beyrouth* 23: 137-142.

Stein, J. K. 1987. Deposits for Archaeologists. *Advances in Archaeological Method and Theory* 11: 337-395.

Škrdla, P. 2003. Comparison of Boker Tachtit and Stránská Skála MP/UP Transitional Industries. *Mitekufat Haeven. Journal of The Israel Prehistoric Society* 33: 37-73.

Tixier, J. 1963. *Typologie de l'Epipaléolithique de Maghreb*. Paris, A.M.G. (Mémoire du C.R.A.P.E., Alger; 2).

Tixier, J. 1982. Techniques de débitage: osons ne plus affirmer. *Studia Praehistorica Belgica* 2: 13-22.

Tostevin, G. B. 2000. *Behavioral Change and Regional Variation across the Middle to Upper Paleolithic Transition*. Unpublished PhD. Dissertation. Department of Anthropology, Harvard University, Cambridge, MA, USA.

Valla, F. R. 1984. *Les industries de silex de Mallaha (Eynan) et du Natoufien dans le Levant*. Paris: Association Paléorient, Mémoires et Travaux du Centre de Recherche Français de Jerusalem, 3.

Valla, F. R. 1987. Chronologie absolue et chronologie relative dans le Natoufien. In Aurenche, O., Évin, J. Hours, F. (eds.) *Chronologies in the Near East*, Oxford, BAR International Series. pp. 267-293.

Valla, F. R. 1989. A propos du Kebarien geometrique de la terrasse d'Hayonim (Fouilles D. Henry (1974-1975). In Bar-Yosef, O., Vandermeersch, B. (eds.) *Investigations in South Levantine Prehistory. Préhistoire du Sud-Levant*, BAR International Series 497. pp. 255-273.

Valla, F. R. 1995. The First Settled Societies – Natufian (12,500-10,200 BP) In Levy, T.E. (ed.) *The Archaeology of Society in the Holy Land*, Leicester University Press, London. pp. 170-187.

Valla, F. R., Khalaily, H., Samuelian, N., Bocquentin, F., Delage, C., Valentin, B., Plisson, H., Rabinovich, R., Belfer-Cohen, A. 1998. Le Natoufien Final et les Nouvelles Fouilles a Mallaha (Eynan), Israel 1996-1997. *Mitekufat Haeven. Journal of the Israel Prehistoric Society* 28: 105-176.

Valla, F. R., Khalaily, H., Samuelian, N., March, R., Bocquentin, F., Valentin, B., Marder, O., Rabinovich, R., Le Dosseur, G., Dubreuil, L., Belfer-Cohen, A. 2001. Le Natoufien Final de Mallaha (Eynan), Deuxieme Rapport Préliminaire: Les Fouilles de 1998 et 1999. *Mitekufat Haeven. Journal of the Israel Prehistoric Society* 31: 43-184.

Volkman, P.W. 1983. Boker Tachtit. Core reconstructions. In Marks, A.E. (ed.) *Prehistory and Paleoenvironments in the Central Negev, Israel, vol. III. The Avdat/Aqev Area, Part 3*, Dept. of Anthropology, Southern Methodist University. pp. 127-188.

Weinstein-Evron, M., Bar-Oz, G., Zaidner, Y., Tsatskin, A., Druck, D., Porat, N., Hershkovitz, I. 2003. Introducing Misliya cave, Mount Carmel, Israel: a new continuous Lower/Middle Paleolithic sequence in the Levant. *Eurasian Prehistory*, 1(1): 31-55.

Williams, J. K. 2003a. *Examining the Boundaries of the Levantine Aurignacian*. Unpublished PhD thesis, Southern Methodist University.

Williams, J. K. 2003b. An Examination of Upper Palaeolithic Flake Technologies in the Marginal Zone of the Levant. In Goring-Morris, A.N., Belfer-Cohen, A. (eds.) *More Than Meets the Eye: Studies on Upper Palaeolithic Diversity in the Near East*, Oxford, Oxbow. pp. 196-208.

Wiseman, M.F. 1993. Lithic Blade Elements from the Southern Levant: A Diachronic View of Changing Technology and Design Process. *Mitekufat Haeven. Journal of the Israel Prehistoric Society* 25: 13-102.

Yaroshevich, A. 2004. *Comparative Analysis between Microlithic Industries from the Kebaran Geometric Sites of Heftziba and Neve David*. Unpublished MA thesis, University of Haifa.

Yizhaq, M., Mintz, G., Cohen, I., Khalaily, H., Weiner, S., Boaretto, E. 2005. Quality controlled radiocarbon dating of bones and charcoal from the early pre-pottery Neolithic B (PPNB) of Motza (Israel). *Radiocarbon* 47(2): 193-206.

Ziffer, D. 1978a. The use of technological and metric data in the study of four Levantine Aurignacian sites in the Mount Carmel region. A preliminary study. *Paléorient* 4: 71-94.

Ziffer, D. 1978b. A Re-evaluation of the Upper Palaeolithic industries of the Kebara Cave and their place in the Aurignacian Culture of the Levant. *Paléorient* 4: 273-293.

Ziffer, D. 1981 Yabrud Shelter II – A reconsideration of its cultural composition and its relevance to the Upper Palaeolithic cultural sequence in the Levant. *Quartär* 31–32: 69-91.